ABOUT THIS VOLUME

Global anti-Asian racism, particularly in the guise of Yellow Peril, has endured for centuries around the world. In Europe and the Americas, Asian immigrants and refugees were, and are, treated as threats to national security. Yellow Peril and anti-Asian racism is also found in Africa, Australia, and in Asian nations as well. Wherever Asian immigrants and refugees found themselves, anti-Asian sentiments quickly followed.

The contributors to *Global Anti-Asian Racism* investigate the varied manifestations of prejudice and violence that Asians have endured through the 17th century to the twin pandemics of anti-Asian racism during COVID-19. From historical case studies in Mexico and Brazil to personal ruminations of people who are Asian German, mixed-race Swedish-Japanese, and adopted Korean American, to graphic narratives and poetic explorations, the essays in this volume illuminate the multifaceted nature of global anti-Asian racism and the resilience of Asians across the world to resist and counter this bigotry and bias.

GLOBAL
ANTI-ASIAN
RACISM

GLOBAL
ANTI-ASIAN
RACISM

Jennifer Ho, Editor

ASIA

SHORTS

Published by the Association for Asian Studies
Asia Shorts, Number 18
www.asianstudies.org

The Association for Asian Studies (AAS)

Formed in 1941, the Association for Asian Studies (AAS)—the largest society of its kind, with over 6,000 members worldwide—is a scholarly, non-political, non-profit professional association open to all persons interested in Asia. For further information, please visit www.asianstudies.org.

Cover: The front cover is an original design by Rivi Handler-Spitz, associate professor and chair of Asian Languages and Cultures at Macalester College and author of "Savage Script: How Chinese Writing Became Barbaric" (see page 72). For further information, please visit https://rivihandlerspitz.com.

Library of Congress Cataloging-in-Publication Data available from the Library of Congress

ASIA
SHORTS

Series Editor: David Kenley
Dakota State University

ASIA SHORTS offers concise, engagingly written titles by highly qualified authors on topics of significance in Asian Studies. Topics are intended to be substantive, generate discussion and debate within the field, and attract interest beyond it.

The Asia Shorts series complements and leverages the success of the pedagogically-oriented AAS book series, Key Issues in Asian Studies, and is designed to engage broad audiences with up-to-date scholarship on important topics in Asian Studies. Rigorously peer-reviewed, Asia Shorts books provide cutting-edge scholarship and provocative analyses. They are jargon free, accessible, and speak to contemporary issues or larger themes. In so doing, Asia Shorts volumes make an impact on students, fellow scholars, and informed readers beyond academia.

For further information, visit the AAS website: www.asianstudies.org.

AAS books are distributed by Columbia University Press.

For orders or purchasing inquiries, please visit

https://cup.columbia.edu

COLUMBIA
UNIVERSITY
PRESS

CONTENTS

FOREWORD

TACKLING THE TABOO SUBJECT

Christine R. Yano

The field of Asian Studies, as it has been conceptualized outside Asia, has been shaped by the historical spectre of public interests. Asia has provided a curio shop of exotica, whether in aesthetics, philosophy, spirituality, political structures, economic systems, or cultural patternings. As a convenient and productive "other," Asia acts as a decorative fan to enflame passions, prod musings, and invite contemplations. In some ways this volume may be thought of in similar light. Given our particular era of Black Lives Matter and heightened anti-Asian racism spurred by the global pandemic, framing Asia and Asians within issues of race can be thought of as yet another refraction of that curio shop. And yet, this framework is fundamentally different: racism represents more than an opportunity to re-examine Asia through our current interests. Racism has been taboo in intellectual approaches to Asia because the subject strikes too close to non-Asian homes. In particular, racism sounds like an American concern, etching black-white divides, even as other colors and mixtures fill immigration lines. Obviously, racism spans far more than US borders, yet the driving forces of critical race theory stem from US civil rights movements and activism. In this light, global anti-Asian racism seems like a side note. Moreover, it is a side note that Asian Studies as a historically conservative field would rather ignore. With too few exceptions, racism and Asia have been a relatively taboo combination in academia (Kowner and Demel 2012).

This volume dispels that taboo and pushes the side note of racism onto center stage with the significant imprimatur of the primary scholarly body of the field, the Association for Asian Studies. In many ways it took the bridging of Asian and Asian American Studies to validate that stage. While I was President of the Association for Asian Studies (2020–2021), as well as in the years surrounding that period, I conferred with Jennifer Ho, then President of the Association for Asian American Studies (2020–2022). Our conversations were facilitated by Tina Chen, founding editor of *Verge: Studies in Global Asias*, dedicated to increasing dialogue between the separate but adjacent fields of Asian Studies, Asian American Studies, and Asian Diasporic Studies. What began as strategizing to bridge fields intensified with the COVID-19 global pandemic that not only isolated individuals and institutions, but also generated widespread, often violent anti-Asian racism. Both Jennifer and I had to pivot to online leadership of our respective organizations. Jennifer in particular was called upon by the media to comment on the increasing cases of anti-Asian violence. I contributed to a pandemic-focused volume of the AAS Asia Shorts series with a chapter, "Racing the Pandemic: Anti-Asian Racism amid COVID-19" (2020). Jennifer developed a much-referenced document, "Anti-Asian Racism and COVID-19," as well as published an article on the topic in *Japan Forum* (see her introduction in this volume). In short, our leadership as heads of Asian Studies and Asian American Studies placed us in the spotlight that demanded reconsidering racism and Asia and Asians.

This is the back story of this collection. When David Kenley, editor of the Asia Shorts series for the Association for Asian Studies, asked for suggestions on who to edit and shape this volume, I could think of no more capable scholar than Jennifer Ho. Indeed, the richness, breadth, and deep insights of this collection reflect Jennifer's personal and professional integrity on the topic of anti-Asian racism. I underscore the fact that the two of us—women of Asian ancestry and commitment—have helped give birth to not only this volume (for which Jennifer receives full credit and admiration), but also a place at the table of concerns for the field of Asian Studies. As Jennifer writes in her introductory chapter, "The personal is political and . . . the political is personal" (p. 12). Thus I take pleasure in offering this foreword driven in part by who I am and what that means. Through its publication as part of the Asia Shorts series intended to make thinking through Asia broadly accessible, this volume announces that any sense of taboo in discussing race and racism in and around Asia and the Asian diaspora is no longer tenable. Jennifer has done a remarkable job of pulling in different parts of the world, different ranges of experiences, and even different modes of presentation. The result is far more than the sum of its parts, but carries the forcefulness of its rich weaving. Global anti-Asian racism affects us all—for the violence that lays in its wake, as well as the critical frameworks that it demands. I thank all those involved in the production of this historic volume for helping sharpen, deepen, and diversify the voices that speak to these issues.

References Cited

Kowner, Rotem and Walter Demel, eds., 2012. *Race and Racism in Modern East Asia: Western Constructions and Eastern Reactions*. Leiden: Brill Publishers.

Yano, Christine, 2020. "Racing the Pandemic: Anti-Asian Racism amid COVID-19." In Vinayak Chaturvedi, ed. *The Pandemic: Perspectives on Asia*. Asia Shorts. Ann Arbor: Association for Asian Studies: 123–136.

ACKNOWLEDGMENTS

I would not be the scholar I am, nor have the awareness of the Asian diaspora, were it not for my family of origin and extended family—both those related to me through networks of kinship and those connected to me through communities of care. I am the daughter of a refugee father from China and an immigrant mother from Jamaica. My paternal grandparents hailed from Chongking and my maternal grandparents originated in the New Territories region of Hong Kong. My YeYe spoke over eight Chinese languages, but as a refugee from Communist China in the 1950s could not master English and as a proud man could not bring himself to do what refugees all over the world did: work menial jobs well below their educational level. Instead it was my Nai Nai, a Shanghai beauty who never worked a day in her life while in China, who made costume jewelry in NYC to help her family survive. My Gung Gung was from a poor farming family and did what poor people do the world over: immigrate to another country in hopes of a better life. My PoPo took a leap of faith in marrying a man who had relocated to Kingston, and she raised nine children in a country in which the majority of the people looked nothing like her and did not eat the same foods she had grown up with as a Hakka woman. Undoubtedly my grandparents experienced global anti-Asian racism, even if they never shared specific stories with me.

So I acknowledge those who have made my life possible and the great number of people that this volume is dedicated to: the Asian people across the globe who have been subjected to anti-Asian racism brought on by xenophobic fears of disease during the COVID-19 pandemic. This volume acknowledges the traumas and losses that all of us have experienced during the global pandemic, and the additional traumas and harms brought about by global anti-Asian racism. I also want to thank everyone who made this volume possible: the Association for Asian Studies, especially Dr. Christine Yano, past president of AAS who recommended me as the special guest editor for this volume. My sincerest gratitude goes to series editor, David Kenley, and AAS Publications Manager, Jon Wilson, for all their labor and support and their affirmation that despite my lack of expertise in Asian

Studies, I was nonetheless the editor that they thought would be the best fit for this particular volume. I am so appreciative to everyone who answered the call for papers for this issue. I wish I could have accepted three times the number of submissions, but the interest in this topic illustrates the need for a volume dedicated to global anti-Asian racism. And I am sincerely thankful for each contributor to this volume; they were all wonderful to work with and inspiring in their dedication to making a valuable contribution to a vital topic.

Finally, as I do in all my acknowledgmens, I have saved my sincerest thanks for my husband, Matthew Grady, who makes me feel like who I am—a fully enfranchised human.

— *Jennifer Ho*

INTRODUCTION

GLOBAL ANTI-ASIAN RACISM

THE PROBLEM THAT NEVER WENT AWAY

Jennifer Ho

When I was in fifth grade, Freddy Sloan called me a chink.[1] It wasn't the first time I had been called this particular racial slur, but it is a memory that is so clearly etched in my mind's eye that I can conjure up specific details of the exact place of this racist harm (outside the Exploratorium museum in San Francisco) and what I was feeling just before this moment (out of breath because I was running and elated because I was going to catch Freddy in a game of tag). I was just about to touch Freddy when he twirled his body out of arm's length and yelled, "Get away from me, chink!" I can still vividly recall what happened next and how it felt hearing someone I thought was a friend call me a chink: I froze and experienced a rush of cold entering my body—it felt like Freddy had slapped me. He said these words not with venom but mocking glee—he was showing me and telling me that I was not going to win where he was concerned, not in this game of tag with our classmates and not in life, since I could so easily be reduced to a "chink" with just one word. Until this moment, I had never had a bad encounter with Freddy: as I said, I thought we were friends. My other clear memory of Freddy is having him sing Weird Al Yankovic's "Another One Rides the Bus" to me because our desks were across from one another, and Freddy liked to entertain me with silly skits and songs. I didn't know who Weird Al was at the time, so I thought that Freddy had brilliantly reinterpreted "Another One Bites the Dust," and I laughed until tears came out of my eyes. So when Freddy casually hurled this racial slur at me, I felt a keen embarrassment that I had so clearly misinterpreted our relationship and that I had been so easily reduced to a slur for Freddy, which also made me wonder about my other non-Asian classmates and whether I was just a chink to them as well—a nonhuman who could be summarily dismissed with a single racist word. It hurt then, and it still hurts now, not to be recognized for who I was then and am now: a fully enfranchised human. Racist slurs are weaponized against people, trying to trick them into believing that they are not fully enfranchised humans, that they do not have the same status or stature as the person hurling the epithet, that they are not deserving of dignity and respect, that they are less than.

The feeling of being "less than" is what so many Asians around the globe experienced and reexperienced during the COVID-19 pandemic. While many believe that anti-Asian racism erupted in March 2020, global anti-Asian racism has been around for centuries, particularly in the form of yellow peril xenophobia. In the months leading up to the March 2020 lockdowns that happened around the world, Professor Jason Oliver Chang at the University of Connecticut posted on Facebook in December 2019 about his concern with the virus emerging out of China and the inevitable backlash against Asians that would soon follow. Dr. Chang called on his network of Asian American Studies friends and colleagues to help him with proactively educating our various campuses and local communities about the history of anti-Asian xenophobia through creating an open-source "yellow peril" syllabus, which was filled with articles about anti-Asian racism, the history of yellow peril rhetoric in the US, and ways to combat the anti-Asian racism that reemerged during the COVID-19 pandemic, including refusing the narrative that this was a "Chinese" disease and falsely equating Chinese and Asian people with the disease.

Despite the best efforts of Dr. Chang and others to educate people about anti-Asian racism, between March 19, 2020, and December 31, 2021, the Stop AAPI Hate coalition documented 10,905 hate incidents against Asian American and/or Pacific Islander people who reported to the Stop AAPI Hate website the occurrences of hate that they or others had experienced.[2] In May 2020, Human Rights Watch released an article documenting the anti-Chinese and anti-Asian racism happening around the globe: in the United Kingdom, France, Italy, Spain, Brazil, Russia, India, Malaysia, Kenya, South Africa, and various regions of the Middle East. During the height of the global pandemic, I was president of the Association for Asian American Studies, which meant that—particularly after March 2021 and the murder of eight people, six of whom were Asian women, in what is widely referred to as the Atlanta Spa Shootings—I was constantly fielding requests from reporters wanting to know more about anti-Asian racism. Over the last three years, I have done roughly one hundred interviews, presentations, and workshops that engage in some manner with educating people about anti-Asian racism.[3] I have received numerous private messages through email, Twitter, and

Facebook from people, almost all of whom are Asian identified, asking me for resources about combatting anti-Asian racism in France, Australia, Spain, the UK, Mexico, and other regions outside of the US. While I did not have many resources to share with people at the time I was contacted, I am very proud to share this collection of essays on global anti-Asian racism because this is the volume so many people have been looking for.

I am honored to be curating and introducing these essays on global anti-Asian racism as part of the Asia Shorts series, particularly since as an Asian American Studies scholar, I am Asian Studies-adjacent rather than someone conversant in the field of Asian Studies.[4] As will be evident in the examples that I share below, I am relying on my expertise as a critical race studies scholar who has taught and researched on race and racism in the United States. However, what the world and I witnessed during the height of the COVID-19 pandemic was anti-Asian racism on a global scale—the intensity of which led to innumerable traumas, both physical (people have been killed and others brutally harmed) and psychological (verbal and emotional abuse leave traumatic scars as well, especially when Asian people carry the tension in their bodies, never knowing if they will encounter venomous attacks when walking down the street). I am grateful to the Association for Asian Studies and the editorial team of the Asia Shorts series for creating a space to discuss global anti-Asian racism, both in its current pandemic manifestation and in terms of the long reach of anti-Asian xenophobia in countries around the world.

I am all too aware that this is a daunting and possibly hubristic task—for any single editor to believe that she has the expertise to tackle a subject like global anti-Asian racism across time and space. Indeed, even trying to talk about "Asian" as a category is problematic because the understandings of the term vary depending on the nation you occupy. For example, Asians in Britain are largely understood to be South Asian, people from India, Pakistan, and Bangladesh, whereas East Asians, such as Chinese, Japanese, and Korean people in the UK, are referred to as "Oriental," a term that has been largely banished from US lexicons. Nonetheless, what the essays in this collection have in common is identifying bias, violence, discrimination, and prejudice that people from Asian nations have experienced, particularly when they are residing in countries outside of their ancestral Asian homeland. The lens that each author uses to talk about anti-Asian racism is particular to the Asian ethnicity that is experiencing discrimination and the country in which this bias takes place; it is necessarily contextualized by place and time as well as by the other present ethnic, racial, and religious groups that create the friction of anti-Asian racism. This makes talking about a single cause of anti-Asian racism impossible because it's overly simplistic to say that all anti-Asian racism boils down to white supremacy, especially when the prejudice that Asian immigrants have been faced with in Africa, South America, and other Asian nations may be the residue of white colonial forces but are definitely also deeply imbricated with specific national contexts and geopolitical forces that don't just devolve into white supremacy versus Asian inferiority. If there is an argument that this collection, as a whole, puts forth, it is that anti-Asian racism has occurred and is occurring on every continent, including Asia, and that there is a reality to global anti-Asian racism that can't be reduced to a matter of global politics, class inequities, religious bigotry, or ethnic nationalism. Anti-Asian racism can be internalized by Asian people themselves as well as externalized by non-Asians, weaponized to demean and delimit Asian people in the nations they have immigrated to or found themselves refugees within. To say clearly and forcefully that global anti-Asian racism is real—at a time when world leaders have engaged in age-old stereotypes of Chinese as rat-eaters and reduced Asians to an exterminable mass—is as good a case as any for having a volume that addresses the breadth and scope of global anti-Asian racism.[5]

It is also clear from the moment I shared the call for papers that many scholars have been reflecting on the capacious nature of global anti-Asian racism. I received such a larger number of abstracts after the original call went out that I could accept only a quarter of them. I wish I could have included so many more essays—ones that talk about being Pinoy/a/x, that discuss the ramifications of the Indo-Chinese War in Southeast Asia, or that engage with intersectional issues of religious bigotry (Islamophobia, anti-Sikhism), homophobia, transphobia, national origin, income, and education. There were personal essays detailing attacks experienced during the global pandemic by authors who were misidentified as Chinese or who were correctly identified by their Chinese heritage (though, of course, the violence and vitriol they experienced was not warranted, whether they were of Chinese descent or not). There were people doing research on Japanese Canadians, on the legacy of incarceration in Canada, and on the complexities of racism within Japan of other Asian people. There were so many brilliant abstracts, and I tried doing academic matchmaking by encouraging people to find a home for their essays or to partner up and lobby journals and other presses to publish their works.

I begin with what is not included because I am very aware of the many omissions in a volume tackling global anti-Asian racism. These essays are strong in and of themselves, and by being in conversation with one another in this volume, the sum is far greater than the separate parts. Yet no single book or set of essays can ever fully capture a topic as ominous and weighty as global anti-Asian racism. This work merely scratches a surface that I hope others will continue to probe and take up—and that, indeed, so many of us have taken up over the past decades. Certainly, this is not the first volume to introduce essays on the topic of global anti-Asian racism. It's just that this volume seems so very relevant, appearing when the memories of the fatal violence of anti-Asian racism are still with us and when the fatalities in the US are not a distant memory. Within a US context (which, as noted above, is the context I know best from both my personal location and my professional expertise), this collection is also particularly relevant because the anti-Asian racism that reemerged in March 2020 was so familiar to those of us who work in Asian American Studies; after all, we have studied and researched and taught the history of yellow peril sentiment and anti-Asian racism that has pervaded the lives of Asian immigrants and Asian Americans from the nineteenth to the twenty-first centuries.[6]

I wish there wasn't a need for this collection of essays. I would love nothing more than to have my area of academic expertise in critical race theory become obsolete and irrelevant to the concerns of contemporary society. But I write this introduction at a time when there are calls for bans on books and curriculum, both in US K–12 settings and at US colleges and universities.[7] Globally, there have been attacks on scholars for doing research in their areas of expertise, whether they are studying disinformation or critiquing Hindutva. In the US, there is legislation that prevents transgender youth from receiving gender affirming care and penalizes educators for giving students accurate information about LGBTQ+ issues. There are so many crises, worldwide, involving fascism, authoritarianism, toxic masculinity, and anti-intellectualism. How can one volume on the subject of global anti-Asian racism adequately address the forces of hate, intolerance, bigotry, and violence that are in our daily news cycles?

The answer, of course, is that no single work can ever comprehensively tackle the violence of fascism and hate, but we also can't not do something. As the essays that follow make clear, global anti-Asian racism is not a new subject; it has been around for centuries on every continent (including Asia), and it impacts both Asian and non-Asian people, though the effects of global anti-Asian racism are felt most profoundly and acutely by Asian people. This volume can perhaps affirm the experiences of people so that they feel less lonely, knowing that the bigotry and discrimination that Asian people in Turkey experience have roots in the anti-Chinese racism toward overseas Chinese in Mexico, which also connects with the present-day racism toward Chinese workers in Kenya and Ethiopia.

While there is no single root cause of global anti-Asian racism, much of the bias, discrimination, and violence that Asians around the world have suffered over the last two centuries can be traced back to yellow peril sentiments and rhetoric. Though the actual coining of the term "yellow peril" didn't happen until the late nineteenth century, the fear, hatred, and mistrust of Chinese that propelled the Page Act (1875) and Chinese Exclusion Act (1882) in the US—laws passed by Congress, which for the first time, named people from a specific nation (China) and marked them for exclusion—existed well before the phrase that defined such xenophobia.[8] But beyond hindering the ability of Chinese and other Asian people to enter the

US, yellow peril sentiment and rhetoric disseminated through racist propaganda in media outlets, which cemented the image of Chinese women as immoral and diseased prostitutes who were a bodily and moral threat to US society. Yellow peril sentiment and rhetoric also depicted Chinese men as effeminate, treacherous, and ratlike laborers who were taking jobs away from white men. The fear, anxiety, and anger that yellow peril sentiment fomented in US society can be traced to the lynchings of Chinese men at the hands of white mobs that proliferated in the US West throughout the late nineteenth and early twentieth centuries.[9] Anti-Chinese sentiment in the US quickly spread to other Asian ethnic groups as Japanese, Filipino/a/x, and Indian immigrants experienced discrimination and bias based on their ethnic origins. Most famously, two Supreme Court cases—*Ozawa v. US* (1922) and *Thind v. US* (1923)—were argued nine months apart and were settled in the same way: denying Asian immigrants, whether they were East or South Asian, the ability to naturalize as US citizens.[10] Yellow peril rhetoric inflamed white farmers in Watsonville, California, who grew angry and agitated when they saw Filipino farm laborers dancing with white women. Up to five hundred white men torched Filipino labor camps in Watsonville, setting off a chain reaction of anti-Filipino sentiment up the West Coast to Seattle, Washington.[11]

Yellow peril ideology most certainly contributed to the incarceration of 120,000 Japanese Americans during World War II. Though Executive Order 9066 never mentioned race or nationality—and only gave the US military the authority to restrict anyone, citizen or noncitizen, from the Western portion of the US—in effect, it targeted people of Japanese ancestry for removal, detention, and incarceration *en masse*. Italian and German men were imprisoned along with Japanese men, yet Italian and German women and children were never incarcerated in concentration camps the way that Japanese families were.[12] In the twenty-first century, yellow peril sentiment, along with Islamophobia, contributed to the wave of anti-Muslim, anti-Middle-Eastern, and anti-Arab violence around the world following the September 11 attacks on the World Trade Center and Pentagon. Balbir Singh Sodhi was the first casualty of yellow peril Islamophobia following September 11, 2001, murdered in Mesa, Arizona, by a white gunman who ranted in a bar that he wanted to kill as many "towelheads" as he could. Yellow peril Islamophobia was also the impetus for the mass killing of Sikh worshipers in Oak Creek, Wisconsin: six people were murdered in their gurdwara (Sikh temple) by a white shooter who wanted revenge for September 11.[13]

Yellow peril rhetoric fueled much of the anti-Asian violence during the COVID-19 pandemic, as around the world, people with East Asian features were targeted as "Chinese" (whether they were of Chinese ancestry or not) and blamed for the global pandemic. In 2020 and 2021, Asian people in France, Australia, Kenya, England, Canada, Germany, and other nations reported being harassed, attacked, and called "corona." In the US, researchers at San Francisco State University created a reporting portal, Stop AAPI Hate, to track the anti-Asian harassment being leveled at Asian Americans. Stories of Asian people being spat on, chased, yelled at, hit, kicked, and punched proliferated on social media, in local and national news outlets, within families, and among friends. A Chinese woman in Brooklyn had acid thrown on her. A Burmese family in Texas was stabbed.[14] A Japanese American man was chased in the parking lot of a Trader Joe's store in Boston, Massachusetts, by a white man who accused him of bringing COVID-19 into the country.[15] A Vietnamese American woman was spat at by a white woman and told to go back to where she came from.[16] The president of the United States referred to COVID-19 as the "China flu," the "Wuhan virus," and "Kung flu," fueling anti-Asian sentiment and yellow peril rhetoric.

The severity of the hostility and violence seen in videos that went viral of a woman being kicked repeatedly in New York City, and of Asian elders being punched in the face and beaten in Chinatowns across Oakland and San Francisco, added to a narrative of anti-Black brutality, since the attackers in many of these cases were Black. However, as researchers discovered from mining the data from news stories, police reports, and the Stop AAPI Hate website, the majority (73 percent) of the harassment and violence directed at Asian Americans was perpetuated by white men.[17] The anti-Black narrative that predominated in the wake of these videos and anti-Asian violent incidents also needs to be addressed head-on because there is a history of tension between Asian and Black people, both in the US and in Asia and Africa. I have written about this previously, as have other scholars.[18] The violence that some Asians experienced at the hands of some Black perpetrators must be condemned, but Black violence against Asians is not the main fuel of yellow peril sentiment. Instead, in the US, as it is in other white dominant nations, it's white supremacy that is the ideological driver of yellow peril and anti-Asian racism. As I have stated in a previous publication, though the perpetrator of violence against Asians may be Black, it is the underlying ideology of white supremacy that fuels anti-Asian harassment, discrimination, and bigotry.[19] The inherent belief in Asian inferiority to European superiority undergirds yellow peril sentiment and white supremacy, whether it occurs in the US, Turkey, Germany, Sweden, Mexico, or Brazil. And even in African nations such as Kenya, Uganda, South Africa, and Ethiopia, or even within Asian nations themselves, anti-Asian sentiment linked to yellow peril rhetoric that is rooted in white supremacy propels the discrimination against Asians in favor of Black nationalism, or the discrimination of specific Asian ethnic groups within Asian nations.

The essays in this Asia Shorts volume span centuries and continents, moving through time and space to talk about the various instantiations of global anti-

Asian racism. They are deliberately short essays (as the series title connotes) so that readers can potentially use them in the classroom or pick up and digest them without needing to be experts in a given field. These essays were selected because of the range of archives, locations, fields, time periods, and genres that each engages with. Some of the pieces are intensely personal and raw, intimately detailing firsthand experiences with anti-Asian racism, sometimes violently so. Others offer a more traditional academic focus, using historical and/or anthropological methods in their analyses of anti-Asian racism. And there are essays that can more accurately be described as art, works that employ visual elements and poetic language and structure. Together, these diverse essays speak to one another, creating a conversation about the constant of global anti-Asian racism across time and space, illustrating that the topic of global anti-Asian racism is both old and new and, sadly—since the essays engage with people from every continent except Antarctica—an ever-present social phenomenon for humans to grapple with.

The volume opens with Rahul K. Gairola's intensely personal ruminations on his firsthand encounters with violent anti-Asian racism. In "Yellow Peril, Brown Terror: The Global Virus of Anti-Asian Racism across Closed Borders," Gairola details the racism he has been subjected to by way of violent verbal harassment and physical attacks in Australia during the COVID-19 pandemic. Images of a carefree, sunshine-laden Australia are replaced by scenes of rampant racism and vitriol that Gairola, an Indian American scholar teaching at an Australian university, finds all too common, linked to a history of white British settler-colonialism and "mateship"—a form of Australian multiculturalism that presumes a common white British heritage and that ignores systemic racism and anti-Indigenous policies. Gairola ends his piece with a transcription of an interview he conducted with the head of an Asian Australia advocacy group, where the two discuss the role of the Asian Australia Alliance in documenting the anti-Asian racism rampant in Australia during the COVID-19 pandemic and the strategies for how Asian Australians and allies can work to end anti-Asian racism.

Sara Djahim's essay, "Don't Hate the Player. Between Essentialism and Resistance: Community Organizing against Anti-Asian Racism in Germany," charts the contemporary manifestation of anti-Asian racism during the COVID-19 pandemic by examining how people of Asian descent in Germany have organized and embraced the label "Asian German" in an effort at coalitional political organizing. Yet Djahim questions the efficacy of this label, pointing to the problematics of the term "Asian" (as noted above in this introduction) and wondering whether this nascent racial term created out of political organizing can be truly subversive if the government begins using it as a demographic marker. This, indeed, is what many activists of Asian descent in the US have debated about the category "Asian American" and how a term created out of radical student organizing can be an effective umbrella label if it is being used by the US government for census data collection and by people of Asian descent who want to dismantle race-based policies like affirmative action. By charting the use of "Asian German" during the COVID-19 pandemic, Djahim insightfully analyzes the complications of how "Asian German" is deployed and the debates swirling around its use by activists who want to combat anti-Asian racism in Germany, aware of the long history of white supremacy in that nation's not-so-distant past. While Djahim ponders who this term is for—who feels included and excluded from this new racial label—she closes on a moment of racial solidarity among three women of Asian descent from three different Asian nations who find themselves sharing a warm moment in Germany. Academic debates can also be illuminated through prosaic experiences of solidarity.

The theme of collective action and racial coalitional politics continues with the cowritten essay, "The Choice of Liberdade: Brazilian Facets of Anti-Asian Racism and the Activism's Response," by Érika Tiemi W. Fujii, Gabriel Akira, Maria Victória R. Ruy, and Mariana Mitiko Nomura, four members of a pan-Asian activist collective in Brazil, Coletivo Dinamene, who came together during the global pandemic, meeting for hours over Zoom to discuss not just anti-Asian racism but various intersectional oppressions in Brazilian society and the ways that they could speak and act to combat multiple forms of oppression. Their essay, in content and form, illustrates the power of collective action and racial collaboration. It details the complexities of identifying as Asian Brazilian and the power of Japanese Brazilians, in particular, to shape certain racial narratives, even as they are combatting a history of white supremacy and anti-Asian racism. As they see it, Asian Brazilians, specifically Japanese Brazilians, can either be aligned with whiteness or with anti-racist solidarity work, which entails denouncing anti-Black racism and settler-colonialism.

Richard Aidoo's essay, "The Political Economy of Anti-Asian Discrimination in Africa," is another contribution about anti-Asian racism in the Global South. As Asian nations have increasingly been doing business with African nations, the number of Asian immigrants to African countries has increased throughout the twentieth and twenty-first centuries. Alongside that labor and immigration history are moments of anti-Asian racism, most violently and distinctly the purging of Asian Ugandans (many of whom were South Asian) from Uganda by Idi Amin in the 1970s. More recently, Aidoo describes the impacts of COVID-19 and anti-Asian racism in Kenya and Ethiopia. Aidoo turns a political and economic lens on anti-Asian racism on the African continent, disentangling the postcolonial histories of various African nations and their relationship with Asian countries in the extraction of resources and the infrastructural labor that Asian bodies, both governmental and corporeal, have played in various African nations' economies.

As resentment grows of Asian countries, anti-Asian racism gets superimposed onto an anti-colonial discourse such that Asian Africans become a scapegoat for both political and economic African forces.

As readers approach the midpoint of the volume, they will discover Rivi Handler-Spitz's graphic narrative, "Savage Script: How Chinese Writing Became Barbaric." Though anti-Asian racism is predominantly understood as a phenomenon that happens outside of Asia, Handler-Spitz's graphic essay wonderfully and provocatively illustrates the ways that Chinese intellectuals and scholars were susceptible to anti-Asian racism and messages that equated Chinese characters with a provincial and brutish past in contrast to the European alphabet that Western intellectuals and scholars believed was a force of modernism and progress. Handler-Spitz's drawings don't just tell this story: they put readers inside the debate over Chinese characters, which became a debate about the character of China and its relationship with the West and the rest of the world. On a two-page spread, readers will encounter citations and images depicting contemporary Yale scholar Jing Tsu alongside Qing dynasty politicians and intellectuals like Tan Sitong and Liang Qichao—a literal illustration of how academic articles put scholars in conversation with one another across space and time. The images that Handler-Spitz uses to tell a story about how Chinese characters prevailed despite calls for modernization by twentieth-century Chinese reformers offer readers a stimulating visual essay that puts them into the action, as it were, and helps them see the ways in which cultural chauvinism and alphabetic supremacy are linked to anti-Asian racism, even within the context of Chinese modernity.

Xuening Kong's contribution, "Racialization from Home: China's Response to the Anti-Chinese Movement in Mexico, 1928–1937," describes the violence that Chinese immigrants in Mexico experienced in the early twentieth century. Kong's essay demonstrates the ways that the overseas Chinese in Mexico, and the racism they experienced, were recounted, in differing ways, depending on whether it was by Mexican reporters who saw the Chinese as undesirable or by Chinese journalists who wanted to emphasize the loyalty that Chinese immigrants had to the nascent nationalist government. Kong also dissects the different causes that Chinese nationalists and diplomats ascribed to the violence and racism that Chinese immigrants in Mexico experienced, showing the complications of how Chinese immigrants in Mexico were regarded and used for various political purposes by both Mexican and Chinese politicians.

Moving from early twentieth-century Mexico to early twenty-first-century Turkey, "The Politics of Anti-Asian Discourses in Turkey" by Irmak Yazici continues analyzing the role of foreign policy on the treatment of Asian immigrants. Yazici observes that given the small size of the Asian population in Turkey, the persistence of anti-Asian racism in Turkey derives from transborder issues related to not just racial or national identities but also to religious affiliations. Though anti-Asian racism, and specifically anti-Chinese racism, proliferated in Turkey during the COVID-19 pandemic, assaults on Chinese in Turkey predated the pandemic and have been driven by the policies toward and treatment of Uyghur Muslims, a large portion of whom are refugees from the Chinese state government's violent suppression of Uyghurs' rights in China. One of the largest Uyghur diasporas can be found in Turkey, and Turkey's reliance on foreign aid and relationships, including its relations with China, complicate the various anti-Asian/anti-Chinese attacks that occur. As Yazici notes throughout the essay, there is no "one-size-fits-all" approach to understanding the many moving parts and complex factors that drive anti-Chinese/anti-Asian racism in Turkey.

Kimberly D. McKee's essay, "The Anti-Asian Racism at Home: Reckoning with the Experiences of Adoptees from Asia," takes us from the realm of international diplomacy between nations to the diplomacy required among family members who are attempting to navigate issues of racism and white supremacy within the domestic sphere of a nuclear family. As an Asian American adult adopted into a white US family, McKee opens her essay by talking about the difficulties that she and other transracial adoptees grapple with when trying to talk about the racism they experienced as people of color in white families. Analyzing two documentaries that feature teen girls returning to their countries of origin—India in one case and China in the other—McKee thoughtfully analyzes the elisions and slippages of the teens' responses to encountering a society and culture they no longer recognize or remember. Noting the difficult place that the teens find themselves in—juggling complex notions of their identities and competing loyalties and the nascent recognition of the micro- and macro-racist aggressions coming from within their adoptive families—McKee concludes her essay with a call for compassion and sensitivity as well as political advocacy in the embrace of an Asian American identity.

Continuing with a gendered analysis of anti-Asian racism, Eileen Chung's essay, "Far-Flung Fetishization: Calling Asian Women to Globally Transcend Hypersexualization," provides both a scholar's analysis of the intersectional oppression that Asian women face due to racism and sexism and a personal reflection on how she, as an Asian American woman, has experienced toxic masculinity and racism not just in the US but also in Cuba and Greece. The hypersexualization of Asian women knows no borders, just like anti-Asian racism. It is a global phenomenon that Asian women have had to navigate across the world, and as the Atlanta spa attacks illustrate, this hypersexualization, combined with discourses of racism and toxic masculinity, has led to fatal consequences for Asian women. Chung ends her essay by sharing the wisdom of her Asian American mother in teaching her not just how to stay alive but how to thrive in the midst of these oppressive forces.

The volume closes with Jennifer Hayashida's poetic musings and reflections in "Translating *Guling*: Technologies of Language, Race, and Resistance in Sweden." Hayashida's work may best be described as a meditation on language, identity, and race, one deeply indebted to the author's poetic voice and sensibilities as much as it is to her rigorous research in Asian American literary and cultural studies. The personal details of Hayashida's life—growing up as the daughter of a Japanese American father from Honolulu, Hawai'i, and a white Swedish mother from Vaxholm, Sweden—are intertwined with historical artifacts from Sweden's past, such as the Swedish Society for Racial Hygiene, whose research was used by Nazis as a justification for the Final Solution. Hayashida's ruminations pivot on her work as a translator as well as the various translations she has had to perform, personally, as a mixed-race woman comfortable with both Swedish and English. Hayashida has lived in and between both countries, yet she is trying to map out where "Asian America" can be found and how anti-Asian racism in Sweden during the pandemic allowed her to visit the anti-Asian racism that predates COVID-19, a space she has had to navigate throughout her life in both Sweden and the US.

I am enormously proud to be the editor of this volume and to share the work of these talented scholars. This is the volume I wished I had access to when I was fielding email messages from people looking for stories and resources about anti-Asian racism outside of the US context. The essays are each brave in their own way, but in particular, the scholars who identify as Asian and who share their personal experiences with anti-Asian racism before and during the global pandemic are a testament to the ways that the personal is political and that the political is personal. Our investments in scholarly research, particularly in research that interrogates power, take on an intimate cast when we find ourselves the actual subjects that we are studying—the victims of racist violence and the survivors of intersectional oppression. Tackling a topic like global anti-Asian racism when one identifies as Asian means revisiting scenes of trauma—for ourselves, our families, and our immigrant and refugee ancestors. None of this is easy or simple—to make ourselves vulnerable and reveal our pain. Yet the personal stories and anecdotes that our contributors have shared, whether they have happened to themselves or others, strengthen the ultimate message of this volume. Yes, there is global anti-Asian racism. But there is also global anti-racism resistance and resilience. There is violence, but there is also beauty and hope—not simplistic hope but one borne out of a belief that we are our ancestors' wildest dream. That in the work that we need to do to fight the forces of fascism and oppression, we must also find time for joy and beauty and the power of words. So I end this introduction with a call to you, dear reader, to find the hope amidst the darkness in these essays and to call forth your inner anti-racism advocate as we all work to end global anti-Asian racism.

Notes

1 This is not the actual name of my former classmate.

2 Stop AAPI Hate released a national report in March 2022 on its website documenting the hate incidents that it received from March 19, 2020, through December 31, 2021; the report can be found at https://stopaapihate.org/2022/03/04/national-report-through-december-31-2021/.

3 One such piece that I wrote following the Atlanta spa shootings, "To Be an Asian Woman in America" on CNN, is the most widely read piece I will have ever written. It has also cemented my commitment to public-facing writing.

4 I should share that this publication isn't my first foray into writing for an Asian Studies venue. I was very proud to be invited to write a piece in July 2020 connecting anti-Asian racism and anti-Black racism by the editor of *Japan Forum*, which resulted in my essay, "Anti-Asian Racism, Black Lives Matter, and COVID-19."

5 As reported in the Human Rights Watch article cited previously, the governor of the Veneto area of Italy said that Italians would do a better job than the Chinese in handling the novel coronavirus because of the attention to hygiene that Italy is known for, "whereas we have all seen the Chinese eating mice alive." For more, see the Human Rights Watch article "COVID-19 Fueling Anti-Asian Racism and Xenophobia Worldwide."

6 The *Journal of Asian American Studies* and *Amerasia Journal* are two US-based journals that have included essays, throughout the decades, that engage with anti-Asian racism.

7 The organization PEN America has been actively tracking various book bans in the United States. In September 2002, they released a report, "Banned in the USA: The Growing Movement to Censor Books in Schools": https://pen.org/report/banned-usa-growing-movement-to-censor-books-in-schools/.

8 A good resource to understand the intersections of yellow peril rhetoric, US immigration policy, and shifting attitudes toward Asian Americans is Madeline Hsu's *The Good Immigrants: How the Yellow Peril Became the Model Minority*.

9 For an excellent accounting of the lynching of Chinese in the US, see Jean Pfaelzer's *Driven Out: The Forgotten War against Chinese Americans*.

10 Ian Haney Lopez's *White by Law* details the cases of Ozawa and Thind.

11 To learn more about the Asian American historical cases referenced in this paragraph and the one that follows, see Erika Lee's *The Making of Asian America* and Catherine Choy's *Asian American Histories of the United States*.

12 For more on the specifics surrounding the incarceration of Japanese Americans during World War II, see Greg Robinson's *A Tragedy of Democracy: Japanese Confinement in North America*.

13 Valarie Kaur chronicles the specific anti-Sikh/anti-South Asian/anti-Muslim sentiments that followed 9/11 in *See No Stranger: A Memoir and Manifesto of Revolutionary Love*.

14 In the *Japan Forum* essay "Anti-Asian Racism, Black Lives Matter, and COVID-19," I provide sources for the anti-Asian racist attacks detailed in this paragraph and the one that follows.

[15] This anecdote was shared by my friend Doug Iishi, and it occurred in June 2020 in Boston, Massachusetts.

[16] Hannah Rose recounts being spat on in a Colorado Public Radio interview, "Anti-Asian Hatred Has a Long History in the US and in Colorado."

[17] A 2021 partnership between the University of Michigan and Stop AAPI Hate resulted in a report, "Virulent Hate: Anti-Asian Hate and Resistance during COVID-19," in which they show that the majority of perpetrators of anti-Asian hate were white men.

[18] Nitasha Sharma is a leading scholar who examines Black and Asian American communities and addresses anti-Black racism in Asian American spaces. She is also one of the coeditors of an Asia Shorts volume, *Who Is the Asianist? The Politics of Representation in Asian Studies*, which addresses the relationship between the Black Lives Matter movement, Black Studies, and Asian Studies.

[19] See "White Supremacy Is the Root of All Race-Related Violence in the US."

Bibliography

Bridges, Will, Nitasha Tamar Sharma, and Marvin D. Sterling. *Who Is the Asianist? The Politics of Representation in Asian Studies*. Ann Arbor: Association for Asian Studies, 2022.

Chang, Jason Oliver. "Treating Yellow Peril: Resources to Address Coronavirus Racism." Google Doc. Accessed July 10, 2023.

Choy, Catherine. *Asian American Histories of the United States*. Boston: Beacon Press, 2022.

Friedman, Jonathan, and Nadine Farid Johnson. "Banned in the USA: The Growing Movement to Censor Books in Schools." PEN America, September 2022, https://pen.org/report/banned-usa-growing-movement-to-censor-books-in-schools/.

Ho, Jennifer. "Anti-Asian Racism and COVID-19." Last modified July 16, 2020, https://www.colorado.edu/asmagazine/2020/04/08/anti-asian-racism-and-covid-19.

———. "Anti-Asian Racism, Black Lives Matter, and COVID-19." *Japan Forum* 33, no. 1 (Fall 2020), 148–159.

———. "To Be an Asian Woman in America." CNN Opinion, March 17, 2021, https://www.cnn.com/2021/03/17/opinions/to-be-an-asian-woman-in-america-ho/index.html.

———. "White Supremacy Is the Root of All Race-Related Violence in the US," *The Conversation*, April 8, 2021, https://theconversation.com/white-supremacy-is-the-root-of-all-race-related-violence-in-the-us-157566.

Hsu, Madeline. *The Good Immigrants: How the Yellow Peril Became the Model Minority*. Princeton: Princeton University Press, 2015.

Human Rights Watch. 2020. "COVID-19 Fueling Anti-Asian Racism and Xenophobia Worldwide." Accessed October 20, 2023, https://www.hrw.org/news/2020/05/12/covid-19-fueling-anti-asian-racism-and-xenophobia-worldwide.

Kaur, Valarie. *See No Stranger: A Memoir and Manifesto of Revolutionary Love*. London: Oneworld, 2021.

Lee, Erika. *The Making of Asian America* (edition with COVID-19 postscript). New York: Simon & Schuster, 2021.

Lopez, Ian Haney. White by Law: *The Legal Construction of Race* (Tenth Anniversary edition). New York: New York University Press, 2006.

"National Report (through December 31, 2021)." Stop AAPI Hate. Accessed October 20, 2023. https://stopaapihate.org/wp-content/uploads/2022/03/22-SAH-NationalReport-3.1.22-v9.pdf.

Pfaelzer, Jean. *Driven Out: The Forgotten War against Chinese Americans.* Berkeley: University of California Press, 2008.

Robinson, Greg. *A Tragedy of Democracy: Japanese Confinement in North America.* New York: Columbia University Press, 2009.

Sharma, Nitasha Tamar. *Hip Hop Desis: South Asian Americans, Blackness, and a Global Race Consciousness.* Durham: Duke University Press, 2010.

———. *Hawai'i Is My Haven: Race and Indigeneity in the Black Pacific.* Durham: Duke University Press, 2021.

"Virulent Hate: Anti-Asian Hate & Resistance During COVID-19." University of Michigan. Accessed July 10, 2023. https://virulenthate.org/.

Warner, Ryan, and Carl Bilek. "Anti-Asian Hatred Has a Long History in the US and in Colorado." Colorado Public Radio, March 19, 2021, https://www.cpr.org/2021/03/19/anti-asian-hatred-has-a-long-history-in-the-u-s-and-in-colorado/.

1

Yellow Peril, Brown Terror

The Global Virus of Anti-Asian Racism across Closed Borders

Rahul K. Gairola

Lingering between Life and Death

On September 24, 2022, I was almost killed when a Caucasian Australian male whom I had never before seen or met demanded "f*ck off back to your own country" and then viciously "king hit/coward punched" me. He did so immediately after mocking my speech with a faux "Indian" accent although I clearly speak with an East Coast American accent. It is here painfully evident that his xenophobic mockery referenced my Brown skin, which signifies the Indian identity of which I am deeply proud. Infamous throughout Australia for killing strangers, a "king hit" or "coward punch" is academically defined as "when a single blow to the head causes a victim to fall to the ground unconscious, either from the punch itself or the impact between the head and ground. This can result in fatal skull fractures and subdural hematomas."[1]

When, splayed on the ground, I finally opened my eyes, a ring of concerned faces peering down at me advised, "Blink if you can hear me," while distant voices asked, "Is he alive?" At that moment, I too was unsure exactly where I was—alive, dead, or transitioning within an interstitial purgatory. With respect to my Hindu and Buddhist upbringings, I questioned whether I had earned this near-death experience due to my sinful karma from a past life: what had I previously done that someone whom I have never before met would punch me so hard that I could die? In retrospect, this was not just a terrifyingly surreal experience for me, but it also traumatized a swath of shocked onlookers including two colleagues who were circumstantially present. Although this attack is by no means the only racist experience I have had in Australia or elsewhere, it is the only one in which I have come closest to experiencing what a police constable called "attempted murder."

After a thorough CAT scan revealed no brain damage, internal bleeding, and/or cranial fluid leakage, the surgeon pulled a chair to my hospital bed, sat down, and gravely locked his eyes onto mine. "You dodged a bullet, son," he said. "It's a miracle that you're not in a coma, brain-dead, or worse." He repeated this before advising that I would require surgery on the right side of my face or else be permanently disfigured; then he left the room. Although my brain is not damaged, I am damaged in other ways. His refrain is seared into my mind for the balance of this lifetime. The edgy panic that strikes my heart when a glass shatters or a loud sound resonates in my vicinity will likely remain with me for many years. This residual trauma ripples throughout my soul like karmic shock waves. To date, the perpetrator has not been caught and the police case, like my previously optimistic sense of justice, is closed.

I open with this unsettling account because it has viscerally transformed my life since it is simultaneously, yet regrettably, endemic to global anti-Asian racism. It has compelled me to more honestly integrate the scholarly abstractions of which I often write into experiences that I, and many other Asians and Asian diasporas, routinely encounter worldwide. For many folks of Asian ancestry, experiences of explicit and covert racism constitute an anticipated itinerary that we often rationalize as the price immigrants to Australia, the US, the UK, Canada, and other post-colonial countries must pay. We do so, however, while often forgetting or ignoring the fact that these countries, and other white, settler colonies, are predicated on manifest destiny fantasies that surreptitiously interweave racism, classism, xenophobia, queerphobia, and nationalism. These fantasies sprout from profitable exclusionary praxes including slavery, colonialism, indentured servitude, eugenics, Jim Crow laws, apartheid, redlining, voter disenfranchisement, border laws, and other exclusionary measures.

Still, the current historical moment of pandemic presents yet another woeful challenge. In Jennifer Ho's words, "The fact that the COVID-19 virus doesn't discriminate hasn't prevented humans from acts of extreme violence. . . . The racism that Asian Americans in the US and Asian people around the globe are experiencing right now is real and acute in ways that hasn't felt real and acute for decades."[2] Ho rightly observes that the coronavirus pandemic, including its mutations, has been characterized as an "Asian disease" by bigots around the globe, the most infamous of whom is most likely Donald Trump. Robin Kurilla notes that between March 13 and September 15, 2020, Trump used the terms "China flu, China plague, China virus, Chinese plague, Chinese flu, Chinese virus, Wuhan virus, and Kung flu" in a total of "38 speeches from Trump's election campaign or rallies, 28 talks at presidential events or meetings, 47 interviews, 37 press conferences, 35 tweets and seven re-tweets as well as selected news media responses."[3]

Here, it is evident that Trump rehearses the casualized trope of characterizing Asians as disease-carrying agents whose Chinese nationality is typologically identifiable by racist stereotypes. As formidably demonstrated by Nayan Shah, this is a nineteenth-century discourse wherein American public health officials alleged that Chinese migrants were unhygienic, unsanitary, and disease-ridden.[4] As such, and as I have elsewhere argued in reference to an anti-Chinese flyer posted on the streets of Brooklyn, New York City, "people from Asia have been targeted at this [historical] juncture in what appears to be anti-Chinese jingoism that alarmingly predicts danger to home, business, neighborhood, and community at the local levels. It [the flyer] is designed to stoke fears of the 'yellow peril' and encourage social and physical exile and violence; it is intended to trigger fear and trauma in the hearts of those who look different, 'Asian.'"[5]

The look of the diasporic Chinese "other," that is, is intimately braided into justified exclusion from national belonging based on invisible pathogens that surge throughout the "Asian" bloodstream. Thus, as I argued in my second book, such contemporary nation-states constitute and mold "home" into a realm of exclusion rather than inclusion. In other words, "the state as the 'homeland' of its citizens wields sweeping power within its borders through inclusionary discourses that can only function in and through the recognitions and exclusions of its others, or those deemed exterior to the nation-state and its interests, especially in the historical and ideological context of Anglo-American neoliberal capitalism."[6] When I initially composed these words, I could hardly fathom that we would face a nightmarish global pandemic merely a few years later or that a stranger would almost kill me. COVID-19 has exacerbated the ways in which bigots render Asian bodies "homeless" in brutal acts historically buttressed by settler colonialist nations that normalize white privilege—and thus white supremacy—while consolidating domestic capital to the benefit of racist, heteronormative nationalism.

The Historical Context of COVID-19 in Australia

In Australia, this is casualized to dizzying heights that compel Asian diasporas to gaslight ourselves into a peculiar modality of self-doubt that I have never before witnessed. At some levels, it is a uniquely racialized mixture of "mateship" and toxic hetero-masculinity that is highly discernable through non-white skin and "foreign" accents. To examine this at a deeper level, we must briefly delve into the contemporary context of Western Australia and Australia's federation as a penal colony of the British Empire. On April 5, 2020, Western Australia sealed its border to domestic and international visitors in what eventually proved to be, in the era of COVID-19, the longest international and domestic border closure in the world. "Come home now" was the ominous message delivered by federal border officials to all citizens and permanent residents of Australia as Western Australia sealed its borders with other countries, states, and even intrastate regions.

While this severe curtailing of movement and interaction across the country was legislated in the interest of public safety and national security, one of its macabre effects was a spike in the number of anti-Asian incidents. This brings me to yet another incident that I encountered in July 2021: As I awaited a bus to go to my office, a visibly disturbed, likely intoxicated white man accosted me and began screaming that I was "a terrorist c*nt." Although I put my headphones on and quickly tried to walk away, he ran up behind me and pushed me over into some chairs and tables outside of a café.[7] He continued abusing me, eventually claiming that he had a knife and was going to stab me to death. This incident was especially jarring because at least fifteen bystanders witnessed it but chose to say and do nothing. Rather, it was another local friend-colleague whom I called who came to my defense despite the arrival of police a while later. Given that even the most well-intentioned white folks may struggle to understand the realities of non-white people, I was fortunate that my account could not be disputed—because there were multiple *white* witnesses who corroborated what had occurred. I shudder to think if I had been alone when this man marked me as a Brown "terrorist c*nt" without cause.

In the words of Sarah Maddison, "Even as Australian society has become increasingly multicultural and ethnically diverse, whiteness, and its alignment with Britishness, has remained a 'treasured quality' for settler Australians."[8] In contrast, policies and popular accounts have historically depicted Asians as deceitful, unhygienic nuisances. The willful transposition of the threat of "disease"—and thus biohazard liability—posed by Yellow Asian bodies, to Brown Asian bodies catalyzing mass murder as on September 11, 2001, in New York City links differing Asian groups through a taxonomy of "national security threat." Indeed, "yellow peril" rhetoric stoked by the global pandemic harkens back to familiar depictions of the dangerous "Oriental."[9] As Jennifer Ho historically notes in her Introduction to this volume, "yellow peril sentiment and rhetoric disseminated through racist propaganda in media outlets" portrayed Chinese women as "immoral and diseased prostitutes" while the same discourse depicted Chinese men as "effeminate, treacherous, and ratlike laborers who were taking jobs away from white men" (Ho 2024, 5–6).

Figure 1.1: Anti-immigration cartoon with Victoria urging the Australian federation to rid itself of the "Chinese pest." *Melbourne Punch*, May 1888.

A brief retrospective of Australia's colonialist history illuminates the violence that I have encountered as per Antonio Gramsci's contention that history deposits within us an infinity of traces sans inventory—that is, that history shapes us in unmapped discourses which we must painstakingly excavate.[10] To make sense—if it is even possible—of these anti-Asian incidents in the context of COVID-19, I would cite the British colonization of Australia and its 1901 federation. Unlike actively resistant colonies like India, the British Crown granted federation to Australia and other white supremacist, settler colonies, including Canada and South Africa. Australia's break from the British Empire, despite its ongoing affiliation with the Commonwealth as a constitutional monarchy, is predicated on its reprehensible "White Australia" policy. Governmental officials enacted the White Australia Policy of 1901 to prevent Asian, especially Chinese, immigration onto the continent. The Sinophobia of the time is evident in caricatures of the era that circulated and cemented in Australians' imaginaries a devious, yellow peril, as in the political cartoon in figure 1.1 above.[11]

In this image, the colonies of Victoria, Tasmania, Queensland, New South Wales, and South Australia deploy "Federation" as a fulcrum to pry away "the Chinese Pest" from the shores of the continent. The visual juxtaposition of the milky skin and flowing dresses of these colonies personified as brave women assailed by a bodiless, buck-toothed, slanty-eyed invader requires little to fuel the racist imagination. This sophisticated media caricature engages intersectional bigotry that combines ethnic typologies, dark skin color, anti-male sexism, and a smutty gaze. Indeed, the high forehead, stringy hair, and lascivious gaze of "the Chinese pest" goads viewers into racialized nationalism that warrants common-sense Sinophobia. Such propaganda powerfully articulates the nationalized Sinophobia embedded in the very constitution of Australia as a federation.

Federation from the British Crown was thus racially predicated on whom to exclude just as it would be with Indigenous Australians, who endured grim genocide while being regarded as subhuman, and who, in October 2023, were overwhelmingly denied a Voice to Parliament by Australian voters. Clearly, for many descendants and beneficiaries of the Crown's diasporic presence in Australia, neither Black, Yellow, or Brown lives have mattered ... except perhaps to remedy postpandemic labor shortages and promote neoliberal and transnational capitalism. Indeed, global devastation can be, as 9/11 showed us, quite profitable. While Asians have since been invited into the land down under through the rhetoric of "diversity" and "multiculturalism," we nonetheless routinely face casual racism that is arguably networked throughout "Aussie mateship" like a subterranean, rhizomatic maze.

Have Asian Australians' cultural and economic contributions stymied widespread, casual racism here? The recent backlash against Opera Australia's 2023 production of *Miss Saigon* as a spectacle of racist, white valorization suggests otherwise on the Sydney and global stages.[12] This debacle merely reflects the startling reality that the Union Jack, the national flag of the UK, is indelibly stitched into Australia's national flag in the latter's upper left hoist quarter. Thus, the historical caricature of East Asians as national security threats to Australia and its nationalist identification with Britannia persists, only intensifying with the global onslaught of COVID-19. In his compelling observation of how contemporary times are manacled to the past, Jon Stratton writes:

> With its shaping in nineteenth-century racial ideologies, the culture that we call "Australian" leads members of that culture to have a range of taken-for-granted assumptions and expectations to differentiate between groupings of people. It is these shared assumptions and expectations that produce the practice of everyday racism. The individuals involved may well claim that they are non-racist, or even anti-racist . . . in Australia everyday racism permeates the dominant institutional order and the social relations of everyday life because race and racialised preferences are core structuring mechanisms of Australian culture.[13]

It is a bittersweet irony that multicultural "mateship" is lauded across the continent along with this nation's unofficial soundtrack: The Seekers' 1987 folk song "We Are Australian." "We are Australian," I suppose, while fervent identification with the British Empire, obsession with the royal family, ongoing rejection and exlusion of Indigenous Australians, and widespread stereotypes of Asians as disease-carriers forfeit our claims to inclusion. In The Seekers' lyrics, it is dubious who the imagined community of "we" is exactly given the rampant racist violence experienced by Asians, other immigrants, Indigenous Australians, and people of color.[14] This is, for many Aussies, their own historical "inventory," proudly linked to a form of subjugation that initially shaped this continent as a British penal colony characterized by "criminality."

But this is not *my* historical inventory or lived experience of Australia. My chronology of how anti-Asian racism flourishes here in the era of COVID-19 follows a familiar pattern of exclusionary practices based on what Etienne Balibar succinctly calls "fictive ethnicity."[15] For Balibar, "fictive ethnicity" is "the community instituted by the nation-state. . . . No nation possesses an ethnic base naturally, but as social formations are nationalized, the populations included within them, divided up among them or dominated by them, are ethnicized, that is, represented in the past or in the future as if they formed a natural community, possessing of itself an identity of origins, culture, and interests which transcend individuals and social conditions."[16] This is precisely, in my view, the problematic ideology instilled in the lyrics of the song by The Seekers.

In contradistinction, my historical inventory of White Australia today includes demonstrated behaviors that often cascade in the following order: (1) *Distance* oneself from the victim politely, sometimes through the rationale of not wanting to "get involved"; (2) *Ignore* racism—say nothing or look the other way; (3) *Frame* racism as "humor," wherein the victim is unable to "take a joke, mate" and is thus prompted to gaslight their own cultural awareness; (4) *Deny* that racism persists in Australia by pointing to "America" (the United States) or other places; (5) *Deflect* the conversation in another form of gaslighting that I have elsewhere called "gas-whiting" to signify racialized psychological manipulation; (6) *Silence* the victim by denying their experience, suggesting instead that they are loud, disrespectful, unprofessional, insubordinate, etc. (i.e., tone policing); (7) *Invoke* "reverse racism," wherein the victim is "in fact, racist" or "anti-Australian" and thus ungrateful to be here and should "go back home"; and (8) *Exclude*, socially ostracize, the victim through silence, gossip, homological tribalism, and other modes of punitive othering mobilized to publicly and privately shame them and/or encourage gang bullying/mobbing and other forms of existential violence that, again, default to "gas-whiting."

This list is by no means exhaustive, but these are the overarching trends that I, as a material witness, have personally experienced and observed with profound pain and disappointment. This is *my* Australia as experienced through its anti-Asian racism over the years and throughout the era of COVID-19. Balibar continues:

> Fictive ethnicity is not purely and simply identical with the ideal nation which is the object of patriotism, but is not indispensable to it, for without it the nation would appear precisely only as an idea or an arbitrary abstraction: patriotism's appeal would be addressed to no one. It is fictive ethnicity which makes it possible for the expression of a preexisting unity to be seen in the state and continually to measure the state against its 'historic mission' in the service of the nation.[17]

This is precisely why my historical inventory combines neocolonial and nationalist ideologies with action words that resist abstraction and, as such, recognize accountable actors who commit racist, xenophobic, anti-Asian acts on a regular basis in all walks of life. That is, I call out in cascading order the negating actions of some Australians who watch and at times engage in exclusionary strategies in contrast to white allies. To be clear, I here observe the trend but do not intend to indict all Aussies.

In what follows, I interview Erin Wen Ai Chew, who spearheads the Asian Australian Alliance, an Asian Australian advocacy group that has compiled a record of Australian anti-Asian racism in the wake of the global COVID-19 pandemic.

Brief Q&A with Erin Wen Ai Chew

What is the main goal of the Asian Australian Alliance (AAA) that you lead, and what have you found with respect to anti-Asian racism in Australia?

AAA is an advocacy group/network and platform that aims to amplify the voices and issues which impact Asian Australians and Asians. Our positions are generally progressive, and we do not side with any political party or philosophy and stay nonpartisan. Our projects are outcomes-driven, as we want to see results and not just a talk fest.

In terms of anti-Asian racism in Australia, the issue is generally always swept under the carpet and is seen as an "American" problem. Though what COVID-19 has unequivocally demonstrated is that racism is, and continues to be, a major issue across Australia. Since its launch in 2020, our COVID-19 Racism Incident Report survey has recorded around six hundred COVID-19-related racist incidents. We must remember, however, that COVID-19 is not the *cause* of racism against Asians in Australia but rather a *symptom* of the bigger problem of racism against Asians in Australia. Whereas such racism has been violent and traumatic for the community, it is also considered "casual racism" and constitutes only one part of the anti-Asian racism our community faces in Australia. Systematic and institutional racism is another major issue, wherein Asians in Australia are hardly visible in areas of corporate and political leadership and holding important positions in the media. Where are we on hiring committees? The unconscious or conscious bias plays into this and is all part of anti-Asian racism.

How has the COVID-19 global pandemic exacerbated pre-existing anti-Asian racism in Australia?

I think I answered part of this in the first question. But elaborating on what I mentioned earlier, the global pandemic has exacerbated pre-existing anti-Asian racism in Australia as it has normalized it. People who hold racist and/or ignorant views in Australia feel more emboldened to be racist toward Asians as the tabloid media and politics (both domestic and global) have given the green light to use terms such as "China flu," etc. It is also, ironically, a good reminder that the issue of anti-Asian racism in Australia remains a major issue and can thus be tracked throughout the past century and beyond Australia.

Could you talk a little about the recent assault of Danny Lim, a senior Asian Australian, at the hands of New South Wales (NSW) police officers?

The incident with Danny Lim occurred in November 2022 when he was one-man protesting near, ironically, the Queen Victoria Building in Sydney City wearing a sign that told people to smile and also had the word "CVNT" [sic] on it. The police appeared and when they tried to arrest him, Danny resisted as anyone who did not commit any crime would do. In that scenario, they violently manhandled him.

We can't ignore the big elephant in the room and must call it out as racial profiling/racism. Danny Lim is an Asian Australian man, and being Asian, he is subjected to certain stereotypes and prejudices—it behooves us to call it as it is. Danny is not a big guy, and he is seventy-eight years old. He poses no threat to anyone and was just exercising his right to peacefully protest. Even if he refused to move from his location, the actions of the police officers were violently excessive. They treated him worse than an animal.

Before both NSW officers brutally forced his arms behind his body and took him down, he pleaded with them while informing them that he has PTSD—and yet they ignored him, which exacerbated his existing trauma. Are NSW police officers not trained on understanding issues around mental health? Do they not have empathy and compassion for those whom they are employed to protect? Would things have gone differently if Danny was a white male? The two NSW police officers who violently and brutally manhandled him in an attempted arrest should be dismissed by the force as they are not serving to protect, but have instead caused trauma and injury to an elderly man.

Finally, this is one of many examples of the prejudices and discrimination that BIPOC (Black and Indigenous People of Color) and CALD (Culturally and Linguistically Diverse) peoples routinely face from the police. Indeed, this example is akin to the discrimination against Indigenous Australians who are incarcerated in Aussie jails or are violently manhandled by the police. It is time to get rid of these prejudices and clean up the bad collateral in the police force—not just in Australia, but also in Canada, the US, and other settler colonialist countries founded upon the British Empire's white supremacy.

In what ways are other oppressed groups complicit in anti-Asian racism in and beyond Australia?

This is an interesting question. I think to answer this, it must be said that the Australian and Western media are to blame. The negative notions and stereotypes of Asians in entertainment over the past century have presented Asian men as awkward, asexual, and/or evil people, or the butt of the joke whereby only a "white savior" can be the hero and save the world. Thus, sadly, and as is well-documented, it is white *women* who quite often become the catalysts of vicious violence against Asian men. Popular media, in contrast, routinely represents Asian women as sex objects who are dependent on the white savior to save them, so white men often see them (Asian women) as lascivious sexmongers.

These negative stereotypes have been normalized for a very long time, with many societies viewing Asians as easy targets. Whether you are white or non-white and of other oppressed groups, these stereotypes remain in societies' minds and, hence, Asians are seen as easy targets for racial abuse, robbery, and physical violence. This is not to suggest that Asian communities are devoid of racism because they too are complicit in racism against other oppressed groups for the same reasons just mentioned by replacing "Asian" stereotypes with other oppressed groups. Anti-Black and negative stereotypes about First Nations/ Indigenous Australians evince that Asians and other non-Asian communities also harbor racial biases.

But to your point, for Asians, the negative stereotypes are what have acutely caused ignorance among other oppressed groups like, for example, South Americans or members of the LGBTQIA+ community. The model-minority myth is also something which has played to a disadvantage to Asians wherein we are perceived as wealthy, comfortable, and well-to-do. We thus will not identify or voice our concerns. So where the intention of model minority narrates the story of Asian migration, it also tells other groups and communities that Asians are rich and easy targets for attacks, etc.

If you are a beneficiary of white privilege and witness an anti-Asian, racist incident, what is the best way to serve as an ally in that moment?

Those who are beneficiaries of white privilege can carefully deploy bystander intervention strategies by interceding in acts of anti-Asian hate when it is safe to do so. Yelling out "Stop!" or calling out racism when it is witnessed are good and responsible paths of action. Checking on victims and asking whether they are okay goes a long way.

Also, in a general sense, they should call out racism when they view it on the news and online on their social media. They can serve as allies by educating their families, friends, and networks that racism is wrong, and this is vital from a local, grassroots lens. They can support efforts by Asian groups on campaigns on racism and continually educate, perhaps even challenge, themselves on the issue by reading about or asking those who experience it or who work in the area. Also, do not doubtfully question or talk over Asians when we are sharing our experiences—instead, learn to listen. In other words, avoid "whitesplaining" racism or, even worse, interpreting the victim's account as a personal criticism or attack.

Do you have any recommended survival strategies for Asian diasporas living in Australia who face casual and covert anti-Asian racism on a regular basis?

- Talk about it over social media or to their own social networks, whether it be family and/or friends. Racism is a traumatic experience no matter the severity, and sharing with others can help.

- Report it to surveys like what the Asian Australian Alliance has open or to any of the state anti-racism regulatory bodies or the Human Rights Commission. Even though a solution may not present itself, reporting adds and contributes to the data. This goes the same for reporting it to the police.

- Seek mental health help if required because of the traumatic nature of racism.

Conclusion: Compassionate Resistance as Pro-Asian Healing

Given the traumatic extremes of my opening and two other reported attacks (there have been more beyond the reported three incidents) that I have endured in Australia as an Indian (ancestry) American (nationality) Australian (residency), this contribution's prose traverses genres to blend two Asian voices together. It enfolds theoretical, academic writing with my personal, ethnographic experiences, and tackles the often unbelievable topic of anti-Asian bigotry in the era of COVID-19 by deploying these varying genres to the service of my account of "global anti-Asian racism." Coward punches, herein, can be understood as racist microaggressions that extend the physical and epistemic violence of empire and the Australian federation upon the bodies of Asian and Black diasporas, as well as Indigenous Australians.

Combined with nostalgia for the British Empire and colonialist symbolism that has exploded throughout media with the passing of Queen Elizabeth II and the accession of King Charles III, a particularly toxic "state of acceptance" has emerged from the "state of exception" forged by this continent's bigoted history and, more recently, sealed borders.[18] In Jennifer Ho's words, the complexity of anti-Asian racism compels us to uncomfortably acquiesce that any monolithic understanding of it is reductive "especially when the prejudice that Asian immigrants have been faced with in Africa, South America, and other Asian nations may be the residue of white colonial forces but are definitely also deeply imbricated with specific national contexts and geopolitical forces" (Ho 2024, 3–4).

So what is the way forward? Loved ones and friends of all backgrounds around the world have asked another valid question: If these incidents keep occurring and the best comfort one can have is the lonely blessing of white witnesses who often watch and say nothing, why stay Down Under? My answer is twofold and simple: (1) in the wake of this terrible event, scores of friends, colleagues, students, and other people amassed by my side. If this is not a sign of magnanimous humanity, then I am unsure what else could be in our mortal coil through such a hellish experience; and (2) if in this violent maelstrom I adopt the view that all Australians are like the one who coward punched me, then I can be no better than him. We must, in other words, empathize with and learn from our communities of care, even, and always, in our darkest hours. I have no desire to myself metaphorically coward punch a place that has given me so much, and in which many of my dreams have come true beyond my wildest imagination.

It is also true that empathy has its limitations; I shudder to consider empathizing with a serial killer or a bona fide racist. I have thus come to believe that there are some with whom I should never fully empathize. Perhaps the most promising glimmer of hope in navigating and surpassing the widespread tempest of global anti-Asian bigotry, then, must be resistance in the most compassionate way—something I have yet to master but pensively meditate on to this day. With each passing moment, my most earnest and naive hope is that we congregate, as a global community, closer to compassionate resistance against anti-Asian racism in ways that reincarnate us all in this very lifetime—even when a bigoted stranger almost obliterates us from it. For such a practice of compassionate resistance, it now seems to me, beyond betrayal, anger, fear, and upset, can potentially transcend anti-Asian racism while together uplifting us to higher states of awakened consciousness.

Acknowledgments

As readers may surmise, this was a very traumatic experience and one that continues to haunt me, but is moreover one that was much alleviated by lovely allies around me. I therefore owe heartfelt thanks to: Debbie Rawlings Barton, Ethan Blue, Erin Wen Ai Chew, Cohen Donaldson, Deborah Gare, Sarah Gately, Steve Grant, Jennifer Ho, Peter Jordan, Sven Kassil, Jacqueline Lo, Courtney Lopez-Edser, Nilesh Makwana, Christian Mauri, Melissa Merchant, Vijay Mishra, Dee O'Connor, Thelma Plum, James Quickfall, Shabnam Rathee, Mignon Shardlow, Michael Slade, Aunty Dawn Smith, Gayatri Chakravorty Spivak, Glen Stasiuk, Edward L. Taylor, Ian and Mileva Tubbs, Rajeev Varshney, Cameron Wiggins, Jon Wilson, Jenna Woods, my supportive colleagues across Murdoch University and the University of Western Australia, and many others in the educational and cultural networks beyond. Again, thank you.

Notes

[1] Pilgrim et al., "King Hit Fatalities in Australia," 119.

[2] Ho, "Anti-Asian Racism," 149–150.

[3] Kurilla, "Kung Flu," 1.

[4] Shah, *Contagious Divides*, 17–18.

[5] Gairola and Jayawickrama, "The 'Asian Pandemic,'" 2.

[6] Gairola, *Homelandings*, 9.

[7] Yang, "COVID-19 Exacerbates Existing Racial Hatred."

[8] Maddison, *The Colonial Fantasy*, 224.

[9] Said, *Orientalism*.

[10] Gramsci, *The Prison Notebook*, 324.

[11] This image comes from the now defunct *Melbourne Punch* from May 10, 1888.

[12] Flux, "Opera Australia Faces Backlash."

[13] Stratton, "Two Rescues, One History," 662–663.

[14] Anderson, *Imagined Communities*, 5–7.

[15] Balibar, "The Nation Form," 349.

[16] Ibid.

[17] Ibid.

[18] Gairola et al., "Viral Stagings across the Globe," 691.

Bibliography

Anderson, Benedict. *Imagined Communities: Reflections on the Origin and Spread of Nationalism* (Revised Edition). London and New York: Verso, 1991.

Balibar, Etienne. "The Nation Form: History and Ideology." *Review* 13, no. 3 (Summer 1991): 329–361.

Flux, Elizabeth. "Opera Australia Faces Backlash over Controversial Production." *Sydney Morning Herald*, January 25, 2023. Accessed March 12, 2023, https://www.smh.com.au/culture/theatre/opera-australia-faces-backlash-over-controversial-production-20230124-p5cf28.html.

Gairola, Rahul K., Lauren O'Mahony, Melissa Merchant, and Simon Order. "Viral Stagings across the Globe: Performing Identity in the Era of COVID-19." *Journal of Intercultural Studies* 43, no. 6 (2022): 691–703.

Gairola, Rahul K., and Sharanya Jayawickrama. "The 'Asian Pandemic': Rethinking Memory and Trauma in Cultural Narratives of Asia." *Memory, Trauma, Asia: Recall, Affect, and Orientalism in Contemporary Narratives*, edited by Rahul K. Gairola and Sharanya Jayawickrama, 1–27. New York: Routledge, 2021.

Gairola, Rahul K. *Homelandings: Postcolonial Diasporas and Transatlantic Belonging.* London: Rowman & Littlefield International, 2016.

Gramsci, Antonio. *The Prison Notebook: Selections.* Trans. and ed. Quintin Hoare and Geoffrey Nowell Smith. New York: International Publishers, 1971.

Ho, Jennifer. "Anti-Asian Racism, Black Lives Matter, and COVID-19." *Japan Forum* 33, no. 1 (2021): 48–159.

Ho, Jennifer. "Introduction: Global Anti-Asian Racism: The Problem That Never Went Away" In *Global Anti-Asian Racism*, edited by Jennifer Ho, 3–6. Ann Arbor: Association for Asian Studies, 2024.

Kurilla, Robin. "'Kung Flu'—The Dynamics of Fear, Popular Culture, and Authenticity in the Anatomy of Populist Communication." *Frontiers in Communication* 6 (2021): 1–19.

Maddison, Sarah. *The Colonial Fantasy: Why White Australia Can't Solve Black Problems.* Sydney: Allen & Unwin, 2019.

Melbourne Punch. Accessed online via Museum of Australian Democracy at Old Parliament House website on March 7, 2023, https://getting-it-together.moadoph.gov.au/victoria/road-to-federation/resource-1.html.

Pilgrim, Jennifer Lucinda, Dimitri Gerostamoulos, and Olaf Heino Drummer. "'King Hit' Fatalities in Australia, 2000–2012: The Role of Alcohol and Other Drugs." *Drug and Alcohol Dependence* 135 (2014): 119–132.

Said, Edward. *Orientalism.* New York: Pantheon Books, 1978.

Shah, Nayan. *Contagious Divides: Epidemics and Race in San Francisco's Chinatown.* Berkeley: University of California Press, 2001.

Stratton, Jon. "Two Rescues, One History: Everyday Racism in Australia." *Social Identities* 12, no. 6 (2006): 657–681.

Yang, Samuel. "COVID-19 Exacerbates Existing Racial Hatred Experienced by Australian Asian Communities, Report Finds." ABC News, July 23, 2021, https://www.abc.net.au/news/2021-07-23/covid-19-racism-australia-report-racial-hatred-pandemic/100316184.

2

Don't Hate the Player. Between Essentialism and Resistance

Community Organizing against Anti-Asian Racism in Germany

Sara Djahim

In August 2020, I was sent by korientation, a network for Asian German perspectives, to the first civil society hearing before the newly appointed Cabinet Committee for the Fight Against Right-Wing Extremism and Racism. On February 19 of that year, nine young people, all of them with a so-called migration background, had been murdered by a right-wing extremist in the city of Hanau.[1] Their names were Gökhan Gültekin, Sedat Gürbüz, Said Nesar Hashemi, Mercedes Kierpacz, Hamza Kurtović, Vili Viorel Păun, Fatih Saraçoğlu, Ferhat Unvar, and Kaloyan Velkov. Shaken to the core, migrant organizations had urged Chancellor Merkel to address structural racism. The Black Lives Matter movement, after the murder of George Floyd, further paved the way for more in-depth discussions on racism in Germany. In June 2020, fifteen thousand people joined the silent demonstration against racism in Berlin.[2] Numerous media outlets took on the issue of racism, focusing mostly on personal experiences of Black people and people of color. The appointment of a cabinet committee seemed like a political turning point.[3] With the chancellor herself and ministers as members of the committee, this was the first time that racism was to be addressed at the highest institutional level.[4]

A number of migrant organizations banded together under the lead of the Bundeskonferenz der Migrantenorganisationen to critically watch the proceedings and evaluate the outcome.[5] For korientation, I took part to "represent an Asian-German perspective."[6] In order to amplify our voices, the group agreed on fundamental demands, which we affirmed at the hearing.[7] I additionally asked that people of Asian descent be named as a vulnerable group in the report to the UN Committee on the Elimination of Racial Discrimination, that there be more diversity training of administration and authorities, particularly police, and that there would be broader funding for research on anti-Asian racism and the history of Asian communities in Germany. Another demand was for more resources for Asian diasporic organizations. At a preliminary hearing for researchers, anti-Asian racism was also named as one of the important issues to focus on. However, the catalog of measures released by the committee in November 2020 did not mention the racist attacks on Asians during the pandemic or name them as a vulnerable group.[8] The work went on: korientation continued archiving media articles that, through imagery and language in their reporting of the pandemic, perpetuated anti-Asian racism; Asian German/diasporic activists and platforms such as Deutsche Asiat*innen, Make Noise (DAMN*) and tiger.riots facilitated community spaces; journalists (Vanessa Vu, Minh Thu Tran, Lin Hierse, and Nhi Le, to name a few) and podcasters (Diaspor.Asia, Rice & Shine) kept raising awareness; and the website Ich bin kein Virus, initiated by Victoria Kure-Wu with a team, gave people affected by anti-Asian racism the space to write about their experiences.[9] When the racist attacks in Atlanta happened and six Asian women were killed, the community in Germany grieved too. Despite the geographical distance, the political differences between the US and Germany, and the assumption that the lives of the victims had probably been very different from the lives of second-generation migrant children in Germany, many of us felt a proximity and personal anguish. As Lin Hierse wrote, "You put into perspective your involvement, you don't have enough in common with the women to be allowed to break apart. How much exactly would be enough then? You think of the differences but feel the commonalities. You see the photograph of a murder victim and think of your mother."[10] The community came together in a digital space, organized by Asian German/diasporic organizations and individual activists, and held a rally in front of the US embassy. An open letter—I was part of the group of authors—against anti-Asian racism and in memory of the victims in Atlanta was signed by 1,216 people and organizations.[11]

One month later, in May 2021, the concluding report of the cabinet committee named five focal issues: antisemitism, antiziganism, anti-Muslim racism, anti-Black racism, and anti-Asian racism. It was the very first time anti-Asian racism was officially acknowledged by political decision-makers.[12] Suddenly, Asians were seen and taken seriously as part of the German population. It seemed like a radiation from the inside to the outside world: the more we talked about ourselves as a community, the more we were seen as such. Of course, activists and scholars have thought, talked, and educated others about being Asian German before. The term "Asian German" was officially coined in 2012 when the book *Asiatische Deutsche: Vietnamesische Diaspora and Beyond* by Kien Nghi Ha was published.[13] It has been in the past three years, within the frame of a general reckoning with racism, that anti-Asian racism as an issue—and with it, the affected group of Asian Germans—have found their way into political discourse. I used the categorization of "Asian," "Asian German," and "Asian diasporic" in my statement before the hearing, following the lead of those scholars/activists who have referred to Spivak's "strategic essentialism" when using "Asian German" as a political positionality that doesn't refer to origin or heritage, colonial geographical borders, or the essentialization of culture.[14] At the heart of this reasoning lies the attempt to deconstruct and break colonial, homogenizing narratives of Asia and what it means to be Asian German. As a "permanent work-in-progress," the political positionality as "Asian Germans" is not meant to be a complete concept; rather, it is supposed to "develop with the changing needs and interests of the community"—"Asian Germans" is therefore to be understood as an "open offer."[15]

In this personal essay, I examine if this categorization that was meant to be fluid and adaptable, but that now marks a homogenous political stakeholder, can still hold subversive power at all. Retracing the events around community organizing against anti-Asian racism during the pandemic, and the theories our action-taking has been based on, I argue that we have arrived at a critical moment to interrogate who we are as a community, who we want to be, and what that means for organizing our anti-racist work. The "we" I write about in this essay means the imagined and real community under the umbrella term "Asian German" and/ or Asian diasporic, the delicate network between individual activists and groups, and the people who don't/can't necessarily identify as part of the community but whose contributions as researchers and activists to the ongoing discussions around a shared identity are invaluable.

Asian German as a Category

Although much of the inspiration for "Asian Germans" was taken from the Asian American movement, the focus increasingly turns to our own migration history, the experience and resilience of the generations before us. A prominent example would be the recruitment of nurses from South Korea in the 1960s and their successful fight for the right to stay in Germany in the 1970s.[16] The knowledge that we have today about the lives, work, and agency of Korean nurses is due to the self-organization of the women themselves as well as the efforts of their children and other scholars, artists, and activists to learn more about their history.

Another important achievement is the Friedensstatue in Berlin, a memorial for the hundreds of thousands of "comfort women" in Japanese-occupied territories during the Second World War. The bronze statue, a girl in a *hanbok* sitting next to an empty chair, inaugurated by the Korean association in 2020, is not only a memorial of past atrocities in Korea but has also become a call to end sexualized violence against women the world over.[17] Vigils for the victims of the shooting in Atlanta have been held here.[18]

Anujah Fernando and Linh Müller researched the presence of people from Asia, specifically from Korea and India, between 1918 and 1938.[19] They trace how revolutionary Asians in Berlin in the 1920s had anti-imperialist perspectives in common and, while they held their own respective spaces, how they used the term "Asian" strategically. Political organizing during that time was indicative of worldwide anti-colonial liberation movements: the Association of Revolutionary Asians, a leftist, anti-imperialist Japanese student group, which presumably was in touch with Korean and Indian activists, published the magazine *Revolutionäres Asien* from 1932 to 1933, with the goal of showing and building solidarity among Asians in Germany and between the German people and the oppressed in Asia. As Fernando and Müller find, the magazine can be interpreted as an attempt to strategically turn around the imperialist Pan-Asianism of Japan by connecting oppressed peoples in Asia, but the term "Asian" has always been unstable, from both the external perspective of authorities, media, and society as well as within the labeled group itself. In this case, however, the self-identification as "Asian" was used strategically in the global anti-colonial struggle.[20]

With growing interest from within the community that still (re)discovers itself, it might be that we revisit what held together Asian collaborative movements in early postcolonial times. As of now, struggles of the present moment in the Global South do not seem to be a point of reference either in the formation of scholarly theory about Asianness in Germany or in Asian German community work. In the daily lives of many Asian families, however, the ties to the Global South play an important role: the felt responsibility toward those "they have left behind" is linked with an awareness of economic inequality and a vigilance for global political unrest. Remittances from migrants in Germany by far exceed official development aid.[21] The discussions around anti-Asian racism and Asian German community building have so far been quite removed from these realities. In light of the pandemic, unequal global vaccine distribution, and worsening economic conditions in both the diaspora and the countries in the Global South, this might seem strange, but it mainly reveals the unpreparedness and pressure under which the specific anti-Asian racism during that time had to be answered. The political purpose and goal of "Asian German," other than a tool for representation and as a reaction to racism, is indeed not quite clear. As a "political practice of self-designation," the term is "connected to extensive transnational, diasporic histories, specifically to the movements of Asian Australians, Asian Britons, or Asian Canadians," and most of all, the Asian American movement that heavily influenced all other Anglophone appropriations."[22] While "only few would identify as culturally or racially 'Asian' and only become so through the demeaning white gaze," "Asian American," as a "political category of anti-racist and decolonial resistance," for Ha, is a form of self-empowerment that "confidently inverts the external racialization."[23]

Ha concludes a similar function and meaning for the German context:

> We are not Asian Germans, too, because we are Asian people who live in Germany. More pivotal is the fact that we are construed by a colonial-racist gaze as "Asian" and are made Asian—independently of how we see ourselves. . . . We are Asian Germans, because *we want* to *collectively* define *ourselves* like that, to recognize our common experiences and our differences . . . and to live political alliances within and outside the Asian diaspora in solidarity and with equal rights.[24]

Much of the community work that is presently done is based on these considerations and, at the same time, is subject to the fragility of a largely theory-derived political collectivity.

While "Asian" is supposed to be an umbrella term under which everyone is welcome who is in some shape or form connected to Asia, being recognized or marked as Asian is not part of the experience for many people who, despite their ties to the Asian continent, aren't addressed in that way; the aforementioned inversion of the white gaze of Asia is not really possible or desirable. Urmila Goel, who noted that Asia is not a reference point for people who are given the label "Indian" in Germany, inquired why the Asian label, another excluding category, is important at all; to address racism, it would rather be necessary to connect all racially marginalized groups.[25] There is an acute awareness of the fraught nature of a blanket term that some people don't want and others aren't afforded. Activists are also sensitive to the fact that the Eurocentric naming of these regions is a problematic issue in itself and connects to conditions of political self-identification as diasporic people in the Global North. This finds expression in simple acts such as carefully worded invitations addressing "BIPoC who (can) strategically choose relations to North/South/East/Southeast/Vorderasien or Central Asia to make visible diverse lived realities and to speak to questions of racism and other exclusions from a specific perspective in solidarity."[26]

None of the existing organizations or initiatives claim representation of the whole Asian community, of course, and there is a constant emphasis on the need for critical self-reflection and the fluidity of the process of identity-building. The fact that parts of the community are underrepresented weighs all the heavier, as it clearly indicates our internalized colonial knowledge about who is Asian in Germany, no matter how hard we try to avoid erasing the experience of less visible, racialized groups. It is very safe to say that when political decision-makers talk about anti-Asian racism, they mean racism against people who look East Asian to them. In our effort to draw attention to the issue within a very short time frame, we inscribed anti-Asian racism and who is affected into the political sphere or, more to the point, we confirmed preconceived notions that existed all along.

The Difficulty of Deconstruction: Visibility in Politics and Research

In March 2022, Reem Alabali-Radovan, the minister of state and integration officer, published the status report "Racism in Germany. Status Quo, Key Issues, Measures."[27] At the press conference, she presented the report as the first federal government document with a comprehensive depiction of racism and its manifestations in Germany.[28] In line with the cabinet committee, it specifically named anti-Black racism, anti-Muslim racism, antiziganism, antisemitism (as "a neighboring phenomenon"), and anti-Asian racism. Referencing the research by Suda, Mayer, and Nguyen, it describes the rising racist attacks on people "perceived as Asian" as being connected to media narratives about China and Asian eating and living habits, which were responsible for the outbreak.[29] Interestingly, it mentions who the affected group is and how many people belong to it: "Around one million people of Asian origin (South, Southeast, and East Asia) and their descendants live in Germany, the number of people potentially affected by anti-Asian racism is therefore high."[30] Sandip Roy, albeit rather cynically, wrote about the "numbers game," the need to present as a quantifiable group in order for funds to be allocated for specific interests.[31] The emphasis that "we" are numerous and a nonnegligible part of the constituency reveals what civil society organizations have come to realize: we don't exist if we don't show up in statistics, and we are believed only if we are backed up by "science," even if we know that Hanau was not a single occurrence; we remember Hoyerswerda, Rostock-Lichtenhagen, Mölln, Solingen, the murders by the NSU, and Halle. Nevertheless, the initiation of the racism monitor was, in large part, a result of the demand for hard data to prove that the experience of racialized people in Germany is real and to enhance evidence-based advocacy.[32]

This "datafication of injustice" that is "the hunt for more and more data about things we already know much about" directly impacts the way we speak of and for ourselves.[33] The way we are visible in statistics, our organizing efforts as a community, and who feels included are, however, very different things. In the survey by Köhler and Suda, mostly people of Southeast and East Asian origin took part, with the authors clarifying that "by people of Asian origin we understand anyone who feels addressed by a survey about anti-Asian racism."[34] But who *can* feel addressed, and who does the addressing, and why? The criticism from within community circles is equally as contradictory as the approach to deploying the label "Asian German" itself. It ranges from disappointment and anger about not being included to a complete rejection of the term as trite or even self-indulgent in the way that the discourse overlooks the ones who are most affected by structural racism, namely refugees (from Asian countries). It is worth noting that there seems to be increasing interest in "Asian Germans" as an umbrella term, with people of Southeast or South Asian origin joining or leading activities, but in many, if not most, instances, an uneasiness remains.

Whether we are "looking at the claim to the word Asia, however historically unjustified" or not, it is still the case that we haven't resolved how to cope with the necessity to self-essentialize within a political framework that insists on categories, however mistaken they are, while also challenging them.[35] Concern about anti-Asian racism directed at East Asians holds a place in research and politics, at least for now. Visibility of and interest in anti-Asian racism rose precisely because of the essentialist view of Asians, their history, and their experiences. The theoretical diversification of the community, paradoxically, has not challenged the political perception but legitimized the cause and led to a subsummation of less visible racialized groups.

Anti-Chinese Racism

In an effort to avoid erasure, some activists have begun to specify the racism they experience as anti-East Asian or as "racism against people perceived as East Asian"—a conscious decision to name the issue rather than one's own identity. Other authors have written before about being labeled "Chinese" and demeaned for it: "Chinese is not a slur—nevertheless, I encountered this label as disparaging or even hostile."[36] The realization that Chinese is a sort of "prototype of the Asian cliché" and a "synonym für Asians" is shared widely.[37] As many East Asians are affected—and also people who are perceived as such—it seems logical to name it accordingly, even though, for instance, members of the Vietnamese diaspora have historically faced different challenges than the Korean community. It is a complicated walk on eggshells, indeed, to get both the white perception and the actual lives right.

European narratives about perceived exotic and dangerous Asians can be traced back to the thirteenth century.[38] In Germany especially, there is a long historical continuity of anti-Chinese racism: the colony of Kiautschou (1897), the send-off of German East Asian Expeditionary Corps to quell the Boxer Rebellion by Kaiser Wilhelm II, who coined the term "yellow peril," and the persecution of Chinese people living in Germany by the Nazis.[39]

Loud echoes of these sentiments still reverberate today. Recently, a video of Norbert Lammert, the former parliamentary president, and Hage Geingob, the president of Namibia, resurfaced. At a meeting in 2018, Lammert questioned the president about the growing influence of China, citing that the number of Chinese people in Namibia was four times as high as the number of Germans.[40] The message that was conveyed was fraught in more ways than one, as Namibia is a former German colony. Nevertheless, German media at the time reported next to nothing about the dressing down that Lammert received from the president, who told him that "every time a Westerner comes, it is about Chinese."[41] The framing of China as the "new colonial master" on the African continent and the alleged endangering of freedom and democracy that only European governments can impede—not despite but because of their colonial history—is a not a completely new narrative twist but one that will become even more prevalent.[42] We will have to assess if our approach to anti-Chinese racism, that so far has been mostly in reference to historical roots of anti-Asian racism, will serve us well or if we have to connect it to wider issues of white supremacy and global inequality.

Conclusion

The concepts of "Asian Germans" and "anti-Asian racism" have been very successful in shining a light on part of the Asian community in Germany. However, the goal of the term "Asian Germans" to serve as an open offer, to be adaptable to the changing interests and needs of the community, has not been achieved. At this time, it doesn't reflect diverse communities, their commonalities and differences. Instead, it levels histories and experiences, lending itself for political decision-makers to mark one homogenous central stakeholder. Although this was certainly not the intention, the deployment of strategic essentialism meant the formalization of who is Asian in Germany. The political whirlwind moment of 2020 and 2021 opened up certain opportunities that the Asian German community had to seize in order to gain political recognition. The responsibility of addressing asymmetries in power within the community got swept up in the artificial urgency that is typical for output-oriented political processes and a funding system that prioritizes fast results. Under these circumstances, challenging the label that we operate under is hardly possible, at least not at the political stage.

Against the backdrop of a heated discourse on racism in Germany and an ever-shrinking space for civil society, the consequences are very real. If funding and public attention are explicitly directed at communities affected by anti-Asian racism, and if we want to keep participating as players in the political arena, the question of who really is Asian will inevitably become central for discussions within the community, not just in terms of identity building but as an existential issue. It remains to be seen what happens once or if large-scale quantitative research on Asians in Germany is implemented. Meanwhile, the organizational landscape is changing, more initiatives are emerging, and ideas about how to practice solidarity, especially outside of neoliberal funding structures, are growing. With the knowledge of past decades, we now have the opportunity to rethink the way we organize our anti-racist work.

Epilogue

A while ago, a good friend and I went to dinner at a Vietnamese restaurant at Kottbusser Tor in Berlin. When the server came to our table, she asked us where we were from. My friend, who was born in Hamburg, said, "Korea." I, born in Frankfurt, said, "Indonesia." "We are all Asian then," the woman said with a broad smile and an arm gesture that encircled the three of us. We smiled back, just as broadly. "Yes, we are." It was a sweet moment. For the past few months, my friend, who does research on racism, and I had been discussing the impossibility of an Asian identity and the futility of this category for community building. But here it was, this feeling of an uncomplicated moment of understanding. I feel that this is where our approach to community building is rooted—these instances of recognition, a togetherness. The question is whether mere political representation, sitting at the (racist) table, and appealing to the public by way of an Asian presence is the right way to go about it.

Growing up, I experienced mostly anti-Chinese racism, with all the accompanying slurs. When it became more common for white people to take backpacking and self-discovery trips to Southeast Asia, their horizon shifted. Suddenly, they attempted to guess the right ethnicity, if only to prove their own cosmopolitanism. The racism was subtly modified; it had less to do with the foreignness or strangeness of China and more to do with the exoticism of tropical countries where tourists from Europe can afford everything. That is maybe why I was (and somehow still am) drawn to the idea of an Asian umbrella, and why I wanted to identify with it even if I could clearly see that we were, in truth, speaking to the experience of being (mistaken as) East Asian. It is a political identity, after all, a means to an end. But I have always sensed the awkwardness around self-essentializing for the cause and felt in these spaces the absence of my friends who are factually Asian and who deal with unspeakable racism but don't get any sort of recognition. I've also found a sense of community in other instances—with chosen family from Iran and Nigeria when they tell childhood stories that are eerily similar to my parents', with friends whose parents grew up in former colonies and feel forever homesick for something they can't name, with coworkers of color in white spaces, in fleeting moments with strangers who know what it is like to be a perpetual foreigner in Germany, as a visitor of the *documenta 15*, which centered artists from the Global South and showed that collective practices around producing art are just as meaningful as the art itself. Resistance to anti-Asian racism alone, at least the way it is defined now, seems to be a shaky ground to build community on. It is fair to wonder, then, if our work should be to aim for political recognition as German Asians. Or do we have to find other ways to become, in the words of Grada Kilomba, the absolute opposition of what the colonial project has determined?[43]

Notes

[1] Migration background ("*Migrationshintergrund*") is an official category of the Federal Statistical Office of Germany. It clusters together very diverse demographic groups: people who don't have German citizenship, people who weren't born with German citizenship (even if they were born in Germany), and people who were born with German citizenship but who have a parent who wasn't.

[2] Zwerenz, "Silent Demo."

[3] Zeit Online, "Neuer Kabinettsausschuss."

[4] While there had been national action plans against racism before, they had mainly centered racism as a problem on the extreme right margins and failed to offer concrete, sustainable measures.

[5] Bundeskonferenz der Migrantenorganisationen, "Pressemitteilung: Kabinettausschuss muss liefern." The Federal Conference of Migrant Organizations is a collective of over seventy NGOs.

[6] Suda, Schindler, and Kim, "Emerging Asian Germany," 361. All translations from the German sources used in this essay are my own.

[7] Bundeskonferenz der Migrantenorganisationen, "Pressemitteilung: Antirassismus Agenda 2025."

[8] Bundesregierung, "Maßnahmenkatalog."

[9] korientation, "Rassismus in der COVID-19-Berichterstattung"; www.ichbinkeinvirus.de.

[10] Lin Hierse, "Atlanta und verbundene Seelen."

[11] korientation, "Offener Brief."

[12] Bundesregierung, "Abschlussbericht des Kabinettsausschusses."

[13] An expanded new edition, *Asiatische Deutsche Extended: Vietnamesische Diaspora and Beyond,* was published in 2022.

[14] Choi and Suda, "Asian Film Festival Berlin: 'Imagine(d) Kinships and Communities.'"

[15] Kien Nghi Ha, "Gegenwart und Konzeption asiatisch-deutscher Präsenzen," 6.

[16] Berner and Choi, "Koreanische Krankenschwestern in Deutschland," 361–362.

[17] Korea Verband, "Die Friedensstatue."

[18] Koreaverband, "In Memory, In Resistance."

[19] Fernando and Müller, "Asiatische Präsenzen im Berlin der Zwischenkriegszeit."

[20] Ibid.

[21] FAZ, "Migranten überweisen 17,7 Milliarden aus Deutschland."

[22] Ha, "Rückblicke und Ausblicke," 14.

[23] Ibid., 15.

[24] Ibid., 15.

[25] Goel, "Vorzeige-Migrant_innen, Rassismus und mögliche Bündnisse—von Asiat_innen und Inder_innen in Deutschland; Goel et al., "Selbstorganisation und (pan)asiatische Identitäten," 96.

[26] korientation,"Netzwerktreffen: Asians in der politischen Bildungsarbeit." "*Vorderasien*" is a summary term for the regions of West Asia and Southwest Asia. Like "Near East," with which the term has geographical overlap, it has a Eurocentric viewpoint.

[27] Integrationsbeauftragte, "Lagebericht Rassismus in Deutschland. Ausgangslage, Handlungsfelder und Maßnahmen." In February 2022, the commissioner for integration was additionally appointed as the first-ever commissioner against racism on the federal level. The biennial report, which usually features information on the state of "integration," in that year focused exclusively on racism.

[28] ZDF, "Pressekonferenz zum Lagebericht Rassismus in Deutschland."

[29] Integrationsbeauftragte, "Lagebericht Rassismus," 39; Suda, Mayer, and Nguyen, "Antiasiatischer Rassismus in Deutschland," 43.

[30] Integrationsbeauftragte, "Lagebericht," 39; Suda, Mayer, and Nguyen, "Antiasiatischer Rassismus in Deutschland," 43.

[31] Roy, "The Call of Rice," 354–356.

[32] MiGAZIN, interview with Yasemin Shooman.

[33] Benjamin, "Viral Justice: How We Grow the World We Want," 56.

[34] Köhler and Suda, "Factsheet," 3.

[35] Spivak, *Other Asias.*

[36] Wienand, "Ethnisiert ≠ identifiziert," 30–33.

[37] Ibid.

[38] Suda, Mayer, and Nguyen. "Antiasiatischer Rassismus in Deutschland," 39–44.

[39] Ibid.

[40] Namibia Press Agency, "Don't Underestimate Our Intelligence."

[41] Ibid.

[42] Die Tagespost, "Neue Kolonialherren kommen aus Namibia"; Stern, "Habeck warnt vor grünem Energie-Imperialismus."

[43] Grada Kilomba, "Becoming a Subject," 22.

Bibliography

Ajayi, Folashade, Noa Milman, Donatella della Porta, Nicole Doerr, Piotr Kocyba, Anna
    Lavizzari, Herbert Reiter, Piotr Płucienniczak, Moritz Sommer, Elias Steinhilper,
    and Sabrina Zajak. *Black Lives Matter in Europe*. DeZIM Research Notes 6. Berlin:
    Deutsches Zentrum für Integrations—und Migrationsforschung, 2021.

Aktionsgruppe Friedensstatue im Korea Verband. Die Friedenstatue. Accessed January 16,
    2023. https://trostfrauen.de/friedensstatue/.

Amadeu Antonio Stiftung. Todesopfer rechter Gewalt. Accessed January 4, 2023.
    https://www.amadeu-antonio-stiftung.de/todesopfer-rechter-gewalt/.

Beauftragte der Bundesregierung für Migration, Flüchtlinge und Integration. Lagebericht
    Rassismus in Deutschland. Ausgangssituation, Handlungsfelder, Maßnahmen.
    Berlin: IntB, 2023.

Benjamin, Ruha. *Viral Justice: How We Grow the World We Want*. Princeton: Princeton
    University Press, 2022.

Berner, Heike, and Sun-ju Choi. "Koreanische Krankenschwestern in Deutschland." In *re/
    visionen. Postkoloniale Perspektiven von People of Color auf Rassismus, Kulturpolitik
    und Widerstand in Deutschland*, edited by Kien Nghi Ha, Nicola Lauré al-Samarai
    and Sheila Mysorekar, 361–362. Münster: Unrast, 2016.

Bundeskonferenz der Migrantenorganisationen. "Pressemitteilung: Kabinettausschuss
    muss liefern—Bundeskonferenz der Migrant*innenorganisationen setzt
    Begleitausschuss ein." July 6, 2020. http://s890498910.online.de/wp-content/
    uploads/2020/07/PM_Begleitausschuss-der-BKMO.pdf.

Bundeskonferenz der Migrantenorganisationen. "Antirassismus Agenda 2025: Wir
    brauchen einen politischen Neustart und keine halbherzigen Maßnahmen." August
    30, 2020. https://bundeskonferenz-mo.de/antirassismus-agenda-2025.

Bundesministerium für Familie, Senioren, Frauen und Jugend. "Kabinettsausschuss zur
    Bekämpfung von Rechtsextremismus und Rassismus." https://www.demokratie-
    leben.de/das-programm/hintergrund/kabinettsausschuss-zur-bekaempfung-von-
    rechtsextremismus-und-rassismus.

Bundesregierung. "Maßnahmenkatalog des Kabinettsausschusses zur Bekämpfung
    von Rechtsextremismus und Rassismus." November 25, 2020. https://www.
    bundesregierung.de/resource/blob/974430/1819984/4f1f9683cf3faddf90e27f09c692a
    bed/2020-11-25-massnahmen-rechtsextremi-data.pdf?download=1.

Bundesregierung. "Abschlussbericht des Kabinettsausschusses zur Bekämpfung
    von Rechtsextremismus und Rassismus." May 12, 2021. https://www.bmi.
    bund.de/SharedDocs/downloads/DE/veroeffentlichungen/themen/sicherheit/
    abschlussbericht-kabinettausschuss-rechtsextremismus.pdf;jsessionid=9A2E6A3DB9
    8397C3A995ADF23CAB7A8E.2_cid350?__blob=publicationFile&v=3.

Choi, Sun-ju, and Kimiko Suda. "Asian Film Festival Berlin: 'Imagine(d) Kinships and
    Communities.'" Heinrich-Böll-Stiftung, January 29, 2014. https://heimatkunde.boell.
    de/de/2014/01/29/asian-film-festival-berlin-imagined-kinships-and-communities#_
    edn5.

Die Zeit. "Neuer Kabinettsausschuss gegen Rechtsextremismus und Rassismus." Zeit Online, March 2, 2020. https://www.zeit.de/gesellschaft/zeitgeschehen/2020-03/integrationsgipfel-kabinettsausschuss-rechtsextremismus-rassismus-angela-merkel-hanau.

Dinges, Serafin. "Einer für Alle. Geldtransfer von Migranten." Deutschlandfunk Kultur, October 9, 2022. https://www.deutschlandfunkkultur.de/einer-fuer-alle-110.html.

Fernando, Anujah, und Linh Müller. "Asiatische Präsenzen im Berlin der Zwischenkriegszeit: Inder:innen, Koreaner:innen und Community übergreifende Begegnungen." Korientation. Accessed January 16, 2023. https://www.korientation.de/projekte/padb/.

Goel, Urmila. "Vorzeige-Migrant_innen, Rassismus und mögliche Bündnisse—von Asiat_innen und Inder_innen in Deutschland," August 7, 2012. http://www.urmila.de/forschung/zuschreibungen/texte/asiatischedeutsche.html.

Goel, Urmila, Jee-Un Kim, Nivedita Prasad, Kien Nghi Ha. "Selbstorganisation und (pan-) asiatische Identitäten: Community, People of Color und Diaspora." In *Asiatische Deutsche Extended. Vietnamesische Diaspora and Beyond*, edited by Kien Nghi Ha, 84–104. Berlin/Hamburg: Assoziation A, 2021.

Ha, Kien Nghi. "Gegenwart und Konzeption asiatisch-deutscher Präsenzen." IDA Überblick 2 (2021): 3–9.

Ha, Kien Nghi. "Rück—und Ausblicke: Dezentrierte Gemeinschaften und transnationale Solidaritäten." In *Asiatische Deutsche Extended*, edited by Kien Nghi Ha, 11–20. Berlin: Assoziation A, 2021.

Hierse, Lin. "Atlanta und verbundene Seelen." *taz* 30, no. 3 (2021). https://taz.de/Betroffenheit-nach-rassistischen-Morden/!5758395/.

Korea Verband. "In Memory, In Resistance: Gedenkveranstaltung Atlanta-Morde." Vigil in Honor for the Victims of the Atlanta Shootings. March 18, 2023. https://koreaverband.de/termin/in-memory-in-resistance-gedenkveranstaltung-atlanta-morde/.

Köhler, Jonas, und Kimiko Suda. "Erste Ergebnisse der Studie Antiasiatischer Rassismus in Zeiten der Corona-Pandemie." DeZIM Factsheet, March 21, 2023. https://www.dezim-institut.de/fileadmin/user_upload/Demo_FIS/publikation_pdf/FA-5558.pdf.

Kilomba, Grada. "Becoming a Subject." In *Mythen, Masken und Subjekte*, edited by Maureen Maisha Eggers, Grada Kilomba, Peggy Piesche, and Susanne Arndt, 22. Münster: Unrast, 2009.

korientation. "Demo am 28.03.2021 um 14 h, Berlin | In Gedenken. In Widerstand: Solidarität mit Atlanta und mit Asiatischen Diaspora Communities." March 25, 2021, https://www.korientation.de/demo-28-03-2021-berlin-atlanta-asian-diaspora-germany/.

korientation. "[Offener Brief] Atlanta—War da was?" April 16, 2021. https://www.korientation.de/positionen/atlanta-offener-brief/.

korientation. "Netzwerktreffen: Asians in der politischen Bildungsarbeit." January 10, 2023. https://www.korientation.de/netzwerktreffen-asians-in-der-politischen-bildungsarbeit/.

korientation. "Rassismus in der COVID-19-Berichterstattung." Accessed April 8, 2023. https://www.korientation.de/projekte/projekte-verein/corona-rassismus-medien/.

korientation. "Über uns." Accessed April 2023, https://www.korientation.de/ueber-uns/.

Shooman, Yasemin. "Wir wollen einen Rassismusmonitor aufbauen," interview in *MiGAZIN*. July 8, 2020. https://www.migazin.de/2020/07/08/yasemin-shooman-wir-rassismus-monitor/.

Namibia Press Agency. "Don't Underestimate Our Intelligence." Filmed November 2018 at the State House in Windhoek, Namibia. Video. https://www.youtube.com/watch?v=Dx-jKMFtkDI&ab_channel=NamibiaPressAgency.

Nguyễn, Thủy-Tiên. "Anti-Asian Racism, Atlanta, Activism," Stories by Thuy Newsletter, March 26, 2021. https://steadyhq.com/en/storiesbythuy/posts/3e5dca7c-955a-400a-872f-da002ee0e0fb.

Rosenkranz, Jan. "Robert Habeck warnt vor 'grünem Energie-Imperialismus.'" *Stern*, December 6, 2022.

Roy, Sandip. "The Call of Rice: (South) Asian American Queer Communities." In *Part, Yet Apart: South Asians in Asian America*, edited by Lavina Dhingra Shankar and Rajini Srikanth, 349–383. Philadelphia: Temple University Press, 1998.

Spivak, Gayatri Chakravorty. *Other Asias*. Malden: Blackwell, 2007.

Statistisches Bundesamt. "Migrationshintergrund." Accessed January 16, 2023. https://www.destatis.de/DE/Themen/Gesellschaft-Umwelt/Bevoelkerung/Migration-Integration/Glossar/migrationshintergrund.html#:~:text=Eine%20Person%20hat%20einen%20Migrationshintergrund,mit%20deutscher%20Staatsangeh%C3%B6rigkeit%20geboren%20wurde.

Suda, Kimiko, Sabrina J. Mayer, and Christoph Nguyen. "Antiasiatischer Rassismus in Deutschland." *Aus Politik und Zeitgeschichte*. (Anti)Rassismus, October 12, 2020: 39–44.

Suda, Kimiko, Sabrina J. Mayer, Christoph G. Nguyen, and Jonas Köhler. *Antiasiatischer Rassismus in Zeiten der Corona-Pandemie. Innenperspektive quantitative Erhebung. Datensatz, Version 1.0.0.* Berlin: Deutsches Zentrum für Integrations—und Migrationsforschung, 2021.

Suda, Kimiko, Sina Schindler, and Jee-Un Kim. "Emerging Asian Germany. Zur Notwendigkeit und den Grenzen der Selbstrepräsentation von Asiatischen Deutschen." In *Asiatische Deutsche Extended. Vietnamesische Diaspora and Beyond*, edited by Kien Nghi Ha, 352–363. Berlin/Hamburg: Assoziation A, 2021.

Wienand, Carmen. "Ethnisiert ≠ identifiziert. Kleine Erzählung über Zuschreibungen und Umgangsstrategien." In *Asian Germany—Asiatische Diaspora in Deutschland*, edited by Kien Nghi Ha, 30–33. Berlin: Heinrich-Böll-Stiftung, 2014.

ZDF. "Pressekonferenz zum Lagebericht Rassismus in Deutschland." Filmed January11, 2023. Video. https://www.zdf.de/phoenix/phoenix-vor-ort/phoenix-lagebericht-rassismus-100.html.

Zwerenz, Milena. "'Silent Demo': 15.000 protestieren in Berlin gegen Rassismus." ze.tt, June 6, 2020, https://www.zeit.de/zett/politik/2020-06/silent-demos-tausende-protestieren-in-berlin-gegen-rassismus.

3

THE CHOICE OF LIBERDADE

BRAZILIAN FACETS OF ANTI-ASIAN RACISM AND THE ACTIVISM'S RESPONSE

Érika Tiemi W. Fujii, Gabriel Akira, Maria Victória R. Ruy, and Mariana Mitiko Nomura

Liberdade ("freedom" in Portuguese) is a district in downtown São Paulo, Brazil, that is best known for its Asian presence. When describing the district, many might mention the red lanterns that adorn its streets, the Shinto-style gateway, the Japanese restaurants, the shops that sell imported goods, or the festivals such as the Lunar New Year (known in Brazil as Chinese New Year)—all referring to Asian iconography. The Japanese influence stands out enough to have motivated a name change for the main square and the local subway station in 2018 to include "Japão" (Japan), renaming them Liberdade-Japão Square and Japão-Liberdade Station, respectively. These changes were supported by local big business owners of Japanese descent, and they reinforced Liberdade's image even more as a place characterized by a Japanese presence.[1]

Another remarkable attempt to bolster this conception came in 2020, when Alberto Nomura, a Japanese Brazilian city councilman, presented a bill intending to restrict the district's famous street market, Feira da Liberdade, to so-called "Oriental" goods only.[2] The main motive for the proposed restriction was the desire to preserve the local cultural heritage. Yet by mentioning "Oriental" products, especially without a definition of what "Oriental" included, it led to the reproduction of stereotypes. The active use of that word meant what mattered most was a product's resemblance to an item that would be recognized as Asian. Therefore, it was clear that what was considered important was preserving the narrative of Liberdade as an Asian district.

This narrative, however, is relatively recent, starting with a municipal government plan in the 1970s with the support of the Japanese Brazilian community in São Paulo to transform the district into a tourist attraction zone similar to what some Chinatowns have become in other countries. A series of renovations were then carried out in order to characterize the streets with elements that referred to Asian imagery, such as the red lanterns by which the district is known to this day.[3]

What the general public doesn't know, however, is that the Liberdade district is also a place of Black history and memory, linked to the resistance of enslaved people against public torture and execution in the nineteenth century. While the square today has been renamed Liberdade-Japão Square, which is the street market mentioned in Nomura's bill, historically, several convicts—mostly poor Black men—were publicly hanged there.[4] Furthermore, in Liberdade, there was a cemetery where the enslaved, poor, and executed convicts—those despised by society—were buried. Although the public cemetery was deactivated in 1885[5] and buildings were constructed on the site, the chapel built in its center, Capela dos Aflitos ("Chapel of the Afflicted"), still exists, hidden in the midst of commercial buildings and unknown to many, even among those who visit the district regularly.[6]

Moreover, it is essential to highlight that Liberdade is home to many immigrants from around the globe, not only from Asia, and the district's popular markets have local vendors whose products relate to various Brazilian cultural manifestations. Many of these vendors have been present at the Liberdade Street Market for several years, selling African Brazilian street food and other traditional goods. Despite being long-standing sellers, since they do not sell Oriental goods, they would be expelled by Nomura's bill. Policies such as changing the names of the local square and the subway station, as well as Nomura's bill, highlight the presence of certain populations over others. To call Liberdade an Asian district is to erase its Black history and the presence of other immigrants who live there.

The Feira da Liberdade episode, therefore, can be perceived as an illustration of Brazilian racial dynamics that reflects the role of Asians and their descendants in the work of maintaining racist structures. For this reason, we chose this episode as a way to explore the topic of racism because the fight against anti-Asian discrimination must include the choice to also fight with Black and Indigenous populations, rejecting white supremacy as a whole. As members of Coletivo Dinamene, an Asian Brazilian activist collective, this case study aims to understand how Asian people are integrated in the country's racial dynamics. The word "Oriental" that was chosen by the bill was meant to encompass not only Japanese Brazilians but also all Asian Brazilians as a racial category, as opposed to white and Black people. Despite the strong historical influence of Japanese immigration, we avoid generalizations that erase other Asian experiences in Brazil. For that reason, Coletivo Dinamene is composed of, and is open to, Asian Brazilians of all ethnic groups. To share our differences means to comprehend what connects us and to create a common ground for anti-racist solidarity. In one sense, that solidarity is also what we seek by writing this essay, as all struggles against global anti-Asian racism are connected.

In this essay, we will first look into the historical background of how Japanese immigrants came to be accepted in Brazil in an ambiguous racial position, full of disputes and contractions. The endeavors to emphasize Liberdade's Japanese heritage, in tandem with the erasure of Black people and other immigrant groups, can be partially explained by the history of Asian immigration to Brazil and the specificities of Asian racialization in the country. We will examine the racial discussions after Brazilian independence in 1822 and how Asian people were inserted into the development of power structures that would turn race into a core category of Brazilian capitalism. By introducing two important concepts in Brazilian racial theory—the racial democracy myth and the whitening politics— we will use Feira da Liberdade's episode as a leading case to demonstrate how Japanese Brazilians, as the most representative Asian group in Brazil, are confronted with a choice between two alternatives: an alliance with whiteness or anti-racist solidarity.

Our story begins in the nineteenth century, after more than three hundred years of Portuguese colonization based on Indigenous genocide and the forced displacement of African populations to the American continent. In the mid-nineteenth century, Brazil had to manage the labor crisis that accompanied the gradual end of the slave trade and slavery itself while aiming at whitening the nation through immigration.[7] The perfect alternative for both concerns would be white immigrants. Plantation lords, however, were used to the low-cost labor of African or African-descendant enslaved people, and they were not willing to pay for the labor of free white workers. European nations wouldn't be pleased with the idea of its citizens working side by side with enslaved laborers either. Amidst the scarcity of white immigrants, the inevitable yet much delayed end of slavery,[8] and the ever-increasing economic demand for labor (the state of São Paulo's coffee exportation more than doubled between the 1880s and 1890s), a heated debate on the labor crisis and immigration policies took over the Brazilian provincial chambers and press for decades.[9]

The "Chinese alternative" was possibly the most controversial proposal at the time. The "coolie traffic," the trade of unfree Asian workers, had its advocates in Brazil.[10] While they never disagreed that "Yellow race" individuals were definitely an undesired ethnic element to compose the nation, men like deputy Martim Francisco claimed that Brazil was between "accepting the substitute closer to the African slave" or "declaring the country's bankruptcy."[11] As pointed out by historian Ana Paulina Lee, the Chinese were perceived as economic, legal, and racial intermediaries between African enslaved workers and European free ones.[12]

Besides needing to replace the labor force, however, another process that was just as important mobilized Brazilian ruling classes at the turn of the century— the construction of a national identity for an emerging republican nation. In the decades prior to the Proclamation of the Republic (1889), republicans were striving to come up with a liberal project for the nation. According to Lee, far from breaking away from the colonial racial hierarchies, the liberal reform gave them continuation with the project of whitening the country through immigration: "Entangled racial, eugenic, and liberal ideologies—and the enactment of these ideologies into policy—were at the core of Brazil's nation-building project, itself an aspect of an emerging global racialized national consciousness that took its own unique turns in Brazil's transition from postcolonial empire to republican state."[13]

Abolitionists and republicans led the opposition against the adoption of Chinese immigration. They argued it would be a continuation of slavery (and it would indeed, since plantation lords were particularly interested in the unfree condition of Chinese labor) and that it would, in their words, "mongolize" the nation's ethnic composition, thus severely compromising a future of progress and freedom for Brazil. These two motivations were deeply intertwined, to an extent that they were rarely supported separately. For historian Rogério Dezem, some abolitionists (like the prominent Joaquim Nabuco) seemed to center the debate around the alleged racial inferiority of the Chinese.[14]

In the end, the total number of Chinese workers brought to Brazil before 1880 probably didn't surpass three thousand individuals.[15] In other words, the opposition to Chinese immigration succeeded in keeping large numbers of Chinese out of Brazil. As demonstrated by Ana Paulina Lee, despite the relatively small number of Chinese, the long and troubled debate around the topic anchored Asian racialization in the Brazilian mentality and reinforced the nation's acceptance of global racial ideologies. The influence of European eugenic theories and the US Chinese Exclusion Act of 1882 were decisive in how the Chinese question unfolded in Brazil. Like it was in the US, racial representations of the Chinese as uncivilized, filthy, dishonest, inapt for assimilation, and therefore dangerous for the nation, preceded and prepared their exclusion.

The stereotypes of the Chinese and the Japanese were never identical, yet they hold many similarities. Rogério Dezem considers that the anti-Japanese discourse originated from the anti-Chinese one, since collective representations of so-called "Yellow-raced" immigrants were, as previously discussed, first drafted on the Chinese. However, the author points out that, at the turn of the century, negative stereotypes about Japanese people were never as hegemonic as they were about Chinese people.[16] It was a period when strengthening diplomatic bonds with Japan was especially desirable: the Meiji empire had just won two wars (against China and Russia) and had consolidated itself as the superpower in Asia. Some of the intellectuals at the forefront of the opposition to Chinese immigration engaged in promoting Japanese immigration, partly buying into Japan's "leading race" discourse, in which the Yamato race was considered morally superior to other Asian races. Moreover, Japanese immigration would turn Brazil away from Chinese immigration and the alignment with China, made precarious by invasions and political uprisings.[17] Because Japanese immigrants belonged to a strong national state, they wouldn't be subjected to unfree labor conditions, since that would lead to a major diplomatic issue. Indeed, these immigrants were closely accompanied by the Japanese government.

Japanese stereotypes were thus pronouncedly ambiguous. Different from the Chinese, they were considered hard-working laborers—disciplined, docile, and efficient. Yet, the yellow peril component was always there because the Japanese were also portrayed as politically and racially dangerous. With the rise of the Meiji empire, these tropes added to the fear of an imperialist threat. In short, the Japanese were taken as preferred substitutes to the Chinese. In the words of historian Elena Camargo Shizuno, these immigrants were the "*indesejáveis necessários*" (undesired but required).[18] Marcia Yumi Takeuchi points out that even though the diplomatic protocols between Brazil and Japan were successful, it still took thirteen years for Japanese immigration to materialize.[19] Takeuchi mentions the correspondence from Brazilian diplomat Oliveira Lima, in which he advises Brazil to ponder the immigration project, since the Japanese empire would require its subjects to be treated with the same consideration as European immigrants, which was apparently not what Brazil had clear intentions of doing. Lima deemed the admission of Japanese workers was undesirable: not only because they were considered an inferior race but also because of the belief that the so-called "Mongolian" races had a different psychological nature and could not assimilate in Brazil.[20]

Eventually, the subsidized Japanese immigration began. Between 1908 and 1941, 188,615 people left Japan and settled in Brazil.[21] After a sharp increase between 1924 and 1935 (due to, among other factors, the US National Origins Act of 1924), the number of Japanese immigrants dropped steeply. In the Constituent

Assembly of 1932, the anti-Japanese strand finally got to approve quotas meant to limit Japanese immigration, taking the equivalent US laws as a model. Takeuchi considers the 1932 assembly's debates and decisions the ultimate result of US immigration policies' influence in that period.[22] The Japanese were portrayed as unassimilable, politically dangerous, and racially undesired. According to Takeuchi, openly discriminatory amendments were not approved due to the intervention of diplomats and President Getúlio Vargas himself, who were worried about an imminent diplomatic crisis with Japan.[23] Conciliation was reached with an amendment that determined a limit of a 2 percent renovation of the past fifty years' total—for immigrants of all countries. Carefully calculated, the amendment, without mentioning the Japanese, would only affect them, which satisfied those who were worried about the alleged genetic formation of the Brazilian population.

Once again in consonance with the US, the exclusion of Japanese immigrants and their families reached its peak during World War II. In 1937, Getúlio Vargas kept himself in power through a coup and ruled Brazil as a dictator until 1945. Like most dictatorships, Vargas's had a strong nationalist component to it, to the extent that some consider it a fascist regime. Immigrants, or foreigners of any kind, were a problem to be closely watched and repressed. Although other national groups, like the Germans, were also under state oppression, the Japanese already had to face racial exclusion, which was added to because they were subjects to an enemy nation. German and Japanese communities were forbidden to speak their languages in public, and they were required to run schools and publish newspapers solely in Portuguese. They couldn't hold meetings of any kind and had their books and radios seized. At some point, some Japanese colonies were entirely moved to internment camps.

As mentioned previously, the subsidized Japanese immigration to Brazil had begun in the first decade of the twentieth century. Early Japanese arrived through racist immigration policies, which had the objective of whitening the population as a postulate. After centuries of slave traffic, the elites saw *miscigenação* as the ultimate solution to limit Black population growth.[24] Supported by the then alleged scientific consensus on race—as having a biological and genetic explanation— white Europeans were considered to have the preferred makeup to shape the population melting pot—in morphological, psychological, and cultural aspects.[25]

The institutional policies aimed at whitening Brazil's population were central to its self-perception of race. The national census's count of the white and "*pardos*" population would increase between the 1870s and the 1950s,[26] while the number of Black people would decrease.[27] This data reflects how the mixed-race population would strive to identify as white and also how the collective imaginary would be consolidated around the racist premise of being seen as white as a distinction that was not only an honor given by the elites but also the most desirable genetic composition for a population.

The immigration policies also accompanied the erasure of Black history. For instance, the incineration of documents in 1889, ordered by Ruy Barbosa, the minister of finance, included statistical and demographic records pertaining to slavery, slave trafficking, and enslaved Africans. The destruction of documents was justified by the desire to erase what was then called the "Black stain" of slavery in Brazil, but it was actually meant to deny Black people the possibility of self-definition.[28] Along with the prohibition of cultural practices, these were some of the mechanisms that limited African descendants from recovering and solidifying their identities.[29]

This Black genocide project, as worded by Nascimento, had, as its institutional varnish, the discourse of "we are all Brazilians" by eliminating Black presence and memory through *miscigenação* and erasure policies.[30] To claim Brazil as a country of supposedly racial harmony meant denying any recognition of race and hindering any public discussion about racism and racial discrimination from flourishing. This idea of one conciliated unity, with no racial conflict, is an ideology known as the racial democracy myth, which still very much structures the country's current mainstream perception of itself.

A purportedly racial democracy, in this sense, means that to talk about race in Brazil—be it in the popular context or the institutional one—is taboo. Gonzales criticizes how, in Brazil, "the first thing that we perceive, in this talk about racism, is that everyone thinks it's natural," as if "Black people should really live in misery" based on the common underlying assumption that "they have some attributes that are nothing of value."[31] As ingrained in the social and cultural fabric, this naturalization also posits discourse at the organs of institutional power (such as government, law, armed forces, and police), as demonstrated by the public policies adopted throughout history.

This is a determining feature of the Brazilian outlook on how race is viewed domestically. As Lélia Gonzales ironically observes, "Racism? In Brazil? Who said that? This is an American thing. Here there is no difference because everyone is Brazilian above all, thank God."[32] Racial democracy paints Brazil as a nation without prejudice or racism, allegedly capable of assimilating anyone who arrives in the country. This myth denies the recognition of race itself, which means it denies people of color of making any claims about racism ever existing in Brazil. As a result of the nonrecognition of a racially diverse country—especially a country whose population is comprised mainly of Black people—the dominant ideology also serves to deny how race determines economic exclusion. In this Brazilian race-class-society labyrinth, to be the "undesired but required" national labor force would result in Asian descendants occupying different positions throughout the decades within Brazil's racial structure.[33] The idea of yellow peril and ambiguous stereotypes would still accompany the Japanese in the 1930s and beyond.

Bruno Hayashi observes how, beginning in the late 1950s, congressmen had shifted from the yellow peril discourse to one in which the Japanese would become the ethnic minority capable of social integration and economic growth.[34] In 1958, one congressman would attest that the Brazilian interest is for ethnic groups to be assimilated "as soon as possible, as completely as possible, in order for them to be integrated in Brazilian communion."[35] In this respect, Nascimento points out how the "monstrous machine" called racial democracy bestows upon Black people a single "privilege"—that is, to become white, inside and out.[36] And the answer to "this imperialism of whiteness, and its inherent capitalism" lies in assimilation, acculturation, and miscegenation.[37]

Given this history, what does assimilation mean for Japanese Brazilians? A prosopography of Japanese Brazilian activists conducted by Lesser[38] shows racial ambiguity, as Japanese Brazilians would not describe themselves as a minority, but their Brazilian-ness would not suffice to avoid racist stereotypes.[39] The end result was that "our Japanese," the Japanese immigrants and descendants who came to Brazil, had an "always fluid national identity," being considered both as "atypical" and as "the best of all the Brazilian."[40]

Due to the confluence of whitening politics and the racial democracy myth, some Japanese descendants came to be, like Alberto Nomura, the "ideal neoliberal subject."[41] In this sense, as a councilman in the largest city in Brazil, Nomura implicitly claims to be a representative of the largest Japanese population outside Japan. To impose a bill to banish so-called "non-Oriental" vendors in a key neighborhood of downtown São Paulo is to accept the model-minority role as an example of meritocracy, a role that does not complain about its sufferings and is capable of erasing other groups' struggles. What Liberdade, as an exclusively Asian neighborhood, shows us is the project of a country without race, a paradox that can only work within the racial democracy myth. Those referred to as "Orientals" (or Japanese, because in a Brazilian Orientalist point of view, both categories are interchangeable) emerge as a modernity vehicle, a symbol of development, a better minority for a better Brazil.[42]

Nevertheless, this Feira da Liberdade episode also shows an opposing yet consistent and historically accurate face of the role Asian people can play in Brazilian society. The bill proposed by Nomura, after having some repercussions on social media and in online communities—mostly from the point of view of affected vendors—drew attention from Asian Brazilian activists and other political groups. Despite its very recent presence and still minor relevance in the national race debate, those groups engaged in a large coalition to raise their voice against the exclusionary bill. As one of them, we aimed to deliver a counter-hegemonic stance within Asian communities in São Paulo, creating both an internal and external dispute over Liberdade's Asian-ness. The coalition stood beside the vendors' claims and the Capela dos Aflitos' denunciation, helping to mobilize a campaign against the bill, particularly on the internet.[43] The diversity of those three groups was relevant enough for the campaign to thrive and reach a large audience. Ultimately, Nomura's bill was dropped.

Asian activism is still a nascent movement in Brazil. Although it is undeniable that Asian Brazilians have been a target of racism, it is also a fact that their position is better than other racial minorities, which has contributed to an acceptance of the model-minority role. However, it is also possible to say this role was imposed on Asian Brazilians, who were struggling to be accepted by a society that still perceives them as a foreign ethnic group, always lacking Brazilian-ness. The first collective groups that started calling for Asian activism in Brazil were born in the early 2010s, mostly online, and they spread awareness about some jokes as racist tropes. Our prognosis in 2023 is that there is incipient political potential, as there is a great number of small groups in different places but still little engagement among them. In this sense, the 2020 coalition was an important step to create common ground that could lead to a more conclusive discussion about the activism's main claims and principles.

Luís de Camões is possibly considered to be the most important writer in Portuguese-language literature. His main work, *The Lusiads*, is an epic poem on the Portuguese journey to the Indies in the so-called "Age of Discovery," celebrating the search for a sea route to Asia—therefore, celebrating Portugal's colonization project. It is said that Camões wrote it when he was exiled in Macau. By reading some poems he wrote about this period of permanence, one can find references to a woman, Dinamene, a muse to the author. Legend has it that Camões met Dinamene in Macau and fell in love with her. Returning to Portugal, he found himself in a shipwreck, during which he was forced to make a great decision: to save the manuscript of his epic poem or to save Dinamene's life. Thus, the greatest poem in Portuguese literature survived.

In colonial projects, a person's life is made commensurate to land as a means to colonial power. As land, people's lives are merely properties that insure the continuity of production based on exploitation, and some sheets containing an ode to the brave sons of Lusus (that is, the Lusiads) are more valuable than a human life. "Forget Camões; our true heroine is Dinamene."[44] When we wrote that in our manifesto in 2020, we wanted to say we would not take part in the construction of Asian people as neither a friend to Camões nor as a better Camões. We reject colonial structures by understanding our complex and contradictory positions within colonialism and by trying to change these structures through political endeavors to force an epistemological turn.

The Feira da Liberdade case is symbolic. On the one hand, we find in Nomura a reproduction of white oppression against other people of color, erasing their history and political struggle and serving whitening politics and racial democracy. Japão-Liberdade, the project of transforming Liberdade into an Asian/Japanese neighborhood, is a step toward colonial white violence obliteration right in the heart of Brazil's biggest metropolis.[45] On the other hand, the groups in the Asian Brazilian activist coalition chose to fight against racism within their communities, putting the new activism's greatest principle into practice: anti-racism solidarity. By preventing our people from supporting white supremacy, we choose to fight the real enemy, which is not white people themselves or meritocratic Asians but systemic white supremacy, racism as a structure within capitalism.

While Alberto Nomura and his allies attempt to fulfill a crucial role in the gears of racism, we reject the breadcrumbs of whiteness. By turning our gaze to other people of color and by choosing solidarity with them, acknowledging the role given to us by whiteness, we aim to break the logic that puts Europe and colonizers at the center of the world. We try to bring into reality what Frantz Fanon said sixty years ago: "For humanity, comrades, we must turn over a new leaf, we must work out new concepts, and try to set a foot a new man."[46] We shall not take on white people's positioning; we must not accept to be either "next in line to be white" or "next in line to disappear."[47] What we truly desire is "that the tool never possess the man. That the enslavement of man by man cease forever. That is, of one by another. That it be possible for me to discover and to love man, wherever he may be."[48] We call for actions in the world to globally achieve this goal. Not as an idealistic humanism, but as an effort of struggle against a cosmogony that has already brought us to a nonreturning point. To destroy colonialism, we must look into ourselves as Asian Brazilians.

Notes

[1] Qiao Yin, "O desenvolvimento do relacionamento civil entre os novos imigrantes chineses e imigrantes japoneses desde os anos 1970: Um estudo de caso sobre a interação social no bairro da Liberdade," 54.

[2] In Brazil, "Oriental" is normally a synonym for Asian, while the use of "*asiático*" is much less common. Although we do not endorse it, it is not a term considered outdated or problematic in the common sense.

[3] Lais de Barros Monteiro Guimarães, *Liberdade*, 91–95.

[4] Yin, "O desenvolvimento," 53.

[5] Odair da Cruz Paiva, "Da Glória à Liberdade: a memória em disputa num território paulistano," in *Anais Eletrônicos do XXV Encontro Estadual de História da ANPUH-SP: História, Desigualdades e Diferenças*, 6.

[6] Social movements have been fighting for the preservation of the chapel's memory, having gained the registration of the former cemetery as an archeological site, recognition and permission from city hall to build a memorial, and the recent approval by the city council to include "Africa" in the name of Liberdade-Japão Square.

[7] Jeffrey Lesser, *A invenção da brasilidade: identidade nacional, etnicidade e políticas de imigração*, trans. Patricia de Queiroz Carvalho Zimbres, 40–45.

[8] Brazil was the last country in the Western world to abolish slavery in 1888. The international slave trade had been abolished (at least legally) since 1850, following the British Aberdeen Act of 1845.

[9] Marcia Yumi Takeuchi, "Entre gueixas e samurais: a imigração japonesa nas revistas ilustradas (1897–1945)," 35; Rogério Dezem, *Matizes do "Amarelo": a gênese dos discursos sobre os orientais no Brasil*, 102.

[10] Mostly, but not only, of Chinese origin.

[11] Dezem, *Matizes do "Amarelo,"* 45.

[12] Ana Paulina Lee, *Mandarin Brazil: Race, Representation, and Memory*.

[13] Ibid., 11.

[14] Dezem, *Matizes do "Amarelo,"* 93.

[15] Takeuchi, "Gueixas e samurais," 36.

[16] Dezem, *Matizes do "Amarelo,"* 58.

[17] Lee, *Mandarin Brazil*, 127.

[18] Elena Camargo Shizuno, *Os imigrantes japoneses na Segunda Guerra Mundial: bandeirantes do oriente ou perigo amarelo no Brasil*.

[19] Takeuchi, "Gueixas e samurais," 42–43.

[20] Ibid., 43.

[21] Lesser, *Brasilidade*, 215.

[22] Takeuchi, "Gueixas e samurais," 185.

[23] Ibid., 188.

[24] *Miscigenação* as racial politics is the plan of mixing races in Brazil with the goal of whitening its population. It presents itself as a pacific, or at least a softer, model of racial identity building, but in fact it is just as violent as racial apartheid or racial extermination.

[25] Abdias do Nascimento, *O genocídio do negro brasileiro: processo de um racismo mascarado*, 64.

[26] Historically, "*pardo*" has been synonymous with mixed Black and white peoples. It is also one of the official racial categories used by the Brazilian Institute of Geography and Statistics (IBGE) for the official national population census, in which the questionnaire

asks respondents to self-identify according to their skin color. In this sense, "pardo" poses almost as a residual identity for Black people who have light skin.

[27] Nascimento, *Genocídio do negro*, 65–66.

[28] Ibid., 69–70.

[29] Ibid., 82–89.

[30] Ibid., 61–68.

[31] Lélia Gonzales, "Racismo e sexismo na cultura brasileira," 225.

[32] Ibid., 226. Jair M. Bolsonaro, Brazil's former president, had as his campaign and government slogan, "Brazil above everyone, God above everything," which is one of the most recent examples of how this idea is still very much alive in Brazil.

[33] Nascimento, *Genocício do negro*, 75.

[34] Bruno Naomassa Hayashi, "Metamorfoses do amarelo: a imigração japonesa do "perigo amarelo" à "democracia racial."

[35] Ibid., 17.

[36] Nascimento, *Genocídio do negro*, 82.

[37] Hayashi, "Metamorfoses do amarelo," 82.

[38] Jeffrey Lesser, *Uma diáspora descontente: os nipo-brasileiros e os significados da militância étnica 1960-1980.*

[39] Ibid., 44–46, 58.

[40] Ibid., 59–61.

[41] Cathy Park Hong, *Minor Feelings*, 185.

[42] Lesser, *Diáspora descontente.*

[43] What once was the center of a cemetery for enslaved people, as previously mentioned.

[44] Originally "Esqueçam Camões. Nossa verdadeira heroína é Dinamene" "Manifesto do Coletivo Dinamene."

[45] In June 2023, after the submission of this essay's first draft, a new law was published in São Paulo, once again renaming the Praça da Liberdade, this time to Praça da Liberdade África-Japão. The dispute over Liberdade's memory is still ongoing and possibly heading in new directions.

[46] Frantz Fanon, *The Wretched of the Earth*, 316.

[47] Hong, *Minor Feelings*, 35.

[48] Frantz Fanon, *Black Skin, White Masks*, 231.

Bibliography

Coletivo Dinamene. "Manifesto do Coletivo Dinamene." Accessed May 4, 2020. https://coletivodinamene.medium.com/manifesto-do-coletivo-dinamene-558a15b3a8a2.

Dezem, Rogério, *Matizes do "Amarelo": a gênese dos discursos sobre os orientais no Brasil*. São Paulo: Fapesp, 2005.

Fanon, Frantz. *Black Skin, White Masks*. London: Pluto Press, 1986.

———. *The Wretched of the Earth*. New York: Grove Press, 1963.

Gonzales, Lélia. "Racismo e sexismo na cultura brasileira." *Revistas Ciências Sociais Hoje* (1984): 223–244.

Guimarães, Lais de Barros Monteiro. *Liberdade*. São Paulo: Secretaria Municipal de Cultura do Município de São Paulo, 1979.

Hayashi, Bruno Naomassa. "Metamorfoses do amarelo: a imigração japonesa do 'perigo amarelo' à 'democracia racial." *Revista Brasileira de Ciências Sociais* 37, no. 108 (2022): 1–15.

Hong, Cathy Park. *Minor Feelings: an Asian American Reckoning*. New York: Oneworld, 2020.

Lee, Ana Paulina, *Mandarin Brazil: Race, Representation, and Memory*. Stanford: Stanford University Press, 2018.

Lesser, Jeffrey. *A invenção da brasilidade: identidade nacional, etnicidade e políticas de imigração*. Trans. by Patricia de Queiroz Carvalho Zimbres. São Paulo: Editora Unesp, 2015.

———. *Uma diáspora descontente: os nipo-brasileiros e os significados da militância étnica 1960–1980*. Trans. by Patricia de Queiroz Carvalho Zimbres. São Paulo: Paz e Terra, 2008.

Nascimento, Abdias do. *O genocídio do negro brasileiro: processo de um racismo mascarado*. São Paulo: Perspectiva, 2016.

Paiva, Odair da Cruz, "Da Glória à Liberdade: a memória em disputa num território paulistano." In *Anais Eletrônicos do XXV Encontro Estadual de História da ANPUH-SP: História, Desigualdades e Diferenças*, edited by ANPUH-SP. São Paulo: ANPUH-SP, 2020, https://www.encontro2020.sp.anpuh.org/anais/trabalhos/trabalhosaprovados.

Shizuno, Elena Camargo. *Os imigrantes japoneses na Segunda Guerra Mundial: bandeirantes do oriente ou perigo amarelo no Brasil*. Londrina: EDUEL, 2010.

Takeuchi, Marcia Yumi. "Entre gueixas e samurais: a imigração japonesa nas revistas ilustradas (1897–1945)." Doctoral thesis, Universidade de São Paulo, 2009.

Yin, Qiao. "O desenvolvimento do relacionamento civil entre os novos imigrantes chineses e imigrantes japoneses desde os anos 1970: Um estudo de caso sobre a interação social no bairro da Liberdade." Master's thesis, Universidade de São Paulo, 2019.

4

THE POLITICAL ECONOMY OF ANTI-ASIAN DISCRIMINATION IN AFRICA

Richard Aidoo

"We want the Chinese out of Kenya. If the Chinese become the manufacturers, distributors, and retailers and even hawkers, where will Kenyans go?"

—Kenyan trader, March 5, 2023[1]

In 2022, Ugandan Asians[2] commemorated fifty years since they were forced out of Idi Amin's Uganda with recollections of castigations, like the one above from a Kenyan trader during a protest of unfair Chinese competition in the East African country.[3] Hundreds of Kenyan petty traders marched in the streets against the unfair trade practices of a major Chinese-owned bargain shop located on the outskirts of Nairobi after the government dismissed a counterfeit goods claim brought against the shop.[4] Over the past two decades, such incidents have characterized the expanding relationships between Asian and African countries, and they sadly perpetuate an increasing trend of anti-Asian discrimination. Particularly with the COVID-19 pandemic, anti-Asian hate has risen in Africa.[5]

Though anti-Asian discrimination has been historically present across Africa's diverse socioeconomic landscape, the recent surge of Asian economic interests has brought more migrants from countries like China, India, South Korea, and Japan, driving anti-Asian resentment and discrimination. As Asian capital and labor enter African communities, the clash among interests, expectations, values, and outcomes often impels discriminatory incidents in both Asian and African communities. Economic partnerships with different Asian countries, particularly China, have expanded trade and transferred technology to ensure the upskilling of African labor. Furthermore, though Asian-African partnerships have also invested in Africa's weak infrastructure, such contributions have come with immense and intense economic competition. The consequences may range from progress on economic development to acts of discrimination and deadly clashes.[6] Such effects are widely harnessed to fuel the political and economic ambitions of diverse domestic political actors. How do these African political entrepreneurs foment discrimination against Asian populations to facilitate their own political and economic ambitions?

Historically, African encounters with Asian countries consist of engagements with a mix of economic and political motives with deep ideological imperatives. These include instances of early twentieth-century Chinese indentured laborers in South African mines, and India and China's roles in pre-independence struggles to end imperialism in Africa. The breadth of these encounters set the stage for rather complex Afro-Asian partnerships after colonial rule, particularly the post-Cold War expansion of China's diplomacy in Africa. With postindependence Africa undergoing persistent political and economic transitions alongside the exemplary rise of Asian economies, Asia has provided instructive cases to serve as guideposts to African economic growth and development. This begs the question: How has the emergent pragmatic economic relationship between Asian and African countries given rise to anti-Asian rhetoric and bias in Africa?

To unravel this puzzle of political-economic opportunism, which has often had dire consequences, this essay draws from the broad concept of political economy that affords us the wisdom of sorting out the interrelationships between politics and economics with wide-ranging outcomes—in effect, how the strands of the struggle for political power in African constituencies enmesh to shape both political and economic development. In this essay, I contextualize examples of anti-Asian (particularly anti-Chinese) discrimination across the main regions of the African continent—southern, northern, eastern, and western—in order to capture the political value of anti-Asian hate, illustrated through specific examples and the outcomes they produced.

Political Economy and Anti-Asian Discrimination in Africa: A Brief

Over the past two decades, two major socioeconomic and political developments have occurred throughout the African continent, fostering significant changes that have enabled the resurgence of Asian economic and diplomatic interests across Africa, with attendant issues like anti-Asian discrimination and populism.[7] The first development is what has become known as the "Africa rising" discourse. This is a renaissance paradigm of African development, different from the postcolonial years of economic stagnation and political indiscipline that stifled economic development from the 1970s through the 1990s. After the turn of the millennium, African countries witnessed an era of inflection, with open economies and spurts of growth signifying a new epoch, that also welcomed a surge in external economic interests and investments. Democratization is the second post-Cold War development in Africa, as the turning of the economic tide was preceded and aided by a changing political order, which constituted Samuel Huntington's third wave of democratization.[8] Most of Africa's political regimes, which have hitherto been largely dominated by military dictatorships and one-party governments, gave way to popular and democratically elected governments.[9] This same political change has also enabled popular protest, an essential part of the democratic process.

Notably, the instances of anti-Asian discrimination throughout the history of various African countries were largely enabled by social and political forces that foment and direct such biases against the resident Asian communities. The recent anti-Asian bias in African communities has been mostly linked to economic imperatives with frequent prospects of fueling popular anger to propel political and economic change. Increasingly, instances of anti-Asian populism and violence are rife in many African communities with the entry of Asian capital, labor, and entrepreneurship. Though there are different nodes of contention that often lead to clashes between Asian and African inhabitants in a community or workplace, these occur with socioeconomic contexts that exist in a political framework.

Anti-Asian Discrimination in Africa: An Introduction

Africanists argue that violence is an inherent character of the African state as it evolved out of the throes of colonization. Consequently, various forms of political violence and struggle have continuously bedeviled political and economic development processes across Africa.[10] Instances of political and economic strife range from civil and ethnic conflicts to extreme starvation and stagnation, insurgencies, and terrorism. Alongside these struggles is the canker of xenophobia, which has increased over recent years, as economic challenges in most African neighborhoods have led to struggles over existing resources, often pitting foreigners or migrants against locals or citizens.[11]

In postcolonial Africa, several examples of openly xenophobic policies were established and enforced by different governments. From Ghana's 1969 Aliens Compliance Order to Nigeria's anti-immigration acts in the late 1980s, these formal frameworks discriminated against noncitizens under the guise of limited economic opportunities for local populations. Unsurprisingly, discrimination against Asians in Africa remains one of the common examples visible in the political-economic evolution of different countries.[12] From south to north and from east to west in Africa, diverse instances depict tales of anti-Asian discrimination that offer relevant connections between the past and present.

One of the historical accounts that roots discriminatory political-economic arrangements against an Asian population in Africa is the tale of the 63,695 Chinese indentured laborers imported to the Transvaal (now South Africa) between 1904 and 1907 to toil in the gold mines of Witwatersrand. The workers had been brought in as an experiment to help rebuild the colony's economy and to raise wealth for debts owed to Britain after the South African War (1899–1902).[13] By 1910, all Chinese indentured laborers had been forcefully repatriated to China.[14] This "use and discard" episode not only shaped South African history but had notable global impacts. Considering the importance of the mining industry to the development of modern South Africa, it revealed and affirmed the timeless construct of government-business relations geared toward the production of capitalist-inspired prosperity with deep undertones of colonization, discrimination, racism, and dehumanization.

The Transvaal experiment was also preceded by South Africa's experience with Indian indentured laborers who were brought by the British in the 1860s to work in the sugarcane plantations under contractual agreements that were slightly better than those of the Chinese indentured laborers.[15] While the Indian indentured workers were guaranteed the freedom and choice of settling in South Africa with a small land grant after a decade of servitude, the Chinese indentured workers were offered a return to China after their laborious stints in the mines of Witwatersrand.[16] The latter's offer was discriminatorily embedded in hostile and racist policy and discourse from a white British colonial government and populace that feared being overrun by Asian laborers. As vividly captured in Yoon Jung Park's *A Matter of Honour: Being Chinese in South Africa*:

> The presence of tens of thousands of these Chinese mineworkers, especially as they roamed about the streets of early Johannesburg on their off-days with their foreign looks and long, plaited pigtails, wreaked fear in the hearts of white South Africans. Fueled by exaggerated reports of desertion and crime, mass protests demanded the repatriation of the Chinese indentured labourers. In response, the government declared open season on the Chinese, empowering white citizens to shoot or arrest any Chinese found outside the mining compounds of the Transvaal.[17]

Such heart-wrenching accounts add to trajectories of xenophobia, racism, and apartheid throughout South Africa's contemporary political-economic history. More startling are the legislative and policy nods that were granted to such arrangements. For instance, in the history of racist legislation in South Africa, the initial industrial color bars were framed specifically to exclude Chinese from skilled occupation and were later extended to cover all Black labor.[18] Some scholars argue that the significance of the government's involvement in the Transvaal scheme goes beyond whether they colluded with the mines and reflects competing ideas about capitalism and the role of government to regulate or modify society.[19] Furthermore, according to Rachel Bright, the obsession with turning the Transvaal into a *white* British colony governed the decision process just as much, if not more, than economic concerns.[20]

Another example of anti-Asian discrimination can be found in the postindependence Africa of President Idi Amin's 1972 mass expulsion of Asians— particularly the Indian population—from Uganda. Beginning in the 1800s, Asians had worked their way to the upper echelons of the Ugandan economy.[21] They provided skilled labor, capital, and entrepreneurship, and in return accumulated large amounts of wealth, widening the socioeconomic gap between them and the Black Ugandan population.[22] Arguably, it was the Asian domination of the commercial sector that drew massive popular resentment and contributed to the push by Amin's military regime to unleash the "war of economic liberation"—a government-driven plan of getting rid of the Indian "exploiters and cheaters" that had monopolized many sectors of the Ugandan economy and that posed an obstacle to Black Ugandan advancement.[23] One of the symbols of Asian supremacy in the Ugandan economy had been the *dukawallahs* (traders), whose daily business transactions in Ugandan neighborhoods incurred the displeasure of the Africans who felt displaced in their own economic locality.

Idi Amin's abrupt and distressful policy of economic liberation drove a sharp wedge between citizens and noncitizens in Uganda in the 1970s. The policy, which was initially targeted at British Indians, quickly included other Ugandan-born Asians who knew no other homeland than this East African polity. The Black Ugandans, who mostly felt slighted by the economic inequities that disadvantaged them, saw immense benefits on the economic horizon, as the policy included a reallocation phase.[24] With the exit of the Asians, the government intended to allocate Asian property—houses, shops, and industries—to the Africans as part of a much more effective plan to implement the policy of the Africanization of commerce, jobs, and wages, which had hitherto been ineffective under previous postcolonial government administrations.[25] To facilitate the process of the African ownership of wealth and production, the war of economic liberation by Amin's populist military regime had to combine the eviction of Asians with the transfer of the means of production to Africans, leaving in place a traumatized socioeconomic order. Despairingly, this anti-Asian popular fervor was sweeping across East Africa, as Uganda's neighbor to the east, Kenya, had made earlier significant formal attempts to deal with the dominance of Indians in its economy.

In the late 1960s, the postcolonial Kenyan government passed two pieces of legislation—the Immigration Act and the Trade Licensing Act. Both were deemed to have detrimentally affected Asian businesses, and hence, they drove out many Asians.[26] Most eerily, Kenya's past expressions of anti-Asian popular sentiments have currently morphed into the tide of anti-Chinese populism during COVID-19. For instance, the expression below by a Kenyan parliamentarian in 1972 is quite akin to the quote highlighted at the opening of this essay, a rebuke during a 2023 protest by petty traders against a Chinese bargain shop in Nairobi: "Look at the Olympic team today. A Singh here and a Patel there—even in the East African Car Safari it's all Singhs. I look forward to the day when there will be no more Singhs in the Olympic team, only Africans."[27]

During the post-Cold War era, African countries have attempted to push their economies past the postindependence economic challenges between the 1970s and the 1990s that strained and stifled African development. As previously discussed, this occurred alongside the renewed popular embrace of resourceful, responsive, and accountable governance: democracy. Generally, the political and economic openness across Africa, particularly in the 1990s, equally revived and increased external interest from both the developed and developing worlds. Scholars and stakeholders have referred to Africa's engagement with the Washington Consensus and Beijing Consensus, intimating the persistence of economic interests from the West and an equally recent surge in China-Africa economic diplomacy. This new era of China's engagement with African countries has reportedly received an enthusiastic continental embrace as China has replaced the West as the largest financier of African development efforts, with heavy investments in African infrastructure, trade, and security, and with China's status as a model for economic development.[28] In short, Beijing has evolved away from its role as an ideological proselytizer during the struggle to end imperialism in African countries to become a pragmatic economic influencer in Africa. These exhortations of China in Africa have also come with an increase in anti-Chinese sentiments across segments of the African population, as Chinese migrants and their economic initiatives compete with the efforts of local Africans.[29]

Across sub-Saharan Africa, the sources or fault lines that foster anti-Chinese populism are largely those economic spaces where African resources and labor often converge or collide with Chinese capital and management. This has often led to popular anger that can sometimes turn deadly in the oil fields or on the factory floors in Ethiopia, as well as in the mining fields in Ghana or Zambia. In 2007, nine Chinese workers were killed during an attack on a Chinese oil field in eastern Ethiopia at the Abole oil exploration facility. This ghastly event was a stain on the renewed relationship between Ethiopia and China under Prime Minister Meles Zenawi, whose Ethiopian People's Revolutionary Democratic

Front administration was inching away from Western overreliance.[30] Having led Ethiopia since 1995—against the backdrop of a complex and messy democratic process fraught with ethnic and national factionalism that undermined Ethiopia's democracy—Zenawi's hard-line approaches and political heavy-handedness led to Western disfavor and criticism. This necessitated deepening relations with other non-Western allies like China to support a government-renewed plan for greater economic and political liberalization beginning in 2001.[31] An increase in Chinese economic interests in Ethiopia saw the development of high-profile projects, such as a hydroelectric dam, roads, and railways, as well as investments in the garments industry, particularly after Ethiopia hosted the second Forum for China-Africa Cooperation.

With the ramp-up of high-level exchanges between Addis Ababa and Beijing at the turn of the millennium, many Ethiopian political elites perceived opportunities while the popular masses clashed with the Chinese within their communities. Some of the remaining points of contention included the employment of Chinese labor instead of Ethiopian workers for high-skilled positions, language and cultural differences that led to clashes over the work ethic of Ethiopian workers, tensions over workers' rights, and the continuous influx of Chinese manufactured goods that competed with local producers.[32] Besides these economic issues, which continue to complicate Ethiopia-China relations, China is often caught in Ethiopia's political crises that are fueled by ethnic and nationalist struggles. In January 2023, nine Chinese came under deadly attack in Ethiopia's Oromiya region, where a separatist conflict continues to impede development efforts.[33]

Finally, another source of anti-Asian sentiment that supports diverse forms of discrimination and deadly attacks is connected to the increasing involvement of Chinese migrants in illegal mining in resource-endowed African communities. Though this problem is present in a few African countries with increasing Chinese migrant communities, the situation in Ghana's artisanal gold mining industry is quite notable. Despite relatively warm China-Ghana diplomacy, which dates back to the 1950s, both countries have struggled to navigate the public diplomacy disaster connected to increasing reports of Chinese engagement in illegal and unregistered artisanal gold mining (locally known as *galamsey*) in Ghana.[34] Though this has been a challenge over the years, it has risen to destructive levels as the unregulated extraction of gold has led to the pollution of Ghanaian rivers and the destruction of forest and soil covers. The environmental destruction comes along with human costs, as armed Chinese and Ghanaian illegal miners often clash with security forces and local inhabitants.[35] With the situation reaching unconstrained levels in 2013, government administrations from the two dominant political parties—the New Patriotic Party and the National Democratic Congress—have both tried different approaches but with very little success.[36] Not even the mass repatriation of Chinese citizens out of Ghana over the years has deterred the increase in this illegal activity. As much as this situation has proven challenging at the government level, it also continues to open avenues of anti-Asian hate and further discriminatory behaviors in some of the communities that bear the brunt of the destruction resulting from this Chinese-aided, unregulated economic activity.[37]

Playing Politics and the Economy with Anti-Asian Discourse in Africa

As shown previously in this essay, as well as through the different cases presented in this volume—which include Turkey, Brazil, Mexico, Germany, and Sweden—it is evident that different forms of anti-Asian discrimination manifest through sociopolitical arrangements. In both the historical examples and the twenty-first-century manifestations of Asian hate across Africa, the common denominator remains the role of political actors (both inside and outside government) in the fomentation and facilitation of the active structures and processes that advance this dangerous phenomenon. For political actors, the function of anti-Asian discourse may be geared toward outcompeting an opponent during an election or in the debate of ideas, with an objective of winning a greater share of the vote. In this bid, the use of anti-Asian discourse or rhetoric that could devolve into hate and discrimination is a perennial feature of African political contests, particularly in recent years. During the 2022 campaign, William Ruto, the current president of Kenya, vowed to deport Chinese nationals engaged in jobs reserved for Kenyans and to make government contracts with Beijing more transparent. Here, anti-Asian political messaging remains a viable platform in Africa for some political-economic purposes.

First, elections, as a means of sorting through political ideas in post-independence Africa, have largely been about the selection of the best path for economic development. In this regard, elections are also about the major political-economic actors who influence the course of economic development in any African country where they occur. Throughout history, diverse Asian actors continue to hold sway over political and economic processes in individual African countries. Accordingly, while African incumbents can claim the political potency of Chinese economic partnership as a key to job creation, access to capital, and infrastructural projects, the opposition parties and candidates relish the opportunity to convert anti-China popular anger into electoral votes. This has become a common practice in numerous competitive elections in Africa. Opposition parties are adept at connecting the failures of the incumbent party to its association or dependence on China, thereby driving up anti-China rhetoric to get angry sections of the electorate to act on their xenophobia at the ballot box. A classic case of this approach is Michael Sata, Zambia's fifth president. After two failed attempts at earlier presidential runs, Sata led the opposition Popular Front to electoral victory during the 2011 elections by vigorously and controversially employing anti-China rhetoric during his political campaign.[38]

Another oft-politicized issue in relations between Asian actors and their African hosts is the extraction of natural resources. This is an age-old economic activity—with connections to Asian communities in Africa—that dates back to nineteenth-century instances of Chinese and Indian involvement in South African mines. Given that natural resource sectors in African countries are often fulcrums of economic development, they logically elicit intense political debates and popular discontent. If the activities of an external actor at the site of the resource or resource-endowed community is considered untoward, or if they undermine the capacity of local dwellers to benefit from a given natural resource, a clash may be imminent. As African political actors engage in competition, localities in areas endowed with natural resources—that are often managed by or that employ Asian labor—often serve as targets in anti-Asian political campaigns. For instance, research shows that the local populations in close proximity to Chinese-operated mines benefit from better socioeconomic amenities; however, anti-Chinese sentiments are also highest in these areas, making them potential strongholds for political opposition in their quest to unseat an incumbent.[39] Regarding the definitive example of Zambia's Sata, the maltreatment of Zambian mine workers in Chinese-owned mines contributed to the increasing anti-China fury that fueled his victory in 2011.[40] Many such incidents exist in both past and present competitive elections in countries like Ghana, Kenya, Sierra Leone, and Zimbabwe.

The political effectiveness of neocolonialism is often dangled over any unequal diplomatic relations with an external global power in Africa. Over the past two decades, as China's influence has increased in Africa, Beijing has been accused of the recolonization of the continent.[41] Though China has warded off the neocolonialism critique, diverse African political stakeholders, such as opposition parties and their sponsors (often from the West), see this line of attack as viable and effective given Africa's colonial past.[42] The anti-China rhetoric is often grafted onto the discourse of anti-colonialism, which often awakens anger and frustration across the African continent and diaspora. Such popular resentment often materializes in emotive political discourses that propel populations to seek or effect political change meant to displace political or economic actors who are deemed supporters of the "neocolonizer." Again, in the model case of the 2011 electoral victory of Zambia's Michael Sata, one of the well-quoted anti-China sound bites that conjured apparitions of colonialism is, "Zambia is becoming a province—make that a district—of China."[43] When such anti-Asian sentiments are stirred up by political agents, the hope is to use them as propellants to electoral victory, yet their impacts are often far-reaching and destructive, lasting beyond a single election cycle.

Finally, the conception and use of anti-Asian discrimination as part of the political discourse is rendered effective because China's new role in Africa is commonly linked to vital issues of economic value. Hence, the political use of anti-Asian discourse has real economic implications. The provision of Chinese capital in the form of loans and other types of financial assistance, the issue of debt, and the allocation of jobs to Chinese laborers while African populations are beset with high unemployment rates are some of the major issues that are often spun to appeal to an anti-Asian base during elections. Paradoxically, once the political candidates are declared winners, they quickly make an about-face to embrace all external political and economic actors, including Asian economic residents in their countries. Such an approach is indicative of the use of anti-Asian (particularly, anti-Chinese) discourse and discrimination as tools of political expediency to pursue and achieve political-economic development objectives, which further propagates this socioeconomic plague in Africa.

Notes

[1] BBC, "China Square."

[2] This is a common reference for the Asian population that resides in Uganda. It is a term that appears especially in popular media to represent the rather diverse Asian population in the country. For an example of such a reference, see "Ugandan Asians Recall the Trauma of Fleeing Their Homes 50 Years On"—a media report by the BBC cited in this essay.

[3] BBC, "Ugandan Asians Recall the Trauma of Fleeing Their Homes 50 years On"; BBC, "China Square."

[4] BBC, "China Square."

[5] Aidoo, "Explaining the Impacts of the COVID-19 Pandemic on China-Africa Relations."

[6] Mohan, Lampert, Tan-Mullins, and Chang, *Chinese Migrants and Africa's Development.*

[7] Aidoo and Hess, "Non-Interference 2.0: China's Evolving Foreign Policy towards a Changing Africa"; Hess and Aidoo, *Charting the Roots of Anti-Chinese Populism in Africa;* Aidoo, "The Political Economy of Galamsey and Anti-Chinese Sentiment in Ghana."

[8] Huntington, *The Third Wave.*

[9] Radelet, "Success Stories from Emerging Africa."

[10] Akinola, "Introduction: Understanding Xenophobia in Africa."

[11] Ibid., 1–4.

[12] Hess and Aidoo, *Charting the Roots of Anti-Chinese Populism in Africa.*

[13] Bright, *Chinese Labour in South Africa, 1902–10.*

[14] Ibid., 1.

[15] Yoon, *A Matter of Honour.*

[16] Ibid., 12.

[17] Ibid., 13.

[18] Wang, "Roots and the Changing Identity of the Chinese in the United States."

[19] Bright, *Chinese Labour in South Africa, 1902–10.*

[20] Ibid., 2.

[21] Jamal, "Asians in Uganda, 1880–1972: Inequality and Expulsion."

[22] Ibid., 602.

[23] Patel, "General Amin and the Indian Exodus from Uganda."

[24] Jamal, "Asians in Uganda, 1880–1972: Inequality and Expulsion."

[25] Ibid., 602–603.

[26] Furedi, "The Development of Anti-Asian Opinion among Africans in Nakuru District, Kenya."

[27] Ibid., 347.

[28] Large, *China and Africa: The New Era.*

[29] Aidoo, "Why Anti-Chinese Sentiment in Africa is on the Rise."

[30] Hess and Aidoo, *Charting the Roots of Anti-Chinese Populism in Africa.*

[31] Ibid., 80–84.

[32] Ibid., 85–86.

[33] Reuters, "One Chinese Citizen Killed in Ethiopia's Oromiya Region—Embassy."

[34] Aidoo, "The Political Economy of Galamsey and Anti-Chinese Sentiment in Ghana."

[35] Ibid., 6.

[36] Hess and Aidoo, "Charting the Impact of Subnational Actors in China's Foreign Relations."

[37] Ibid.

[38] Hess and Aidoo, *Charting the Roots of Anti-Chinese Populism in Africa*; Hess and Aidoo, "Charting the Roots of Anti-Chinese Populism in Africa: A Comparison of Zambia and Ghana."

[39] Wegenast, Strüver, Giesen, and Krauser, "At Africa's Expense? Disaggregating the Social Impact of Chinese Mining Operations."

[40] Lee, *The Specter of Global China: Politics, Labor, and Foreign Investments in Africa.*

[41] Chau, *Exploiting Africa: The Influence of Maoist China in Algeria, Ghana, and Tanzania.*

[42] Aidoo, "African Countries Have Started to Push Back against Chinese Development Aid. Here's Why."

[43] Michel and Beuret, *China Safari: On the Trail of Beijing's Expansion in Africa.*

Bibliography

Aidoo, Richard. "The Political Economy of Galamsey and Anti-Chinese Sentiment in Ghana," *African Studies Quarterly* 16, no. 3–4 (December 2016): 55–72.

———. "Explaining the Impacts of the COVID-19 Pandemic on China-Africa Relations." In *Teaching about Asia in a Time of Pandemic*, edited by David Kenley, 69–77. Ann Arbor: Association for Asian Studies, 2020.

———. "Why Anti-Chinese Sentiment in Africa is on the Rise," *Sixth Tone*, July 18, 2016. https://www.sixthtone.com/news/1076.

———. "African Countries Have Started to Push Back against Chinese Development Aid. Here's Why." *Washington Post*, October 16, 2018. https://www.washingtonpost.com/news/monkey-cage/wp/2018/10/16/african-countries-have-started-to-push-back-against-chinese-development-aid-heres-why/.

Aidoo, Richard and Steve Hess. "Non-Interference 2.0: China's Evolving Foreign Policy towards a Changing Africa," *Journal of Current Chinese Affairs*, 44, no. 1 (2015): 107–139.

Akinola, Adeoye O. "Introduction: Understanding Xenophobia in Africa." In *The Political Economy of Xenophobia in Africa*, edited by Adeoye O. Akinola, 1–7. Cham: Springer International Publishing, 2018.

Barma, Naazneen H. and Steven K. Vogel., ed. *The Political Economy Reader: Contending Perspectives and Contemporary Debates*. New York: Routledge, 2022.

Bates, Roberts H. "Political Economy of Africa's Economic Performance in the Post-Independence Period." In *The Oxford Companion to the Economics of Africa*, edited by Ernest Aryeetey et al., 224–231. Oxford: Oxford University Press, 2012.

BBC. "China Square: The Cheap Chinese Shop at the Centre of Kenya Row," *BBC News*, March 6, 2023. https://www.bbc.com/news/world-africa-64809423.

———. "Ugandan Asians Recall the Trauma of Fleeing Their Homes 50 Years On," *BBC News*, August 4, 2022. https://www.bbc.com/news/uk-england-coventry-warwickshire-62390725.

Bright, Rachel K. *Chinese Labour in South Africa, 1902–10: Race, Violence, and Global Spectacle*. Basingstoke: Palgrave Macmillan, 2013.

Chau, Donovan C. *Exploiting Africa: The Influence of Maoist China in Algeria, Ghana, and Tanzania*. Annapolis: Naval Institute Press, 2014.

Furedi, Frank. "The Development of Anti-Asian Opinion among Africans in Nakuru District, Kenya." *African Affairs* 73, no. 292 (July 1974): 347–358.

Hess, Steve, and Richard Aidoo. "Charting the Impact of Subnational Actors in China's Foreign Relations: The 2013 Galamsey Crisis in Ghana," *Asian Survey* 56, no. 2 (March–May 2016).

———. *Charting the Roots of Anti-Chinese Populism in Africa*. Cham: Springer International Publishing, 2015.

———. "Charting the Roots of Anti-Chinese Populism in Africa: A Comparison of Zambia and Ghana," *Journal of Asian and African Studies* 49, no. 2 (2014): 129–147.

Jamal, Vali. "Asians in Uganda, 1880–1972: Inequality and Expulsion." *Economic History Review* 29, no. 4 (Nov. 1976), 602–616.

Large, Daniel. *China and Africa: The New Era.* Cambridge: Polity Books, 2021.

Lee, Ching Kwan. *The Specter of Global China: Politics, Labor, and Foreign Investments in Africa.* Chicago: University of Chicago Press, 2017.

Michel, Serge, and Michel Beuret. *China Safari: On the Trail of Beijing's Expansion in Africa.* New York: Nation Books, 2009.

Mohan, Giles, Ben Lampert, May Tan-Mullins, and Daphne Chang. *Chinese Migrants and Africa's Development: New Imperialists or Agents of Change?* London: Zed Books, 2014.

Patel, Hasu H. "General Amin and the Indian Exodus from Uganda." *Journal of Opinion* 2, no. 4 (Winter 1972): 12–22.

Radelet, Steven. "Success Stories from Emerging Africa." *Journal of Democracy* 21, no. 4 (2010): 87–101.

Reuters. "One Chinese Citizen Killed in Ethiopia's Oromiya Region—Embassy," *Reuters,* January 31, 2023. https://www.reuters.com/world/africa/one-chinese-citizen-killed-ethiopias-oromiya-region-embassy-2023-01-31/.

Vogel, Steven K, "Introduction." In *The Political Economy Reader: Contending Perspectives and Contemporary Debates,* edited by Naazneen H. Barma and Steven K. Vogel, 1–23. New York: Routledge, 2022.

Wang, Ling-chi L. "Roots and the Changing Identity of the Chinese in the United States." In *The Living Tree: The Changing Meaning of Being Chinese Today,* edited by Tu Wei-ming, 185–212. Stanford: Stanford University Press, 1994.

Wegenast, Tim, Georg Strüver, Juliane Giesen, and Mario Krauser. "At Africa's Expense? Disaggregating the Social Impact of Chinese Mining Operations" GIGA Working Papers, No. 308, 2017.

Yoon, Jung Park. *A Matter of Honour: Being Chinese in South Africa.* Auckland Park: Jacana Media (Pty), 2008.

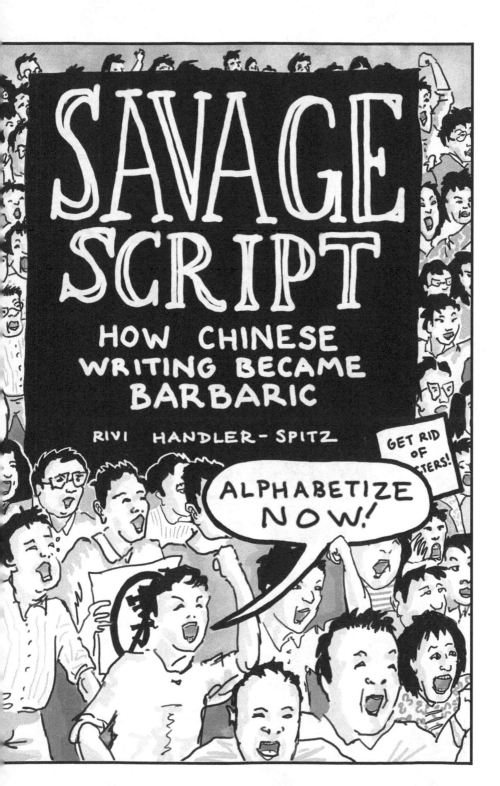

POLITICAL CARTOONS LIKE THIS ONE FROM THE PERIOD ILLUSTRATE THE FEAR THAT COLONIZERS WOULD DIVIDE CHINA AMONG THEMSELVES.

ACCORDING TO YALE PROFESSOR JING TSU,

IN THE EARLY YEARS OF THE TWENTIETH CENTURY, THE QUESTION OF WHETHER TO

ADOPT THE ROMAN ALPHABET WAS REGARDED "AS A PRACTICAL MATTER... SEPARATED FROM THE STAKES OF CULTURALIST DEBATES."

TAN SITONG ↓

AN ALPHA-BET IS MORE LOGICAL, EFFICIENT AND ECO-NOMICAL THAN CHINESE CHARACTERS. ANYONE CAN LEARN 26 LETTERS IN A MORNING, BUT MASTERING CHINESE CHARACTERS TAKES YEARS.

A LIFETIME.

CAI YUAN PEI

CHINESE CHARACTERS ARE ELITIST AND UNDEMOCRATIC!

WHO HAS THE LEISURE TO MEMORIZE THOUSANDS OF INDIVIDUAL GRAPHS?

CHINA MUST HAVE A LITERATE POPULATION!

LIANG QICHAO

THE NEED IS URGENT. THE FATE OF THE NATION DEPENDS ON IT!

INDEED, AT THE TURN OF THE 20th CENTURY, CHINA'S

LITERACY RATE WAS UNDER 20%, WHEREAS LITERACY IN GERMANY AND THE UNITED STATES WAS OVER 95%.

EVEN THE LUCKY FEW WHO DO LEARN TO READ AND WRITE WASTE THEIR WHOLE LIVES AT IT.

QIU TINGLIANG

THIS RETROGRADE, PICTO-GRAPHIC SCRIPT HAS RENDERED THE CHINESE PEOPLE BLIND, BENIGHTED, AND

... RETARDING OUR INTELLECTUAL DEVELOPMENT AND LEAVING NO TIME FOR

SCIENTIFIC INQUIRY.

QIAN XUANTONG

SUSCEPTIBLE TO BELIEVING THE MOST PREPOSTEROUS SUPER-STITIONS: SOME EVEN THINK CHARACTERS WERE GIVEN TO HUMANITY BY A MYTHICAL TURTLE!

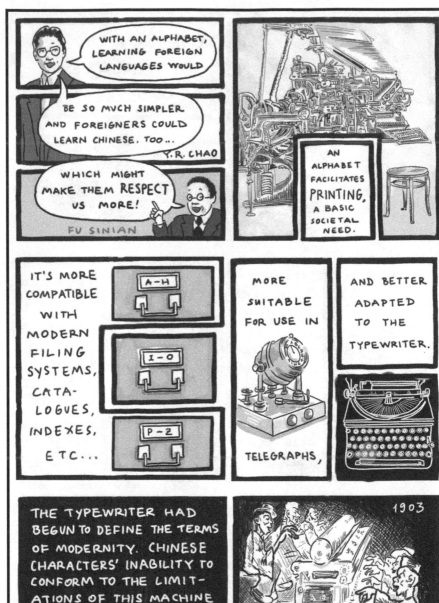

WITH AN ALPHABET, LEARNING FOREIGN LANGUAGES WOULD

BE SO MUCH SIMPLER AND FOREIGNERS COULD LEARN CHINESE, TOO...

Y.R. CHAO

WHICH MIGHT MAKE THEM RESPECT US MORE!

FU SINIAN

AN ALPHABET FACILITATES PRINTING, A BASIC SOCIETAL NEED.

IT'S MORE COMPATIBLE WITH MODERN FILING SYSTEMS, CATA-LOGUES, INDEXES, ETC...

A-H

I-O

P-Z

MORE SUITABLE FOR USE IN

AND BETTER ADAPTED TO THE TYPEWRITER.

TELEGRAPHS,

THE TYPEWRITER HAD BEGUN TO DEFINE THE TERMS OF MODERNITY. CHINESE CHARACTERS' INABILITY TO CONFORM TO THE LIMIT-ATIONS OF THIS MACHINE MADE THE CHINESE LANGUAGE SEEM MONSTROUS, OUT-DATED, AND RISIBLE. RACIST IMAGES IN THE WESTERN PRESS MOCKED THE VERY IDEA, AND DEEMED THE

1903

CHINESE TYPEWRITER "OUT OF THE QUESTION."

JOSEPH DE GUIGNES THOUGHT HE PERCEIVED VISUAL LIKENESSES BETWEEN THE SHAPES OF CERTAIN CHINESE CHARACTERS AND EGYPTIAN HIEROGLYPHS.

EUREKA!

CHINESE CHARACTERS MUST HAVE DERIVED FROM EGYPTIAN HIEROGLYPHS. IT'S CLEAR THE ANCIENT EGYPTIANS COLONIZED CHINA!

HE WASN'T TAKEN VERY SERIOUSLY...

GUIGNES

DIVINE LEGATION OF MO

BUT WILLIAM WARBURTON (1697-1779) WAS.

SURVEYING ACCOUNTS OF THE WRITING SYSTEMS OF THE NEW WORLD, AFRICA, AND ASIA, WILLIAM WARBURTON ALIGHTED UPON AN EVOLUTIONARY HYPOTHESIS.

"THE FIRST AND MOST NATURAL WAY OF COMMUNICATING MEN'S CONCEPTIONS

LASCAUX →

MUST HAVE BEEN BY TRACING OUT IMAGES OF THINGS. TO EXPRESS THE IDEA OF A MAN OR A HORSE, ONE WOULD DELINEATE ITS FORM."

"THE FIRST WRITING WAS A MERE PICTURE."

"WE MAY SEE THIS THEORY PLAINLY VERIFIED IN THE CASE OF THE MEXICANS."
~ WARBURTON

WARBURTON, *DIVINE LEGATION OF MOSES*

PRECISELY! INDEED A PICTOGRAPHIC SCRIPT IS STILL IN USE AMONG THE

"SAUVAGES DU CANADA!"

NICOLAS FRÉRET (1688-1749)

WHEREAS PRIMITIVE SOCIETIES EMPLOY RUDE PICTURE WRITING, THE MORE INGENIOUS, CIVILIZED NATIONS ABRIDGE THEIR WRITING, **TURNING PICTURES INTO LETTERS...**

... THIS PROCESS OF **VISUAL ABSTRACTION** ATTESTS TO THE **PROGRESS OF HUMAN CIVILIZATION.**

I TOLD YOU CHARACTERS WERE BARBARIC!

QIAN XUAN TONG

SHOULD THEY BE TAKEN TO TASK FOR THEIR OWN **INTERNALIZED PREJUDICE**, OR REGARDED WITH **EMPATHY?**

THE REFORMERS SAW THEMSELVES AS ARDENT PATRIOTS.

SAVING CHINA

FROM POLI-TICAL DOMI-NA-TION OR EVEN *ANNIHIL*

AS POWER-HUNGRY COLONIAL NATIONS SOUGHT TO CARVE CHINA UP LIKE A MELON.

ONLY *IN EXTREMIS* DID THEY PUSH CHINESE CHARACTERS

HELP!

TO THE BRINK OF *EXTINCTION*,

BUT THE REFORMERS' PROPOS WERE NO MERE PRAGMATIC SOLUTIONS TO PRACTICAL PROBLE

FAR MORE WAS AT STAKE IDEOLOGICALLY WHEN A MAJORITY OF PROGRESSIV CHINESE INTELLECTUAL UNDERTOOK TO DEMOLISH THIS TOWERING SYMBOL O CHINESE CULTURAL HERITA

BIBLIOGRAPHY

Chao, Y.R. 趙元任 [Zhao Yuanren], Yuanren. "The Problem of the Chinese Language: Scientific Study of Chinese Philology." *Chinese Students' Monthly* 11, no. 8 (1916):572-93.

Chappell, Hilary, and Lamarre. *A Grammar and Lexicon of Hakka.* Paris: Ecole des Hautes Etudes en Sciences Sociales, 2005.

DeFrancis, John. "A Missionary Contribution to Chinese Nationalism." *Journal of the North Asia Branch of the Royal Asiatic Society* 83 (1948): 1-34.

————. *Nationalism and Language Reform in China.* New York: Octagon Books, 1972.

Fréret, Nicolas. *De La Langue Des Chinois,* 1718.

Fu Sinian 傅斯年. "漢語改用拼音文字的初步談." In 中國新文學大系, edited by Hu Shih 胡適, 147-64. Shanghai: Shanghai wenyi chubanshe, 2007.

Hegel, Georg Wilhelm Friedrich. *The Philosophy of Right; The Philosophy of History.* Translated by J. (John) Sibree. Vol. 46. Great Books of the Western World. Chicago, 1952.

Hudson, Nicholas. *Writing and European Thought, 1600-1830.* Cambridge: Cambridge University Press, 1994.

Kaske, Elisabeth. *The Politics of Language in Chinese Education, 1895-1919.* Leiden: Brill, 2008.

Kuzvoglu, Ulug. "Capital, Empire, Letter: Romanization in Late Qing China." *Twentieth-Century China* 46, no. 3 (2021): 223-46.

Liu, Lydia H. "Scripts in Motion: Writing as Imperial Technology, Past and Present." *PMLA* 130, no. 2 (March 2015): 375-83.

Lu Xun 鲁迅 "病中答救亡情報訪員." In 拉丁化中國字運動二十年論文集, edited by Ni Haishu 倪海曙, 119. Shanghai: Shidai chubanshe, 1949.

Medhurst, Walter Henry. *China: Its State and Prospects.* Boston: Crocker & Brewster, 1838.

Mullaney, Thomas S. *The Chinese Typewriter: A History.* Cambridge, MA: The MIT Press, 2017.

Nash, Eveleigh. *China As It Really Is.* London, 1912.

Qian Xuantong 錢玄同 and Chen Duxiu 陳獨秀. "中國今後之文字問題" 新青年 4, no. 4 (April 15, 1918).

Richard, Timothy. "Non-Phonetic and Phonetic Writing Systems." *The Chinese Recorder* 19, no 11 (1898): 540-45.

Tsu, Jing. *Kingdom of Characters: The Language Revolution That Made China Modern.* New York: Riverhead Books, 2022.

Vico, Giambattista. Translated by Thomas Bergin and Max Fisch. *The New Science of Giambattista Vico.* Ithaca: Cornell University Press, 1984.

Wagner, Rudolf. "'Dividing up the [Chinese] Melon, Guafen 瓜分': The Fate of a Transcultural Metaphor in the Formation of National Myth." *The Journal of Transcultural Studies* 8, no.1 (October 10, 2017): 9-122. https://doi.org/10.17885/heiup.ts.2017.1.23700.

Walfred, Michele. "'The Coming Man' 1881." *Illustrating Chinese Exclusion* (blog), April 3, 2014. https://thomasnastcartoons.com/2014/04/03/the-coming-man-20-may-1881/.

Warburton, William, *The Divine Legation of Moses,* (2 volumes), London, 1742.

Zhang Binglin 章炳麟. "駁中國用萬國新語說." 民報 21, June 10 (1908).

Zhong Yurou. *Chinese Grammatology: Script Revolution and Chinese Literary Modernity, 1916-1968.* New York: Columbia University Press, 2019.

NOTE ON ACCURACY: ALL EXACT QUOTATIONS ARE INDICATED WITH QUOTATION MARKS. OTHER WORDS APPEARING IN SPEECH BUBBLES ARE CONSISTENT WITH VIEWS EXPRESSED BY THE SPEAKERS. (I HAVE ALTERED THE WORDING TO FACILITATE DIALOGUE). ALL PORTRAITS ARE DRAWN FROM HISTORICAL IMAGES.

ACKNOWLEDGMENT: SPECIAL THANKS TO MATTHEW BOOKER, PENELOPE GENG, BRYNA GOODMAN, LORRI HAGMAN, ELLEN HANDLER SPITZ, JENNIFER HO, ANDREW HUI, EMMA KIPPLEY-OGMAN, ANDREA LIU, HELMUT PUFF, MAYA SCHAEFER-FIELLO, ROBERT SCHINE, BRIGID VANCE, & JON WILSON,

CODA

AS I WADE IN DEEPER,

THIS ESSAY REPRESENTS SIMPLY MY FIRST FORAY INTO THIS MATERIAL.

I'M NOTICING MANY MORE ASPECTS OF THIS HISTORY THAN I CAN ADDRESS HERE.

FOR INSTANCE, THE ROLE OF MISSIONARY SCRIPTS, ORIGINALLY DEVISED BY EUROPEANS

NO THANKS

PHONETIC SYMBOLS INITIALS

TO FACILITATE THEIR OWN MASTERY OF CHINESE PRONUNCIATION,

AND LATER USED FOR TRANSLATING THE BIBLE INTO REGIONAL VERNACULARS. OR THE QUESTION OF WHETHER TO USE A NON-ALPHABETIC SYSTEM TO TRANSCRIBE SOUND.

SO I'VE STARTED DRAWING A BOOK-LENGTH GRAPHIC NARRATIVE THAT TAKES INTO ACCOUNT THE HISTORICAL DEVELOPMENT OF CHINESE CHARACTERS AND COMPARES DEBATES ON CHINESE

SCRIPT REFORM TO CONTEMPORANEOUS 20TH C DISCUSSIONS OF NATIONALISM, PHONETICIZATION, AND ALPHABETICIZATION IN TURKEY, VIETNAM, JAPAN...

...THE U.S.S.R., AND ELSEWHERE.

STAY TUNED!

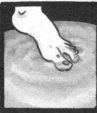

6

RACIALIZATION FROM HOME

CHINA'S RESPONSE TO THE ANTI-CHINESE MOVEMENT IN MEXICO, 1928–1937

Xuening Kong

"*Se calcula que no menos de cinco mil chinos se encuentran en el territorio mexicano, sin haber llenado los requisitos de inmigración. Esta fabulosa cantidad de individuos deseables, que ha logrado introducirse en nuestro país.*" (According to the statistics, there are no less than five thousand Chinese in Mexico without having fulfilled the immigration requirements. This large amount of undesirable individuals who have managed to enter our country.)

—"5,000 Chinese Will be Expelled from Mexico," *Hispano-América*, January 18, 1928

"Nankin telegrams to the 'Eastern Times' states that the Chinese residents abroad in Mexico and South America have made a contribution of $39,000 to the financial support of the Nationalist Government."

—*The North-China Herald and Supreme Court & Consular Gazette*, August 18, 1928

The two newspaper articles quoted above were published in the same year—one in Shanghai and one in San Francisco—and they covered overseas Chinese in Mexico. The first article depicted Chinese people as undesirable laborers who competed for jobs with Mexicans. Facing expulsion, five thousand Chinese migrants' personal safety was under threat, which was consistent with US newspaper reports and the scholarship on Chinese Mexicans in the early twentieth century. However, the second article highlighted that the Chinese settlers were sufficiently comfortable and capable of donating crucial military materials to their motherland to show loyalty. The two articles offer contradictory portrayals of Chinese settlers in Mexico during the late 1920s. How could Chinese migrants provide considerable financial support to their native country with their lives in turbulence? Why did the Chinese newspaper patriotically portray the overseas group?

This essay focuses on different understandings of overseas Chinese in Mexico and the anti-Chinese movement. It examines how the state-sponsored press of the Chinese Nationalist Party (GMD), Chinese diplomatic personnel, and contributors to the independent press disparately responded to Sinophobia between 1928 and 1937 as the Nationalists nominally united China on the eve of the Second World War. As China experienced factional conflicts, overseas Chinese in Mexico suffered from a state-supported anti-Chinese movement during and after the Mexican Revolution (1910–1920). I argue that when Chinese migrants were victims of racism overseas, their home country actively denounced the anti-Chinese persecution by the Mexican government and nativists. The Chinese Nationalist government used the phrase "Chinese migrants in Mexico" to signal its power to other states and its influence over Chinese emigres in international affairs. Chinese diplomats and independent newspapers employed the phrase to critique Chinese authorities. Chinese intellectuals used the phrase to establish a broad Chinese identity dependent upon political participation. All three groups politicized the phrase for their own purposes without necessarily taking direct action to alleviate the racial violence facing Chinese Mexicans.

Chinese Migrants to Mexico

Economic considerations shaped the communications between China and Mexico regarding the plight of Chinese migrants. In 1899, the Qing government (1663–1912) and the development-minded Mexican dictator Porfirio Díaz signed the Treaty of Amity and Commerce, marking the beginning of formal diplomatic relations between Mexico and China and confirming Chinese migrants' rights to work and invest in Mexico.[1] Amid increasing industrialization, Díaz recruited and welcomed Chinese laborers to build railroads. After the railroads were completed, the Chinese laborers found new occupations as small business owners, allowing them to permanently settle in Mexico. Their hardworking attitudes and skill sets brought them prosperity but also caused resentment among Mexican nativists.

After overturning the Díaz regime (1876–1880, 1884–1911), they claimed that Chinese migrants stole Mexicans' job opportunities and gained huge profits.

Beginning in Sonora, the anti-Chinese sentiment evolved from regional racism into a government-sponsored, anti-Chinese movement with popular support across Mexico. In 1911, jealous of Chinese small businessowners' success, disgruntled revolutionary soldiers murdered 303 Chinese civilians in Torreón, Coahuila. Economic nationalism continued to drive antagonism against the Chinese over the following two decades.[2] The "80 percent law" in Ley de Trabajo, or Work Law, in 1919 required all Chinese businesses to ensure that 80 percent of their staff were ethnic Mexicans. Chinese migrants were victims of economic nationalism, and they were also racially alienated from the nation-sponsored mestizo identity in the postrevolutionary era.[3] The new leadership embraced its indigenous, as well as its mestizo, character and denigrated other unwanted foreigners, including Chinese. Political figures and the media proclaimed that Chinese people were undesirable. In newspapers and through public speeches, proponents of the anti-Chinese movement also portrayed Chinese men as brutal people who enslaved Mexican women and had concubines, which contradicted the Catholic beliefs held by the majority of Mexicans.[4] The anti-Chinese movement gained further traction when numerous Mexican workers returned from the US, peaking when former president Plutarco Elías Calles publicly supported the exclusion of Chinese people. Calles's son, Rodolfo Elías Calles, who was also Sonoran governor at the time, ordered the expulsion of all Chinese in Sonora in August 1931.[5] Wing S. Wong, a Chinese migrant living on the other side of the Arizona-Sonora border, recorded that he saw many Chinese "kicked out of the border fence and arrested by Mexicans."[6] Chinese Sonorans' property was confiscated, and the majority migrated to other Mexican states, the US, or China.[7] The Chinese population in Mexico reached 24,222 in 1927 but decreased to 4,856 by 1940.[8]

Mexican and US newspapers reported on Chinese migrants' misery and highlighted the pressure Chinese immigrants felt to survive. A report in 1930 from *Excélsior* covered the actions of an anti-Chinese committee aimed at prohibiting the marriage between Mexican women and Chinese men. Their rationale was that intermarriage would "degenerate our race," and the committee proposed to "establish similar groups throughout the state, in order to carry out an active anti-Chinese campaign."[9] On March 7, 1932, the *Fort Worth Star-Telegram* announced its receipt of reports from patrolmen that "Chinese crossing the border from Mexico had complained they were forced to cross by Mexican officials."[10] The newspaper reports thus verified the broad influence of the anti-Chinese movement in Mexico and its blow to Chinese migrants as undesirable aliens targeted by racist critiques.

When Chinese migrants experienced persecution in Mexico, the newly-born Chinese Nationalist government in Nanjing was aware of the political importance of overseas Chinese in North America. After Chiang Kai-shek (1887–1975) launched the Northern Expedition against warlords, the Nationalist government nominally unified China in 1928, though it continued to fight against political opponents and counterrevolutionaries, especially the communists. The GMD also restricted freedom of speech to consolidate its power. The need to centralize state power turned the GMD's attention to overseas Chinese communities, who historically provided financial support to the Nationalists in the late nineteenth century before they became the dominant power. After seizing power domestically, the Nationalists needed the political endorsement of overseas Chinese—especially wealthy ones—to legitimize their government in the eyes of the international community. Support from the overseas community grew more imperative as Japan posed an increasing threat to China in the late 1920s. Chinese migrants in the Americas were one of the overseas communities with whom the Nationalists sought to strengthen relations. In 1928, an influential senior Nationalist general telegraphed Chiang to assign a delegate who could appeal to the overseas Chinese community in the Americas to "endeavor to national affair" (*jinli guoshi* 盡力國事).[11] Overseas Chinese in Mexico, therefore, became constituents with whom the Nationalists strived to seek support and maintain connections.

The Nationalists under Chiang recognized the necessity for an institutionalized way to extend its administration to overseas Chinese. In 1926, the Overseas Chinese Affair Commission (OCAC) was founded in Guangzhou as a result of decisions at the Nationalist Party's Second National Congress. The OCAC became an executive branch in 1932, subordinated to the Executive Yuan, which empowered the OCAC to negotiate overseas affairs with the Ministry of the Interior, Foreign Affairs, Finance, and Education.[12] Rather than simply offering outreach services to the overseas community, the OCAC represented progress in terms of the Nationalists' political goals involving overseas Chinese. Through the OCAC, the Nationalists not only requested assistance in the name of patriotism but also offered services to support their legitimacy as a government—a reciprocal relationship that would prove central to mobilization.[13] For example, offering Chinese-language classes was a way in which the Nationalists cultivated a connection with Chinese overseas. Yü Shouzhi 余受之 (1910–unknown), an educated urbanite, participated in the training program offered by the OCAC and became the president of the Nationalist-sponsored Chinese Language School in Mexico City to engage the local Chinese residents in 1937.[14]

Responses to the Anti-Chinese Movement, 1928-1934

When the Nationalists built up their international recognition and institutionalized their administration to the overseas Chinese, the state-sponsored press highlighted their efforts to maintain political and Chinese cultural connections with the

Chinese migrants in Mexico. The state-sponsored press of the Nationalists believed that factionalism among multiple Chinese communities and disconnection with the Nationalists led to the persecution and vulnerability of the overseas Chinese. *Review of Chinese and Foreign Affairs* commented, "inside Chinese immigrant community was full of factionalism. . . . [Each part] jostled against each other for their own interests and created troubles. . . . These villains violated the law [in Mexico] without considering the standing of China internationally . . . [and] did not follow the lead of the Nationalist Party."[15] The critique of factionalism reflected the Nationalists' intention to extend their influence and administration over the Chinese diaspora, even though their intended subjects were not currently within Chinese territory. Nationalists incorrectly assumed that communism was another factor dividing the overseas community and impeding the association between the local Chinese people in Mexico and the Nationalist government's influence on the Chinese diaspora. Perceived Communist Party members became an urgent concern for Nationalist chapters in Mexico as they developed connections with Chinese migrants. This paranoia, despite no evidence that communism was in Mexico, led to political persecution against some Nationalist members in Mexico. Several consular officers in Tampico, a city on Mexico's east coast, faced accusations of being "reactionary members" due to their participation in communist actions in the local community.[16] A direct decree from the Executive Yuan (*xingzheng yuan* 行政院) ordered the Ministry of the Military to arrest the "traitors" and send them back to China.[17] The cooperation between the Nationalist government and the military demonstrated that the Nationalists took a zero-tolerance approach to any separatist issues and were willing to use force to achieve unity.

State-sponsored newspapers also attributed the experiences of mistreatment by overseas Chinese to global political chaos instead of to the decline of the Chinese government's international influence stemming from constant internal warfare. An author writing in *Central Daily News* attributed the issue of "bullying and humiliating Chinese" (*qiru huaren* 欺辱華人) to imperialism (*diguo zhuyi* 帝國主義), a worldwide problem that both overseas and mainland Chinese had to resolve.[18] In other words, the Nationalists did not ignore xenophobic actions but downplayed the overseas Chinese's suffering. Nor did the Nationalists provide any effective measures to solve the problem that Chinese migrants faced. Instead, the Nationalist press emphasized the resemblance between the misery of the Chinese residents in Mexico and concurrent events in China—imperialist suppression of the Chinese people and factionalism hindering the authority of the Nationalists. The Nationalists thus linked these threats to create empathy and forge unity between the Chinese diaspora and their homeland.

The state-sponsored newspaper articles reflecting that desire for unification captured the imperative of the Nationalists' state-building efforts during the

Nanjing decade (1927–1937) from the perspectives of both domestic and diplomatic affairs.[19] The Nationalists found it necessary to display their power and an image of unity to the mainland Chinese public through the provision of significant administration of overseas affairs. Even though the migrants in Mexico did not directly aid the Nationalists' larger goal of unifying China, any perceived divisions were intolerable to the Nationalists' goal of consolidating their control over their subjects. The establishment of the OCAC and the Nationalist overseas chapters in Mexico revealed that the Nationalist government actively incorporated the overseas subjects into its building of the nation.[20] The claim that the Nationalists had centralized the nation and developed their power in military, political, social, and economic terms was crucial following the rise of Japanese imperial ambitions and aggression around 1931. As Hans van de Ven points out, a clear and cohesive Nationalist strategy developed after the Northern Expedition ensured that China would fight as one entity led by the Nationalists if war occurred.[21] The Nationalists' press in Mexico spread their political and military ambitions from the homeland to the overseas community on the eve of war, using stories about Chinese migrants to further consolidate political influence overseas.

While the state-sponsored press used the anti-Chinese movement in Mexico for propaganda at home, diplomats struggled to help the overseas Chinese through negotiations with the Mexican government. They acted as mediators, delivering Chinese current affairs news in Mexico, and they relayed policies from China between the embassy in Mexico and the Nationalist government. However, the diplomacy was rarely effective. Xiong Chongzhi 熊崇志 (1883–unknown), the Chinese envoy plenipotentiary in Mexico from 1930 to 1933, reported that the Mexican Ministry of Foreign Affairs promised to combat Sinophobia, but the central government in Mexico City was too weak and did not take any real action.[22] Amid the powerlessness of diplomatic negotiation, the Ministry of Foreign Affairs turned to the US for help and cooperated with transporting immigrants back to China from San Francisco in September 1931, leading many Chinese people to flee to California.[23]

Unlike the state-sponsored press, the disappointed diplomats regarded acts of persecution as foreign relations issues that required the Chinese government's condemnation. An essay from *Immigrants Semimonthly*, a publication attached to the OCAC, reported that "the anti-Chinese movement . . . resulted from the ignorant envying our compatriots' bearing hardship and diligence. . . . For saving the Chinese immigrants, it is necessary for the Mexican government and its public to understand [and accept] our people, and our Chinese government should use diplomacy to protect them."[24] The essay reflected the plight diplomats faced in the process of negotiation. The diplomats believed that attaining cooperative relations with other states was the primary goal of international diplomacy and that it would ensure national security and protect the overseas Chinese.[25] However, they also knew that China's incompetence prevented it from more effective methods, such as military intervention, to resolve the anti-Chinese movement. The essay also expressed an implicit complaint against the lack of support from the Chinese government for diplomacy, which increased the difficulty of negotiations with Mexico. For the diplomats, China's instability, its dearth of military power, and its limited influence with other nations rendered China at a disadvantage on the international stage.[26] Instead of turning the affairs of overseas Chinese into propaganda in support of the unification of China, diplomats regarded Sinophobia in Mexico as an issue that plagued China's national strength.

Reports from Ji Zhuqing 嵇翥青 (dates unknown), a secretary of the Chinese embassy in Mexico, confirmed the complex relationship between Chinese domestic affairs and diplomacy. He reported that the Mexican government did not pay the indemnity or stop the anti-Chinese violence as they had promised to the Nationalist government.[27] "The endless internal political chaos after the Revolution of 1911," according to Ji's report, "afforded the Mexican government an excuse to reject paying off the indemnity."[28] Instead of projecting the experiences of overseas Chinese to domestic Chinese politics as the state-sponsored press did, Ji regarded the anti-Chinese movement both as an international and domestic issue. The inability of the Mexican government to stop the anti-Chinese violence impeded the effectual rescue of overseas Chinese. At the same time, Chinese diplomats tried diplomacy, but that ultimately was not effective due to China's internal political instability.[29] Through negotiating the issue of Chinese in Mexico, diplomats expressed their political opinions and implicit critiques of the Chinese government.

Sinophobia in Mexico attracted the attention of the Chinese independent newspapers and periodicals as well. Their descriptions of the experiences of overseas Chinese in Mexico were broader in perspective than those of either the state-sponsored press or diplomatic personnel. The scramble for leadership in postrevolutionary Mexico, the weakness of China's national power, and disunity among Chinese communities in Mexico allowed Sinophobia to continue unchecked. Articles in the *Eastern Miscellanies* and *Da Gong Bao* insightfully commented that Chinese migrants were scapegoats for Mexican civil strife.[30] The misery that overseas Chinese suffered also triggered the Chinese media's critiques of the Nationalist government's powerlessness. In a newspaper article, "Reflection of the Anti-Chinese Movement in Mexico," the unnamed author highlighted that "the destitution of the Chinese government" (*neizheng shixiu* 內政失修) was the main cause that led to the failure of diplomatic negotiations to end the anti-Chinese violence.[31] These journalists argued that readers should attribute the anti-Chinese violence in Mexico to both the Nationalist government and Mexican racists.

Covering the anti-Chinese movement, independent Chinese newspapers exposed China's situation and disadvantage on the world stage and expressed their understanding of China's domestic and international politics. As Xiaobing Tang argues, independent newspapers in the Republican era mainly functioned as a forum for Chinese intellectuals to express their opinions of building up a modern Chinese nation.[32] Different understandings of Sinophobia, and direct critiques of the Chinese government, also helped the independent press resist the ideological unification narrative of the Nationalists and defend the independence of public opinion. Commentaries on the racist movement thus provided an opportunity to resist the GMD's centralized political ideology and serve the public.

The anti-Chinese movement served as common ground for gathering different political views on how to deal with both overseas Sinophobia and the domestic Chinese national crisis. The reporting of anti-Chinese violence functioned as propaganda for the Nationalists. The proposals of diplomats and the commentary of independent press writers indicated that these two groups believed that China's domestic incompetency had a direct negative impact on the lives of the overseas Chinese in Mexico. For the Nationalists, diplomats, and independent newspapers, "Chinese migrants in Mexico" was not just a term describing one group of migrant people living in a remote Latin American country unrelated to China's domestic affairs. Instead, the term had symbolic meaning and served as a medium for different social groups to express their political claims, causing the anti-Chinese movement in Mexico and garnering the attention of the three groups by the middle of the 1930s. The following section suggests that the phrase "Chinese in Mexico" continued to serve political purposes between 1934 and 1937 as Japan became a military threat on the eve of World War II.

Mexico as an Amiable Ally: Tao Xingzhi's Travel and His Anti-Japanese Mobilization in 1937

The escalating tension between China and Japan in the 1920s and 1930s increased the urgency to mobilize as many Chinese people as possible to fight against Japanese imperialist ambitions. Anti-Japanese boycotts and the denial of Manchukuo were two of the Chinese public's responses to condemn Japan's actions. Chinese antagonism toward Japan generally intensified following China's defeat during the First Sino-Japanese War (1894–1895) and Japan's seizure of the German concessions in Shandong after World War I. In September 1931, Japanese garrisons destroyed part of the railway near Mukden and further invaded all of Manchuria, which contained 15 percent of China's territory. Japan's encroachment violated the integrity of Chinese territory and inflamed Chinese people's anger toward Japanese troops that were marching unrestricted through Chinese territory.[33] Anti-Japanese sentiment and Chinese patriotism promptly rose throughout the country after the Mukden Incident. When Japan continued to invade South China, the unification of all possible Chinese forces—including domestically and overseas—to fight against Japan became a priority for Chinese people from many different backgrounds.

One activist mobilizing overseas Chinese to resist Japan was educator Tao Xingzhi (陶行知, 1891–1946), who flew to Mexico to spread anti-Japanese propaganda in 1937 after visiting the UK and the US.[34] Known for advocating for mass education and establishing a classless society, Tao believed that the Chinese should act as one to build up a great Chinese community of social harmony based on nationality.[35] The rise of the Japanese military was a timely catalyst to achieve this goal, and he endeavored to mobilize Chinese people to resist Japan. In July 1936, Tao began his self-appointed mission as a Chinese people's ambassador to the world in order to advance collective Pacific security and an international united front—which included overseas Chinese—against Japan's military aggression.[36] Tao made a concerted effort to unify as many Chinese groups as possible without political division. As a nonpartisan representative, he met with delegates of Chinese immigrants, GMD members, and leaders of the Chee Kong Tong, a powerful fraternal association fighting for the leadership of overseas Chinese with the GMD in Mexico. The impartial contacts with various Chinese social groups paralleled the concurrent political trend in China—aligning diverse Chinese communities without political partisanship in an effort to defend against Japan.

To gain anti-Japanese support, Tao publicly highlighted anti-fascism as the common goal that China and Mexico worked to achieve, and he downplayed the adversity and suffering Chinese migrants experienced. At a banquet speech he gave to delegates of Chinese immigrants and the local government in Manzanillo, a mid-south port city near Mexico City, Tao proclaimed, "We [China and Mexico] are friends in many aspects. . . . Mexico and China unite as one and stop providing port service to Japan fascist country. . . . Please use the fight with the common enemy [Japan] as the beginning of our friendship."[37] The speech had a significantly positive tone regarding Sino-Mexican relations and omitted the Sinophobia that Tao had personally witnessed and recorded in his diaries.[38] Tao conflated Japan's imperialist ambitions with fascism to unite Mexican authorities and Chinese migrants so that both groups would consciously identify with the Chinese crisis. Through his speech, Tao's anti-Japanese political drive encouraged the Chinese diaspora in Mexico to forget the racial violence in their lives and to feel a sense of responsibility to resist Japan's invasion as *Chinese nationals.*

The threat of Japan thus enlarged the scope of national identity beyond territorial boundaries. The delineation of who was Chinese became more inclusive than before. Not based on *jus sanguinis* or birthplace, political participation and common struggle were the dimensions of citizenship and Chinese identity for

Tao and other Chinese intellectuals in the Republican era.[39] By calling for their participation in the anti-Japanese campaign alongside the masses in China, Tao endowed Chinese settlers in Mexico with membership in a political community and incorporated different political factions into a broad Chinese national community. Even though the number of Chinese migrants was low and Chinese Mexicans were under the threat of racial exclusion, Chinese Mexicans were still an important group to mobilize and win support from. Tao thus politicized the overseas Chinese in Mexico by intentionally downplaying the anti-Chinese violence in Mexico.

Conclusion

In addition to establishing a mestizo national identity in postrevolutionary Mexico, the Mexican government's propagandized anti-Chinese movement contributed to the establishment of an extensive Chinese nationalist identity incorporating overseas Chinese into a broad wartime community that found a common enemy in Japan. This enlarged Chinese identity, however, did not help Chinese migrants in Mexico overcome persecution. Instead, it implicitly maintained racism by shifting the overseas Chinese's attention away from local violence toward a unified Chinese diasporic nationalism. Anti-Chinese racism was useful for Mexican politicians looking to craft new national identities and policies, but they were not alone in finding it convenient for political gain. China also used Sinophobia abroad for domestic political purposes without intending to take measurable actions to relieve the suffering of Chinese migrants.

Notes

[1] For a brief introduction to the anti-Chinese movement, see Hu-Dehart, "Indispensable Enemy."

[2] Romero, *Chinese in Mexico*; see also Schiavone-Camacho, *Chinese Mexicans*.

[3] As for the establishment of mestizo identity through racializing Chinese migrants, see Chang, *Chinos*.

[4] Schiavone-Camacho, *Chinese Mexicans*, chapter 2.

[5] He, *Paihua Shiliao* I, 3–5.

[6] Wong, interview.

[7] Sonnichsen, *Tucson*, 240.

[8] Campos, *Segregación*, 20.

[9] "Committee."

[10] "Chinese Forced to Leave Mexico."

[11] He Yingqin's telegram to Chiang Kai-shek.

[12] Concerning the history of OCAC, see Ji, "Committee of Overseas Business," 94–101; and Chen, "Overseas Chinese Affairs," 64–73.

[13] Phillips, "National Legitimacy," 67.

[14] Yü, *Anthology*.

[15] Cheng, "Current Situations," 27.

[16] "Report from Party Chapter," 26–27.

[17] "Decree no. 4441," 26–27.

[18] "Mexico Mistreated Chinese Immigrants."

[19] Strauss, *Strong Institutions*.

[20] Scholarship on the Nanjing government has challenged the old narrative that it was politically incompetent. See Xiang, "From Diplomatic to Domestic." For monographs on this topic, see Strauss, *Strong Institutions*, and Halsey, *Quest for Power*.

[21] van de Ven, *War and Nationalism*, 131–132.

[22] He, *Paihua Shiliao* I, 158–159.

[23] Ibid., 248, 264.

[24] "National Conditions," 28–30.

[25] Stephen Craft's monograph about V. K. Willington Koo gives a good explanation of the ideologies of Koo and other diplomats to deal with international disputes. See Craft, *Koo*.

[26] Ibid., chapters 2–4.

[27] "Negotiation about Anti-Chinese Movement."

[28] He, *Paihua Shiliao* I, 6.

[29] China in the early twentieth century suffered from turf wars of various military powers, unequal treaties with Western colonialist powers, and Japan's military threat to annex whole China.

[30] "Mexico Experienced Another Revolution"; and "The Authority."

[31] Wang, "Reflection."

[32] Tang, *Gonggong Yulun*, 108–109.

[33] Japan invaded Manchuria and renamed it as Manchukuo (滿洲國).

[34] *Tao Xingzhi Rizhi*, 67.

[35] Yao, "National Hero," 254.

[36] Yao, "National Salvation," 207.

[37] *Tao Xingzhi Rizhi*, 75–76.

[38] In his notes on Chinese labor in Chihuahua and Mexico City, Tao recorded Chinese migrants' unemployment under racist persecution, extra taxes charged on Chinese people, and racial violence against Chinese people. See *Tao Xingzhi Rizhi*, 68–69.

[39] Culp, *Articulating Citizenship*, 7–9.

Bibliography

Campos, Ivonne. *Segregación, Racismo y Antichinismo: La Ley 27 de 1923 y el Caso de los Barrios Chinos de Sonora*. Ciudad de México, México: Suprema Corte de Justicia de la Nación, 2019.

Chang, Jason O. *Chinos: Anti-Chinese Racism in Mexico, 1880–1940*. Urbana: University of Illinois Press, 2017.

Chen, Guo-wei. "The Overseas Chinese Affairs Commission of Republican China, 1932–1945: A Survey." *Overseas Chinese History Studies*, no. 4 (2010): 64–73.

Cheng, Yan "Current Situations of Mexico" (Moxige Xianzhuang 墨西哥現狀)." *Review of Chinese and Foreign Affairs* (*Zhongwai Pinglun* 中外評論) (Nanjing) 20, 1930, 27.

"Chinese Forced to Leave Mexico." *Fort Worth Star-Telegram*, March 7, 1932.

"Committee against Marriage with Chinese" (Comite Contra El Matrimonio de los Chinos). *Excélsior*, March 14, 1930.

Craft, Stephen G. *V. K. Wellington Koo and the Emergence of Modern China*. Lexington: University Press of Kentucky, 2004.

Culp, Robert. C. *Articulating Citizenship: Civic Education and Student Politics in Southeastern China, 1912–1940*. Cambridge: Harvard University Asian Center, 2007.

"Decree of the Executive Yuan no. 4441 (Xingzheng Yuan Ling Di Si Si Si Yi Hao 行政院令第四四四一號)." *Military Bulletin* (Jun Zheng Gongbao 軍政公報), no. 34 (1929): 26–27.

Halsey, Stephen R. *Quest for Power: European Imperialism and the Making of Chinese Statecraft*. Cambridge: Harvard University Press, 2015.

He, Fengjiao. ed. *Paihua Shiliao Huibian: Moxige* 排華史料匯編：墨西哥. Collection of Sources of Anti-Chinese Movements: Mexico. Taipei: Guoshiguan, 1991.

"He Yingqin's Telegram to Chiang Kai-shek Regarding Assigning Shao Yuanchong to Europe and America to Connect and Appreciate Overseas Chinese" (He Yingqin dian Jiang Zhongzheng kefou pai Shao Yuanchong fu oumei zuo guoji lianluo bing weilao huaqiao 何應欽電蔣中正可否派邵元冲赴歐美做國際聯絡宣傳並慰勞華僑) March 6, 1927, Academia Historica, https://ahonline.drnh.gov.tw/index.php?act=Display/image/2696887nMmDDbj#e5F.

Hu-Dehart, Evelyn. "Indispensable Enemy or Convenient Scapegoat? A Critical Examination of Sinophobia in Latin American and the Caribbean, 1870s to 1930s." In *The Chinese in Latin America and the Caribbean*, edited by Walton Look Lai and Tan Chee-Beng, 65–102. Leiden and Boston: Brill, 2010.

Interview of the Wing S. Wong's family [unpublished interview], Special Collection, University of Arizona Library.

Jangsu Sheng Tao Xingzhi Yanjiuhui, ed. *Tao Xingzhi Rizhi* [陶行知日誌, *Daily Logs of Tao Xingzhi*]. Nanjing: Jiangsu Jiaoyu Press, 1991.

Ji, Man-hong. "The Committee of Overseas Business of the Nanjing National Government before the Anti-Japanese War." *Jinan Journal (Philosophy and Social Sciences Section)* 178, no. 11 (2013): 94–101.

Lai, Look Walton and Tan Chee-Beng. eds. *The Chinese in Latin America and the Caribbean*. Leiden and Boston: Brill, 2010.

"Mexico Experienced Another Revolution." (Moxiege youyan yici geming 墨西哥又演一次革命) 26, *The Eastern Miscellanies* 东方杂志, no.4 (1929): 2–4.

"Mexico Mistreated Chinese Immigrants." (Moxige Kedai Huaqiao墨西哥苛待華僑) *Central Daily News* (*Zhongyang Ribao* 中央日報), May 5, 1928.

"National Conditions of Mexico." (Moxige zhi guqing 墨西哥之國情) *Immigrants Semimonthly* (*Huaqiao Banyuekan* 華僑半月刊) 7 (1932): 28–30.

Phillips, Steven. "National Legitimacy and Overseas Chinese Mobilization." *Journal of Modern Chinese History* 7, no. 1 (2013): 64–86.

Romero, Robert C. *The Chinese in Mexico, 1882–1940*. Tucson: University of Arizona Press, 2011.

Schiavone-Camacho, Julia M. *Chinese Mexicans: Transpacific Migration and the Search for a Homeland, 1910–1960*. Chapel Hill: University of North Carolina Press, 2012.

Sonnichsen, C. L. *Tucson, the Life and Times of an American City*. Norman: University of Oklahoma Press, 1982.

Strauss, Julia. *Strong Institutions in Weak Polities: State Building in Republican China, 1927–1940*. Oxford: Clarendon Press, 1998.

Tang Xiaobing, *Xiangdai Zhongguo de Gonggong Yulun: yi Da Gong Bao "Xingqi Lunwen" he Shen Bao "Ziyou Tan" weili* (現代中國的公共輿論: 以《大公報》「星期文論」和《申報》「自由談」為例). Beijing: Shehui kexue wenxian Press, 2012.

"The Anti-Chinese Movement in Mexico: The Authority Ordered to Punish the Leaders." (Moxige Paihua'an: Dangju Xialing Chengxiong 墨西哥排華案: 當局下令懲凶) *Da Gong Bao* 大公報, July 28, 1931.

"The Negotiation about the Anti-Chinese Movement." (Moxige Paihua Jiaoshe 墨西哥排華交) *News Reports* (Xingwen Bao 新聞報), August 17, 1931.

Van de Ven, Hans. J. *War and Nationalism in China, 1925–1945*. London and New York: Routledge Curzon, 2003.

Wang, Mingwo. "Reflection of the Anti-Chinese Movement in Mexico." (Moxige Paihua Ganyan 墨西哥排华感言) *Shanghai News* [Shanghai Bao, 上海報], September 7, 1931.

Xiang, Hongyuan. "From a Diplomatic to a Domestic Issue: China's Struggle with Church Properties in the Nanjing Decade (1927–1937)." *Twentieth-Century China* 45, no. 1 (2020): 66–84.

Yao, Yusheng. "National Salvation through Education: Tao Xingzhi's Educational Radicalism." PhD diss., University of Minnesota, 1999.

———. "The Making of a National Hero: Tao Xingzhi's Legacies in the People's Republic of China." *Review of Education, Pedagogy & Cultural Studies* 24, no. 3 (2002): 251–281.

Yü, Shouzhi. *Yü Shouzhi Shiwenji*. [余受之詩文集, An Anthology of Yü Shouzhi]. Chengdu: Chengdu kanben, 1999.

7

THE POLITICS OF ANTI-ASIAN DISCOURSES IN TURKEY

Irmak Yazici

Introduction

Anti-Asian sentiment has been on the rise since the COVID-19 pandemic hit. Much ink has been spilled on how the hate targeting Asian people took its forms in various places. Although news outlets were saturated with the images of such hate that occurred mostly in the United States, similar attacks on Asian people were reported across the world. Approaching anti-Asian attitudes from a global outlook requires taking a diversified set of contextual—social, cultural, historical, and political—factors into consideration. This essay discusses two key elements, religious identity and foreign policy, in relation to Turkey; uses historical and discourse analyses; and draws on verbal and written statements of government officials, policy briefs, reports, newspaper articles, and secondary literature—all of which aids in understanding the underlying reasons for the diverse manifestations of anti-Asian discourse within particular sociopolitical settings.

More specifically, this essay considers anti-Asian discourses in relation to the treatment of Uyghur Muslims in China. It is important to consider these contextual factors when discussing anti-Asian hate in order to refrain from a one-size-fits-all approach that may overlook important nuances in addressing the complex causes of such hate, as well as the utilization of such causes by political actors. This essay also offers insight into how anti-Asian discourses emerge and persist in countries like Turkey, where Asian immigrants are only a small portion of the population.

This suggests that there are also transborder factors—other than the number or presence of immigrants—such as an imagined global religious identity and foreign policy concerns, that can substantially determine the scope and direction of such discourses.

Anti-Asian Discourses in Turkey and Uyghur Muslims in China

As they were in many other countries across the world, Asian people were targeted in Turkey during the COVID-19 pandemic.[1] There have been cases of Asian kids at school being harassed about whether they eat bats, or of Asian people not being allowed in restaurants.[2] Research shows that there has been an increase in hate speech against Chinese and Asian people in Turkey during the COVID-19 pandemic.[3] Hashtags and trending topics on social media, such as #batsoup (#yarasaçorbası) and #Chinesevirus (#Çinvirüsü), were used to disseminate misinformation about Asian eating habits and to emphasize the origin of the virus. These social media posts dehumanized Asian people in a variety of ways, including by invoking abjection or appealing to feelings of disgust based on eating habits or cultural cuisine (e.g., "How do they eat these disgusting things?") and "scapegoating" or accusing a particular group of all the negative aspects of the pandemic (e.g., "The pandemic happened because of what they ate.").[4]

Nevertheless, anti-Asian attacks predate the COVID-19 pandemic in Turkey. For instance, according to a survey conducted in 2019, 44 percent of Turkish people held unfavorable opinions toward China as opposed to 37 percent who held favorable opinions.[5] Research on the production of hate speech in Turkey points out that certain political events—such as national commemorations of military operations and massacres against Turkic peoples or Muslims—as well as state officials' statements on matters concerning immigrants and genocide allegations, trigger hate speech against particular groups that are associated with these events.[6] Along these lines, anti-Asian sentiments expressed in the form of hate speech or physical attacks are mainly directed at Chinese people as a retaliative response to the Chinese state's oppressive policies toward Uyghur Muslims.

In one such incident in 2015 that received substantial media attention, Istanbul police launched an investigation after a youth organization with links to the far-right ultranationalist political party, Nationalist Movement Party (Milliyetçi Hareket Partisi, MHP), reportedly attacked a group of Korean tourists in the historic district of Sultanahmet in Istanbul following a march to protest China's restrictions on the religious freedom of ethnic Uyghur Muslims in Xinjiang.[7] The leader of the party defended the attackers for having been provoked by what had been going on in China and for mistaking Koreans for the Chinese, saying, "both have slanted eyes."[8] Three days before the attack, a Chinese restaurant in Istanbul was vandalized by ultranationalists, although ironically, the restaurant owner was indeed Turkish, and the chef was of Uyghur descent.[9]

Such incidents that predate the pandemic are directly related to the developments in the Xinjiang Uyghur Autonomous Region (XUAR) in China since 2009. About eleven million Uyghurs—a predominantly Sunni Muslim, Turkic-speaking ethnic group—live in the region.[10] Riots first broke out in the regional capital of Urumqi in 2009, and there is only partial information about the causes and aftermath of the protests.[11] However, the history of unrest in the region can be traced back to the 9/11 attacks in the United States, after which "China began to portray its security campaigns in Xinjiang as a contribution to the global war on terror."[12] Some suggest that 9/11 "triggered a major shift in the Chinese Communist Party's view of the Uyghur people" and that "the Chinese government produced a lot of documents suggesting that it faced a serious terrorist threat from Uyghurs."[13] The Chinese government's continued efforts "to combat terrorist threats" led to the Strike Hard Campaign, and by 2019, China had "destroyed 1,588 violent and terrorist gangs, arrested 12,995 terrorists, seized 2,052 explosive devices, punished 30,645 people for 4,858 illegal religious activities, and confiscated 345,229 copies of illegal religious materials" in the XUAR.[14] Under the strict measures of the campaign, Turkic Muslims were not only banned from using their mother tongue, pursuing Qur'anic studies, or studying abroad, but many also "have been interned, imprisoned, or forcibly 'disappeared' since 2017."[15]

In light of these events that predate the COVID-19 pandemic, such as the attack on Korean tourists in a touristy area and the vandalization of a Chinese restaurant in 2015, the sections that follow discuss the links between anti-Asian discourses in Turkey and China's treatment of Uyghur Muslims. China has long claimed that Uyghurs are part of the "great family of the Chinese nation" and hence sees Xinjiang as "an integral piece of Chinese national territory," whereas Uyghurs see themselves as a distinct nation "with its own rightful homeland, history, culture, and language."[16] In the early twentieth century, the Uyghurs declared independence for a brief period until China's new Communist government took control in 1949. To counter the continued Uyghur resistance against Chinese assimilation, the Chinese government has adopted several strategies. For example, as a result of government incentives to promote Han migration and therefore dilute Uyghur domination in the XUAR, the composition of the region's population has changed drastically: over the last seventy years, since the first census in 1953, the Uyghur population in the region declined from 75 percent to 45 percent, while that of the Han Chinese increased from 7 percent to 42 percent.[17] As such, the history of the relationship between the Uyghurs and the Chinese government has been a key factor in Turkey's defense of the Uyghurs as a Muslim minority on the basis of their Turkic origins and shared cultural elements, such as religion and language, while government officials have strived to maintain good relations with China given its importance as a strategic partner. Hence, it is important to discuss how religious identity and foreign policy concerns have shaped the scope and course of negative attitudes toward Asian people in Turkey.

Anti-Asian Discourses and Religious Identity

In the case of Turkey, a discussion of anti-Asian discourses in relation to religious identity necessitates briefly mapping the secular nationalist ideology in Turkey, since Sunni Muslim religious identity developed as an essential component of this ideology. In addition, contemporary nationalist ideology promoted by the Justice and Development Party (Adalet ve Kalkınma Partisi, AKP), the political party that has been in power since 2002, draws on the historical role of the Ottoman Empire as the leader of the *umma* and hence assumes the role of a protector when other Muslim communities are oppressed, as in the case of Uyghur Muslims in Xinjiang.[18] The appeal of the imagined global religious identity, as an extension of this religious nationalist outlook, manifests itself not only in the official discourse of the Turkish government in critique of China's oppressive treatment of the Uyghurs but also in the attacks that targeted Asians during and prior to the COVID-19 pandemic.

Sunni Islam was designated as the state-approved religious affiliation for the citizens of the secular republic in Turkey—following the dissolution of the Ottoman Empire and the caliphate—as a unifying element under the nation-state rather than a strict formulation of religious practice and piety. More specifically, Sunni Muslimness was presented as the nation's religious identity and legitimized by the Presidency of Religious Affairs (Diyanet İşleri Başkanlığı), which was established in 1924 and assisted the state in regulating the practice of Islam in a "Turkish" way.[19] The Diyanet facilitated the shift "from Islamic civil being to state Muslimness," promoting a "pure" form of Islam that excluded non-Sunni practices under the assumption that this would prevent sectarian or religious threats to the secular state structure.[20] This so-called "pure" Islam of the state was uniform in structure and was subordinate to the nation's "Turkishness," which was adopted as the primary identifier only toward the end of the Ottoman Empire.[21]

This was also in line with the ethno-nationalist politics pursued by the revolutionary Young Turks to form an exclusively Muslim-Turkish class of businessmen in the Ottoman Empire during the first quarter of the twentieth century, and later, with the reforms imposed by the founding elite under the leadership of Atatürk in order to replace the "superstition and ignorance" of the "old ways of life," as they saw it.[22] Morin and Lee argue that by reformulating Islam as a secular state-approved religious affiliation, "Kemalism in Turkey negotiated the tensions between religious tradition and secular ideology, formulated a distinct

Turkish identity beyond the boundaries of umma and successfully transformed an empire to a nation-state."[23] Thus, Islam was redefined by the state as "Turkish Islam," a secular interpretation and accommodation of the religion in its Sunni form. In this sense, religious nationalism was embedded in the state's secular modernization program.

Under the AKP government over the past two decades, this national Sunni Muslim identity has been emphasized more explicitly. The AKP has adopted a "neo-Ottomanist" discourse that involves evoking victorious as well as tragic moments and "the heroes and the pageantry that accompanied them from a Turkish past before the establishment of modern Turkey."[24] President Erdoğan uses this discourse frequently in public speeches to make the point that Turkish people "are the heirs of a unique and historically important civilization," of which Sunni Islam is an indispensable component.[25] This "Ottoman romanticism" also manifests itself in the government's emphasis on restoring Ottoman monuments, giving Ottoman or Ottoman-inspired names to buildings, streets, schools, and bridges, and using Ottoman Turkish vocabulary.[26] For instance, the reopening of Hagia Sophia for prayer as a mosque in 2020 under the AKP, after it had been a museum since 1934, is also part of this neo-Ottomanist approach.

Neo-Ottomanism has fueled the protective language used by the government when addressing or referring to Muslims elsewhere, as in the case of the Uyghur Muslims. In the official statements from the Turkish Ministry of Foreign Affairs, Uyghurs are sometimes referred to as "our kinsmen"[27] or "brothers."[28] Similarly, at an *iftar* (fast-breaking) meeting during the holy month of Ramadan in 2015, in reference to the developments in the XUAR, President Erdoğan said:

> We have kin all over the world. Incidents, taking place in all regions from Balkans to Central Asia, from Crimea to North Africa, directly concern us. In this regard, allegations that our brothers, living in the Xinjiang Uyghur Autonomous Region of the People's Republic of China, are oppressed have caused sensitivity among our people. . . . I would like to express that Turkey stands by the Uyghur Turks in China just like it stands by all its brothers and kin. We voice the problems concerning our brothers living in the Xinjiang Uyghur Autonomous Region at the highest level and will continue to do so.[29]

Erdoğan also acknowledged the incidents that took place in Istanbul earlier in 2015, where Korean tourists were attacked and a Chinese restaurant was vandalized, and highlighted that these incidents were a direct outcome of what had been going on in the XUAR. Moreover, neo-Ottomanism has also been an important component of the ultranationalist movement in Turkey. The statements of Devlet Bahçeli—the leader of the oldest nationalist party in Turkey, MHP, and a political ally of the ruling AKP—defending the attackers for having been provoked by what had been going on in China, in response to the incidents that targeted Asians in Turkey in 2015, manifests the religious nationalist element in neo-Ottomanism.

Nationalist discourse was also utilized to gain political advantage by opposition parties by appealing to these sentiments of kinship. The leader of the Good Party (İyi Parti, IYIP), an offshoot of the MHP, criticized the AKP government for breaking its promise to protect Uyghur citizens when Turkey initiated arrest and extradition processes for numerous Uyghur activists who had been living in the country.[30] A report prepared by the party highlights the importance of protecting their "Uyghur brothers and sisters," and the party leadership accuses the government of ignoring the issue.[31] IYIP leader Meral Akşener proposed that the case should be acknowledged as genocide.[32] In June 2022, during a volleyball game between Turkey and China, where Akşener was present, protesters from IYIP displayed the Uyghur flag.[33] Using these issues and nationalist discourse to gain political advantage and as a point of pressure for the government can trivialize the treatment of Asian peoples under the overarching label of "Chinese," as illustrated by the numerous attacks against them.

Anti-Asian Discourses and Foreign Policy

Looking at anti-Asian discourses through the lens of foreign policy also provides insights into how the nature and scope of such discourses can shift. Changing attitudes in international relations show that despite the religious nationalist roots of anti-Asian discourse in Turkey, diplomatic and economic concerns have altered the course of such discourse that is at times adopted by the government. For example, in 2009, Erdoğan described the incidents in the XUAR as "genocide," positioning himself as a protector—"a defiant Muslim leader willing to speak truth to totalitarian power."[34] Additionally, since 1949, Turkey had been a "safe haven" for Uyghurs who escaped persecution under the communist Chinese government, hosting one of the largest Uyghur diaspora populations in the world. However, in 2016, the Turkish government initiated the extradition process of Uyghur political activist Abdulkadir Yapcan, who had been living in Turkey since 2001. Following this, Turkey and China signed an agreement "allowing extradition even if the purported offense is only illegal in one of the two countries," and since early 2019, Turkey has arrested hundreds of Uyghurs and sent them to deportation centers.[35] These changes in the Turkish government's attitude signal that foreign policy can be a key factor in understanding the responses to anti-Asian discourses.

Diplomatic relations between Turkey and China were established in 1971 and gained momentum in the 1980s with the opening up of both countries. Bilateral relations reached the level of "strategic cooperation" in 2010, and multiple visits by Chinese and Turkish officials took place between 2010 and 2012.[36] Trade volume between the two countries has also increased between 2015 and 2021 from 27.27 to 35.9 billion USD, and China has become Turkey's second-largest import partner after Russia.[37] Turkey aims to realize the Trans Hazar-Middle Corridor Project, complementing the North Line from China to Europe and opening a new connecting corridor between China and Europe. In this regard, to align the Belt and Road Initiative with the Middle Corridor Project, a memorandum of understanding was signed on July 1, 2016, on the margins of the G20 Hangzhou Summit. The Baku-Tbilisi-Kars railway, a main component of the Middle Corridor, was officially inaugurated on October 30, 2017.[38]

Turkey-China relations also developed further on the cultural front. 2018 was celebrated as the Turkish Tourism Year in China, and different cultural events were organized. In 2018, the number of Chinese tourists in Turkey increased by 60 percent compared to the previous year, and in 2019, the number of Chinese tourists exceeded 565,000.[39] Furthermore, the Yunus Emre Institute—a cultural nonprofit organization that promotes Turkish language, history, and art—opened in Beijing in May 2021.[40]

By contrast, in February 2019, following reports that Abdurehim Heyit, an Uyghur folk musician with a popular following in Turkey, allegedly died in detention in China, the Turkish government called China's "systematic assimilation against the Uyghur Turks" a "great embarrassment for humanity" and stated that "this tragedy has further reinforced the reaction of the Turkish public opinion towards serious human rights violations committed in the Xinjiang region."[41] Turkey has also acknowledged that the fundamental human rights of "Uyghur Turks" and other Muslim communities in the XUAR have worsened. Between eight hundred thousand and two million Uyghurs and other Turkic Muslims have been detained in so-called political reeducation centers—or, more accurately, concentration camps—in Xinjiang in addition to students, scholars, artists, and journalists who have been interned, imprisoned, or disappeared since April 2017.[42] The incarcerated are allegedly "being cleansed of extremism and taught how to be good citizens" and are "free to leave whenever they like."[43]

Nevertheless, it did not take long for Ankara to take a step back and change its course. This was partly due to the immediate response from Beijing. After Ankara's statement, China's ambassador declared that if such criticism continued, it "will be reflected in commercial and economic relations."[44] In a precautionary manner, to prevent further friction, during his visit to Beijing in July 2019, President Erdoğan warned against the supposed exploitation of the issue to damage Turkey's relationship with China. This was a crucial step, since tensions between the United States and Turkey increased after Turkey announced that it would consider buying Russia's S-400 system in 2017. Subsequently, in 2018, a Chinese state bank loaned Turkey $3.6 billion during the economic crisis triggered by the diplomatic issues with the United States as the Turkish lira crashed.[45] Eventually, following Ankara's deal with Russia for the S-400 missile system, the Trump administration imposed sanctions on Turkey in 2020.

The economic hardship Turkey has been facing since late 2017, and its reliance on foreign support, has been a determining factor in the changing government attitude toward anti-Asian, and particularly anti-Chinese, sentiment. It seems that the initial response that came from the Ministry of Foreign Affairs in 2019 condemning Beijing's actions was a political move to prevent criticism from the public. Meanwhile, Erdoğan made another strategic move to ensure that China could be relied on as an ally, while Western powers on the other end of the political spectrum, such as the United States, may impose sanctions not only as a response to emerging alliances with countries like Russia but also as a response to declining conditions of freedom as the country has gradually become more authoritarian under the AKP regime.

Concluding Remarks

Turkey's shifting foreign policy strategies that favor China as an ally have indirectly legitimized Chinese oppression of Uyghur Muslims, while its religious nationalist domestic politics have paved the way for public displays of anti-Asian hate and prejudice as a reaction to the Uyghur issue. Acknowledging the historical shifts in the relationship between Turkey and China and the strategic reasons underlying these shifts can be helpful in thinking beyond the limits of the anti-Asian tropes that are commonly used in the United States and elsewhere, where Asian peoples form a certain portion of the population. Most of the time, these anti-Asian discourses are invoked to complain about immigration. During the COVID-19 pandemic, for example, Asian people, including Asian Americans, were told to "go back to where they came from."[46] In a country like the United States, where there is a history of anti-Asian immigration sentiment fueled by policies like the Chinese Exclusion Act of 1882, we should also consider this history against the backdrop of the attacks on Asian peoples during the COVID-19 pandemic.

In a similar way, in a country like Turkey, where Asian immigration has never been an issue, understanding anti-Asian sentiment necessitates considering other factors, such as the history of Uyghur-Turkish relations, China's treatment of the Uyghur minority, and the domestic political strategies that may foster anti-Asian discourses and attacks. In other words, a one-size-fits-all approach—such as anti-immigration sentiment—to understand the underlying reasons of anti-Asian sentiment in different social and political contexts can be misleading. The examples discussed throughout this essay demonstrate that it is important to consider contextual factors when discussing anti-Asian hate, as a one-size-fits-all approach may overlook important nuances in addressing the complex roots of anti-Asian discourses across the globe. The case of Turkey demonstrates that different aspects, such as religious identity and foreign policy, can determine the nature and scope of Anti-Asian discourses and negative attitudes toward Asian peoples in different social, economic, and political contexts.

Notes

[1] Congar, "Koronavirüs Çin'i dünyadan tecrit etti."

[2] Tekin, "Türkiye'de yaşayan Çinliler."

[3] İlden and Gökçen, "COVID-19 PANDEMI SÜRECINDE SOSYAL MEDYADA NEFRET SÖYLEMI RAPORU."

[4] See Kristeva, *Powers of Horror*. Cited in İlden and Gökçen, 17.

[5] Silver et al., "Attitudes toward China."

[6] Hrant Dink Foundation, "Medyada Nefret Söylemi İzleme Raporu."

[7] Kacmaz, "Sultanahmet'te Çinli sandıkları Koreli turist grubuna saldırdılar."

[8] *Hürriyet*, "Bahçeli'nin 'çekik göz' sözleri olay oldu."

[9] *Hürriyet Daily News*, "Istanbul Chinese Restaurant Attacked in Protest at Uighur Suppression."

[10] Other predominantly Muslim ethnic groups living in the region include Hui, Kazakh, Kyrgyz, Mongol, and Tajik peoples. See UNHR, "OHCHR Assessment of Human Rights Concerns in the Xinjiang Uyghur Autonomous Region, People's Republic of China," 4.

[11] Protests started peacefully against the killing of Uyghur workers at the Guangdong toy factory, but it is unclear how the protest turned violent. Uyghur sources accused the riot police of "excessive use of force against the protestors," while Chinese officials stated that the riots were handled "decisively and properly." See Human Rights Watch, "We Are Afraid to Even Look for Them," and Yinan and Xiaoxun, "Urumqi Riot Handled 'Decisively, Properly.'"

[12] Human Rights Watch, "We Are Afraid to Even Look for Them."

[13] Arablouei and Abdelfatah, "Who the Uyghurs Are and Why China Is Targeting Them."

[14] UNHR, "OHCHR Assessment of Human Rights Concerns in the Xinjiang Uyghur Autonomous Region, People's Republic of China," 5. See also the State Council Information Office of the People's Republic of China, White Paper on "The Fight against Terrorism and Extremism and Human Rights Protection in Xinjiang."

[15] According to an AAS statement, at least 386 Uyghur intellectuals and scholars have "disappeared," including twenty-one staff of Xinjiang University, fifteen staff of Xinjiang Normal University, thirteen staff of Kashgar University, six staff of Xinjiang Medical University, six staff of the Xinjiang Social Sciences Academy, four staff from Khotan Teachers' College, and 101 students. AAS, "AAS Statement on Extra-Judicial Detention of Turkic Muslims in Xinjiang, PRC." See also UHRP, "Detained and Disappeared: Intellectuals under Assault in the Uyghur Homeland."

[16] Bovingdon, *The Uyghurs*, 3.

[17] UNHR, "OHCHR Assessment of Human Rights Concerns in the Xinjiang Uyghur Autonomous Region, People's Republic of China," 4.

[18] The imagined community of Muslims across the world.

[19] The Presidency of Religious Affairs reframed the role and duties of the previous religious authorities of the Ottoman Empire within the boundaries of secularism by providing guidance on faith-related matters. In theory, it promoted a modern, secular understanding of religion and separated it from its Arabic origin, creating a unique and strictly Turkish experience of the religion. The elimination of the caliphate that had served as a tool to legitimize the Ottoman Sultanate—as well as the banning of various religious venues of denominational worship and education, namely *tekkes* (dervish lodges), *zaviyes* (Islamic monasteries), and *medreses* (theological schools)—were part of the secular nationalist ideology that underlies the founding of the Turkish Republic. For further reading, see Gözaydın, *Diyanet*.

[20] Cangızbay, *Çok-hukukluluk, laiklik ve laikrasi*, x.

[21] İlber Ortaylı, "Mülakat."

[22] Eligür, *The Mobilization of Political Islam in Turkey*, 159; Andrew Davison, *Secularism and Revivalism in Turkey*, 87.

[23] Morin and Lee, "Constitutive Discourse of Turkish Nationalism," 487.

[24] M. Hakan Yavuz, *Nostalgia for the Empire: The Politics of Neo-Ottomanism*, introduction.

[25] Ibid.

[26] Ibid., chapter 1. For further reading, see Halil İnalcık, "Comments on 'Sultanism' Max Weber's Typification of the Ottoman Polity" and "Turkey between Europe and the Middle East."

[27] Republic of Türkiye Ministry of Foreign Affairs, "Press Release Regarding Thailand's Refoulement of Uyghur Turks."

[28] Republic of Türkiye Ministry of Foreign Affairs, "Statement of the Spokesperson of the Ministry of Foreign Affairs, Mr. Hami Aksoy in Response to a Question Regarding Turkey's National Statement on the Xinjiang Uyghur Autonomous Region Delivered at the Third Committee Meeting During the 75th Session of the UN General Assembly."

[29] Presidency of the Republic of Türkiye, "Turkey Stands by the Uyghur Turks in China Just Like It Stands by All Its Brothers."

[30] This issue is discussed in the next section in relation to foreign policy.

[31] Yılmaz et al. "Çin Uygur Özerk Bölgesi İnsan Hakları Raporu."

[32] *Euronews*, "İYİ Parti lideri Akşener: TBMM, Uygur Türklerinin yaşadıkları soykırım olarak tanımalı."

[33] *Karar*, "İYİ Parti'den Çin'e protesto: Maçta Uygur bayrağı açtılar."

[34] Altay, "Why Erdogan Has Abandoned the Uyghurs."

[35] Alemdaroğlu and Tepe, "Erdogan Is Turning Turkey into a Chinese Client State."

[36] "Relations between Türkiye and People's Republic of China."

[37] Alemdaroğlu and Tepe, "Erdogan Is Turning Turkey into a Chinese Client State."

[38] "Türkiye-People's Republic of China Economic and Trade Relations."

[39] Ibid.

[40] This is a "public foundation" established "to promote Turkey, Turkish language, its history and culture and art, make such related information and documents available for use in the world, provide services abroad to people who want to have education in the fields of Turkish language, culture and art, to improve the friendship between Turkey and other countries and increase the cultural exchange." See "Yunus Emre Institute."

[41] Republic of Türkiye Ministry of Foreign Affairs, "Statement of the Spokesperson of the Ministry of Foreign Affairs, Mr. Hami Aksoy, in Response to a Question Regarding Serious Human Rights Violations Perpetrated against Uighur Turks and the Passing Away of Folk Poet Abdurehim Heyit."

[42] UHRP, "Detained and Disappeared: Intellectuals under Assault in the Uyghur Homeland."

[43] Altay, "Why Erdogan Has Abandoned the Uyghurs."

[44] Farooq, "Uighur Dissident in Turkey Fights Effort to Extradite Him to China."

[45] Yackley, "Erdoğan Finds Warm Welcome, 'Shared Vision' in Beijing."

[46] CPR News, "Fear, Avoidance, Being Told to Go Back to Their Country: What It's Like to Be Asian in Colorado in the Time of Coronavirus."

Bibliography

Alemdaroğlu, Ayça and Sultan Tepe. "Erdogan Is Turning Turkey into a Chinese Client State." *Foreign Policy*, September 16, 2020. https://foreignpolicy.com/2020/09/16/erdogan-is- turning-turkey-into-a-chinese-client-state/.

Altay, Kuzzat. "Why Erdogan Has Abandoned the Uyghurs." *Foreign Policy*, March 2, 2021. https://foreignpolicy.com/2021/03/02/why-erdogan-has-abandoned-the-uyghurs/.

Arablouei, Ramtin, and Rund Abdelfatah. "Who the Uyghurs Are and Why China Is Targeting Them." NPR.org. Accessed on March 18, 2023, https://www.npr.org/2021/05/31/1001936433/who-the-uyghurs-are-and-why-china-is-targeting-them.

Association for Asian Studies. "AAS Statement on Extra-Judicial Detention of Turkic Muslims in Xinjiang, PRC." March 28, 2019. https://www.asianstudies.org/aas-statement-on-extra-judicial-detention-of-turkic-muslims-in-xinjiang-prc/.

Baijie, An. "Trust Highlighted in Turkey Ties." *China Daily*, July 3, 2019.

Bovingdon, Gardner. *The Uyghurs: Strangers in Their Own Land*. New York: Columbia University Press, 2010.

Cangızbay, Kadir. *Çok-hukukluluk, laiklik ve laikrasi*. Ankara: Liberte Yayınları, 2002.

Congar, Kerem. "Koronavirüs Çin'i dünyadan tecrit etti, ırkçılık eylemleri arttı." *Euronews*, February 1, 2020. https://tr.euronews.com/2020/02/01/koronavirus-cin-i-dunyadan-tecrit-etti-irkcilik-eylemleri-artti.

Davison, Andrew. *Secularism and Revivalism in Turkey: A Hermeneutic Reconsideration.* New Haven: Yale University Press, 1998.

Dirini, İlden and Özsu, Gökçen, "COVID-19 PANDEMİ SÜRECİNDE SOSYAL MEDYADA NEFRET SÖYLEMİ RAPORU" (Ankara: Alternatif Bilişim Derneği, 2020), https://ekitap.alternatifbilisim.org/pdf/covid19-nefret-soylemi-raporu.pdf.

Eligür, Banu. *The Mobilization of Political Islam in Turkey.* Cambridge: Cambridge University Press, 2010.

Euronews. "İYİ Parti lideri Akşener: TBMM, Uygur Türklerinin yaşadıkları soykırım olarak tanımalı," March 1, 2021. https://tr.euronews.com/2021/03/01/iyi-parti-lideri-aksener-tbmm-uygur-turklerinin-yasad-klar-soyk-r-m-olarak-tan-mal.

Farooq, Umar. "Uighur dissident in Turkey Fights Effort to Extradite Him to China." *Los Angeles Times*, March 29, 2019. https://www.latimes.com/world/asia/la-fg-turkey-uighur-extradition-20190329-story.html.

Freedom House. "Turkey: Transnational Repression Host Country Case Study." 2022. https://freedomhouse.org/report/transnational-repression/turkey-host.

Gözaydın, İştar. *Diyanet: Türkiye Cumhuriyeti'nde Dinin Tanzimi.* İstanbul: İletişim, 2009.

Human Rights Watch. "We Are Afraid to Even Look for Them." October 20, 2009. Accessed on March 20, 2023. https://www.hrw.org/report/2009/10/20/we-are-afraid-even-look-them/enforced-disappearances-wake-xinjiangs-protests.

Hürriyet. "Bahçeli'nin 'çekik göz' sözleri olay oldu." July 11, 2015. https://www.hurriyet.com.tr/gundem/bahcelinin-cekik-goz-sozleri-olay-oldu-29525168.

Hürriyet Daily News. "Istanbul Chinese Restaurant Attacked in Protest at Uighur Suppression." July 2, 2015. https://www.hurriyetdailynews.com/istanbul-chinese-restaurant-attacked-in-protest-at-uighur-suppression--84846.

Hrant Dink Foundation. "Medyada Nefret Söylemi İzleme Raporu," May–August 2019. Accessed on March 19, 2023. https://hrantdink.org/attachments/article/2375/MNS%C4%B0-rapor-may%C4%B1s-a gustos-2019.pdf.

İnalcık, Halil. "Comments on 'Sultanism' Max Weber's Typification of the Ottoman Polity." "Polity," *Princeton Papers in Near Eastern Studies* 1 (1992): 49–73.

Kaçmaz, Yasar. "Sultanahmet'te Çinli sandıkları Koreli turist grubuna saldırdılar." *Milliyet*, July 4, 2015. https://www.milliyet.com.tr/gundem/sultanahmet-te-cinli-sandiklari-koreli-turist-grubuna-saldirdilar-2083240.

Karar. "İYİ Parti'den Çin'e protesto: Maçta Uygur bayrağı açtılar." June 3, 2022. https://www.karar.com/spor-haberleri/iyi-partiden-cine-protesto-macta-uygur-bayragi-actilar-1668969.

Kristeva, Julia. *Powers of Horror: An Essay on Abjection.* New York: Columbia University Press, 1982.

Morin, Aysel, and Ronald Lee. "Constitutive Discourse of Turkish Nationalism: Atatürk's Nutuk and the Rhetorical Construction of the 'Turkish People,'" *Communication Studies* 61, no. 5 (2010): 487.

Ortaylı, İlber. "Mülakat," *Türkiye Günlüğü* 11 (1990): 26–29.

———. "Turkey between Europe and the Middle East," *Perceptions: Journal of International Affairs* 3, no. 1 (1998): 5–18.

Presidency of the Republic of Türkiye, "Turkey Stands by the Uyghur Turks in China Just Like It Stands by All Its Brothers," July 9, 2015. Accessed on March 26, 2023, https://www.tccb.gov.tr/en/news/542/32895/cumhurbaskani-erdogan-buyukelcilerle-iftar-yapti.

"Press Release Regarding Thailand's Refoulement of Uyghur Turks," Republic of Türkiye Ministry of Foreign Affairs, July 9, 2015. Accessed on June 24, 2023, https://www.mfa.gov.tr/no_-199_-9-july-2015_-press-release-regarding-thailand_s-refoulement-of-uyghur-turks.en.mfa.

"Relations between Türkiye and People's Republic of China," Republic of Türkiye Ministry of Foreign Affairs. Accessed on March 20, 2023. https://www.mfa.gov.tr/relations-between-turkiye-and-china.en.mfa.

Sanchez, Hailey. "Fear, Avoidance, Being Told to Go Back to Their Country: What It's Like to Be Asian in Colorado in the Time of Coronavirus," *CPR News*, March 31, 2020. https://www.cpr.org/2020/03/31/fear-avoidance-being-told-to-go-back-to-their-country-what-its-like-to-be-asian-in-colorado-with-coronavirus/.

Silver, Laura, Kat Devlin, and Christine Huang. "Attitudes toward China," Pew Research Center. December 5, 2019. Accessed March 21, 2023. https://www.pewresearch.org/global/2019/12/05/attitudes-toward-china-2019/.

State Council Information Office of the People's Republic of China, White Paper on "The Fight against Terrorism and Extremism and Human Rights Protection in Xinjiang," March 2019. http://geneva.chinamission.gov.cn/eng/ztjs/aghj12wnew/Whitepaper/202110/t20211014_9587980.htm.

"Statement of the Spokesperson of the Ministry of Foreign Affairs, Mr. Hami Aksoy, in Response to a Question Regarding Serious Human Rights Violations Perpetrated against Uighur Turks and the Passing Away of Folk Poet Abdurehim Heyit," Republic of Türkiye Ministry of Foreign Affairs, February 9, 2019. Accessed March 20, 2023. https://www.mfa.gov.tr/sc_-06_-uygur-turklerine-yonelik-agir-insan-haklari-ihlalleri-ve-abdurrehim-heyit-in-vefati-hk.en.mfa.

"Statement of the Spokesperson of the Ministry of Foreign Affairs, Mr. Hami Aksoy in Response to a Question Regarding Turkey's National Statement on the Xinjiang Uyghur Autonomous Region Delivered at the Third Committee Meeting During the 75th Session of the UN General Assembly," Republic of Türkiye Ministry of Foreign Affairs, October 7, 2020. Accessed June 24, 2023. https://www.mfa.gov.tr/sc_-96_-bm-75-genel-kurulu-toplantisinda-ulkemizin-sincan-uygur-ozerk-bolgesiyle-ilgili-beyani-hk-sc.en.mfa.

Tekin, Aynur. "Türkiye'de yaşayan Çinliler: Bizi restoranlara ve otellere almıyorlar." *Gazete Duvar*, February 25, 2020. https://www.gazeteduvar.com.tr/gundem/2020/02/25/turkiyede-yasayan-cinliler-bizi-restoranlara-ve-otellere-almiyorlar.

"Türkiye-People's Republic of China Economic and Trade Relations," Republic of Türkiye Ministry of Foreign Affairs. Accessed March 18, 2023. https://www.mfa.gov.tr/turkey_s-commercial-and-economic-relations-with-china.en.mfa.

United Nations Human Rights (UNHR) Office of the High Commissioner. "OHCHR Assessment of Human Rights Concerns in the Xinjiang Uyghur Autonomous Region, People's Republic of China," August 31, 2022. Accessed on March 15, 2023. https://www.ohchr.org/sites/default/files/documents/countries/2022-08-31/22-08-31-final-assesment.pdf.

Uyghur Human Rights Project (UHRP). "Detained and Disappeared: Intellectuals under Assault in the Uyghur Homeland." March 25, 2019. https://docs.uhrp.org/pdf/Detained-and-Disappeared-Intellectuals-Under-Assault-in-the-Uyghur-Homeland.pdf.

Yackley, Ayla Jean. "Erdoğan Finds Warm Welcome, 'Shared Vision' in Beijing." *Al-Monitor*, July 2, 2019. https://www.al-monitor.com/originals/2019/07/erdogan-visit-chinaeconomic-political-ties.html - ixzz7vx5CjgC1.

Yavuz, M. Hakan. *Nostalgia for the Empire: The Politics of Neo-Ottomanism*. Oxford: Oxford University Press, 2020. https://academic-oupcom.stanford.idm.oclc.org/book/36837.

Yılmaz, Hüseyin Raşit, İlderya Avsar, Mehmet Yeğin, and Rabigül Hacımuhammed. "Çin Uygur Özerk Bölgesi İnsan Hakları Raporu." December 14, 2021. https://iyiparti.org.tr/cin-uygur-ozerk-bolgesi-insan-haklari-raporu.

Yinan, Hu and Lei Xiaoxun. "Urumqi Riot Handled 'Decisively, Properly.'" *China Daily*, July 18, 2009. https://www.chinadaily.com.cn/china/2009-07/18/content_8444365.htm.

"Yunus Emre Institute," Yunus Emre Enstitüsü. Accessed March 21, 2023. https://www.yee.org.tr/en/corporate/yunus-emre-institute

8

THE ANTI-ASIAN RACISM AT HOME

RECKONING WITH THE EXPERIENCES
OF ADOPTEES FROM ASIA

Kimberly D. McKee

In conversations with my white adoptive father, he always said reassuringly that he does not see me as Korean or Asian, only as his daughter, even though I claim both identities. This is stated as fact and not as something mutable. He also is aware of racism that I may encounter in that he recounts how people would come up to him when I was a child and ask him if I knew Bruce Lee or karate. As his political leanings became more conservative when I entered my mid-twenties and continued into my thirties, I found myself negotiating what it means to engage in conversations about racial injustice with him. My experience is similar to other adoptees of color who are grappling with what it means to be a person of color in a white family that fails to acknowledge racism. Adoptees of color swap stories about adoptive family members who believe it's "not all white people" without recognizing the tangled web of white supremacy shaping the systems and institutions we—adoptees of color—engage with in our everyday lives.

The transracial, transnational adoptions of Asian children were seen as one method to transcend the color line in the US, and in light of anti-Black racism, it offered an alternative to white prospective adoptive parents interested in expanding their families as the market in healthy, white infant children decreased.[1] In the twentieth century, Asian adoptees entered the US as a result of their proximity to whiteness.[2] Even today, international adoptees circumvent xenophobic immigration laws and are seen as integral to the reproduction of the (white) family. While not all Asian adopted infants and children entered white families in the US, the majority did, and those families never envisioned themselves as part of a racial project, even as they participated in the creation of a new strand of the Asian American family.[3] Some may have embraced the ideals of multiculturalism and racial liberalism, while others may not have recognized that their families were seen as progressive bastions of a post-racial ideal. And even as this essay discusses those children raised in the US, Asian adoptees are not immune to racism in other contexts.[4]

The accounts of Asian adoptees offer a glimpse into the interiority of the insidiousness of anti-Asian racism. For many, the family is the first site of anti-Asian racism. That racism may not manifest in the use of language denigrating Asian ethnics, or even the use of racial slurs; rather, it could result in internalized Orientalism, whereby the adoptee creates a false binary that aligns Asia with the backward East.[5] And, if it is not a site of racial microaggressions, the family does not provide protection from anti-Asian racism writ large. Nor does the family offer adoptees skills to navigate such racism, for we are seen as exceptional Asians.

This essay traces the voices of Asian adopted teenage girls to help tell the story of racism, belonging, and kinship through an analysis of *Calcutta Calling* (2006) and *Found* (2021). Deciding to turn my attention toward youth voices vexes me. I wonder, as I raise elsewhere, "What does it mean to document the [voices] of teenagers on the cusp of adulthood?" and I ask, "What would the story be told of me, or others like me, if only rooted in one snippet of our teenage girlhoods?"[6] To simply ignore documentaries that chronicle the lives of adopted youth discounts the importance of these films in capturing a particular moment in time. Interrogations of adopted Asian girlhood from the perspective of teenage girls, as opposed to adult adoptees recalling their youth, offer a lens to sift through the ways these children articulate a sense of self while simultaneously negotiating what it means to disclose dissonance surrounding their adoptions under the gaze of their white adoptive parents.

To Be Asian American and Adopted

In an effort to intentionally engage what it means to film adopted minors as they navigate some of the most complex questions of identity (e.g., return to their countries of origin, birth family search) that sometimes results in casting adult adoptees in harsh light, I consider adoptees' divulgences to non-adopted people. Adoptees have learned to manage the tensions produced by potentially being *too willful* in order to maintain their place within adoptive families.[7] The caveats adoptees offer about their families (e.g., they are supportive, loving, or trying their best) before offering an anecdote that exists in opposition to such adjectives exemplify this balancing act. Adoptees take a risk when we share incidents of racism. This is especially true when the perpetrators of those harms are our adoptive families, friends, or members of our communities. We may be told we cannot take a joke or that the harassment we underwent was not how we remember it. In other words, we are told that our own lived realities are untrue. No one wants to acknowledge this form of gaslighting, as it runs contra to the notions of adoptive families as a site of love and care.

To interrupt these adoption fantasies risks losing our place in our families, or at the very least, it results in adoptees doing additional emotional labor to reassure our families that we know they love us. In *Disrupting Kinship: Transnational Politics of Korean Adoption in the United States*, I assert, "The good, happy subject, or in this case, the happy, grateful adoptee, must then employ a particular affect conveying their joy. To fail to do so results in the adoptee's positioning as both unhappy and ungrateful. This sets the stage for the emergence of the "adoptee killjoy," building upon Sara Ahmed's discussion of the feminist killjoy."[8] In failing to play their part in this affective performance, adoptees "[refuse] to engage an affective performance of gratitude" and are cast as "unfaithful betrayers of the nation," in turn betraying their families.[9]

My analysis of *Calcutta Calling* and *Found* considers adoptees' self-awareness of what it means to mediate their own stories for public consumption. While Liz Stanley writes about auto/biography and the "public woman," her discussion of the "divergence between actual people and the audit selves they are organizationally supposed to be or become" is helpful when exploring adoptees' performative identities in documentaries.[10] Adoptees may engage in "deliberate self-presentations of incomplete fragments" as a method to mediate tensions produced in delving into the minor feelings produced by adoption.[11] Here, I borrow from Cathy Park Hong's discussion of minor feelings, alongside Sianne Ngai's concept of ugly feelings, to interrogate adoptee subjectivity because adoptees' tone, animated behavior, and anxiety, for instance, ensure they may be written off as *too willful*, *too angry*, or *too much*, even as these particular registers of affect reflect adoptees' interior selves.[12]

Consumers of these films, and others featuring adopted teens (e.g., *Girl, Adopted* [2013], *Off and Running* [2009]), should ruminate over questions of agency and wrestle with the ethics of representation. Documentary, like other forms of biography, involves the mediation of voices to craft a compelling storyline.[13] Recognizing the mediation that occurs within a documentary—by the subject (the adopted person) and the director—ensures that we move toward a more ethical consumption of these films as artifacts without risk of pathologizing or eliding them as three-dimensional subjects. Adoptees become characters of their own lives, or, as Stanley writes about audit selves, "quintessentially public selves, publicly created profiles which act as measures and prophecies of what a range of 'types' of selves are and can be."[14]

The adoptees in *Calcutta Calling* and *Found* leave a trail of crumbs for viewers to draw their own conclusions. Yet instances of racism are refracted through other anecdotes or accounts of identity negotiation. These slippages reveal incidents of bigotry or bias within the family and may be mentioned in passing, illustrating the ordinariness of such occurrences in their lives. Consumers of these adoption stories must hold ourselves accountable to situate these narratives within broader histories of adoption and recognize the role color-blind love, multiculturalism, and the circumstances in which we were raised inform our perspectives on adoption as teenagers living with our adoptive parents.

A Letter to My Younger Self

Before I turn my attention to the two documentaries, I employ an introspective lens on my contribution to *YELL-Oh Girls! Emerging Voices Explore Culture, Identity, and Growing Up Asian American* as an opportunity to reflect on what it would mean to only take a snapshot of an adopted teen's life and extrapolate information devoid of larger context. An ethical analysis of youth disclosures on adoption necessitates my own reflections. To be sure, this is not an attempt at navel-gazing; rather, casting a critical eye in reading the documentaries against the grain requires me to employ that same lens to my own narrative. After all, it's been nearly twenty years since the release of *Calcutta Calling* and contributors to *YELL-Oh Girls!* were interviewed to celebrate that collection's twentieth anniversary in 2021.[15]

My essay, "The Other Sister," marks the first time I publicly wrote about my own adoption. Looking back at what I wrote more than twenty years later, I think about how I was fifteen when I first wrote the essay and sixteen when it was published.[16] My adoptive parents were not aware of my submission until the published book and promotion materials arrived at our home.

In the space of slightly more than two pages, my contribution to the volume is chock-full of examples of encounters with microaggressions. This includes an adopted Asian friend accusing me of "being white," my discomfort for not looking like my white adoptive family, and the reduction of Asian ethnic groups to a single, flattened "Asian" category. I disclose, "People in my family have jokingly called me 'Chinese girl' and I'm secretly offended by their remarks. How can my own family be so insensitive, I wonder. I understand that they're only joking, but why can't they imagine how it would feel if I made a mockery of them?"[17] As I analyze these passages, my scholar self would trace the vulnerability in the adopted teenage girl's identity struggles and her desire to be seen solely as herself. I would consider how her longing is tied to a color-blind ideology: "But I look forward to the day that I'll stop having to explain and teach others all the time. A time when people truly begin to see me for who I am—me—and not someone who's different from them on the outside."[18] There is a youthful idealism that aligns with turn-of-the-century multiculturalism.

As I ruminate on the memories divulged in my *YELL-Oh Girls!* contribution, I also see someone who had yet to interrogate anti-Blackness and its role in shaping the white supremacist society in which I was raised. I disclose my response and frustration to my younger sister's question of whether I was Black, because why must I be the one to explain the different histories that led to the arrival of Asian and Black people to the US? I proclaimed an Asian American identity at the expense of an explanation that was devoid of nuance, oversimplifying histories of anti-Blackness, imperialism, and settler colonization, among other forms of state violence. The nearly forty-year-old me wishes that her fourteen-year-old self knew better and did better talking to a three-year-old as I increased my awareness of police brutality and anti-Blackness. This reflection reminds me that one still may perpetuate systems of oppression even as one becomes politicized and stands with marginalized communities.

To overlook this part of that story would mean ignoring the messiness of what it means when adopted youth tell our stories. I remain uncomfortable about that line, but this is my discomfort to both acknowledge and work through, while committing to do better as an adult and educator. This includes considering what's at stake when we capture the voices of teenagers. I would not change contributing to *YELL-Oh Girls!* because adoptee representation is important when interrogating Asian America's heterogeneity; rather, I am hoping that we can hold ourselves accountable and ask whether the adopted person whose voice is captured evolved as they grew up. Doing so facilitates an ability to examine Asian adoptees' internalized anti-Blackness and Orientalism. As ethical consumers of these materials, we must admit that these moments freeze adoptees' voices in a particular moment in time.

The Vulnerability of Speaking Our Truths

The mundane is what tells you the truths of adoption. Our everyday interactions with family, friends, neighbors, and strangers reveal the limitations of fantasies of adoption as the ultimate act of color-blind love. The lived realities are different, which begs the question: Why has no one listened, beyond other adoptees, in the more than twenty years transnational Asian adoptees have publicly recounted our experiences? The vast commonalities across time and space recall Kat Turner's words: "I was truly shocked a few years ago when I learned that the adopted Korean daughter of one of my neighbors was living my *dejà vu*. However, this wasn't Iowa in the 1970s, but progressive Minneapolis in the mid 1990s. I couldn't believe this generation of girls on the edge of a new millennium were not only faced with the same issues and insecurities, but to the same degree I had faced them almost twenty years before."[19] Although published in 1999, Turner's reflection remains relevant, as evidenced in the similarities concerning adoptees' racial, ethnic, and cultural identity formation and encounters with racism and microaggressions in *Calcutta Calling* and *Found*, despite fifteen years separating the films' releases. What has evolved in the intervening years has more to do with the description of birth families—as selfless subjects in *Calcutta Calling* versus subjects who made constrained choices in *Found*. My attention rests on adoptees' articulation of discomfort and the insertion of those moments within the documentaries' larger narrative structures.

Calcutta Calling follows three adopted Minnesota teens—Kaylan Johnson, Anisha Pitzenberger, and Lizzie Merrill—leading up to and during their trip to India as part of a 2003 homeland tour offered by the Ties Program, which operates tailored, planned heritage trips for adoptive families. As viewers are introduced to the three young women, we witness them and their parents vacillate over the adoptees' identities as both culturally white and ethnically Indian. The liminality produced by transnational adoption comes to the fore alongside inflections of multiculturalism and racial liberalism. Exemplifying this sentiment, Kaylan's mother comments directly, "I don't think of Kaylan as Indian at all. She's just my daughter. I don't see the color difference. . . . I don't know how she sees herself."[20] This statement underscores the operationalization of color blindness in adoptive families and reveals the potential lack of communication between adoptees and adoptive parents about adoptees' racial and/or ethnic identification. The latter is evident when contrasting it with Kaylan's proclamation—"I love Indian food. Indian food is so good"—and that she ordered a sari online that was shipped directly from India. While these parents may be more "progressive" in supporting their adopted children around their birth countries, it's unclear whether they recognize the influential role of race in shaping their daughters' identities and interactions with the world around them.

The ruptures produced by adoption are profound in statements by the girls. For example, when viewers first meet Anisha, she notes, "I always just tell myself, you know I'm not supposed to be here." After all, adoption is arbitrary and filled with happenstance. The adoptive parents reflect on the randomness of placements in adoption at the end of the short film. This is also brought to the fore while they are in India, as Lizzie notes:

You got this feeling that you were seeing someone that you could have been. It just makes you feel really isolated too, like, also I don't fit in anywhere. Like, I don't have, I can't fit in at home, and I can't fit in here. It's just, like, that because, like, I had this picture of, like, you know, I'm going to get over there. And, like, I'm going to feel like I'm part of something again, like to me, like, I'm surrounded with Indians, you know. But, like, you get here and you're not, you're still isolated. Like you're still, like, treated different.

The teens' candor about their racial, ethnic, and cultural identities reflects what Richard M. Lee describes as the transracial adoption paradox.[21] Anisha claims an "Indian background" and follows that proclamation with, "but I think I am completely American. I'm just Brown." I read her use of the word "American" as coded for cultural whiteness, given the location of her family and community in a predominately white Scandinavian community. Similarly, Lizzie asserts, "I identify more as white, but I'm not quite as materialistic I think as a lot of Americans are." Again, whiteness and American identity become interchangeable. Even as they're ambivalent about their identities, Bakirathi Mani writes, "For the viewer, racial difference becomes a primary means of 'seeing' the film, as the camera pans across a high school auditorium full of white midwesterners in the opening scene, finally settling on Anisha's brown body."[22] It's through the non-adopted viewers' eyes that we witness the transracial adoptee subject of color disrupting the racial tableau of their communities, even as they also operate as honorary whites.

Calcutta Calling replicates adoptees' existence at the margins in that the filmmaker, Sasha Khokha, creates a narrative that emphasizes internalized Orientalism and positions adoption as a better option. Khokha acknowledges this in an interview, stating:

I was also aware that the tour provided but a superficial glimpse of a complex country. . . . This experience both confirmed and challenged the girls' conceptions of India as a place from which they were "rescued." In the end, I had to reconcile the fact that my film may underscore Western notions of India as a place of desperate poverty. But as a documentarian, I had to remain true to the girls' experience. I hope the film captures not only India as seen through Western eyes, but also the poignancy and humor of three families struggling to make sense of themselves.[23]

As a result, the twenty-six-minute film, drawn from forty-five hours of tape, features statements by Kaylan's mother saying, "It was such a relief to get into the safety of that bus," coupled with adoptees' utterances, "Doesn't it feel good knowing that we get to go home to Minnesota?" and, "Seriously, if I ever had to live here, I would die." Perhaps the inclusion of these moments would not have occurred if Khokha filmed other parts of the trip, but she asserts, "the families decided not to let us film any sessions with the social workers chaperoning the trip and asked us to avoid filming the girls during particularly emotional moments, like visiting the orphanage."[24] Nonetheless, Khokha's response fails to consider her role in constructing the final narrative. Instead, the film, as Mani so aptly asserts, "reinforces not only their salvation from India but also the fact that their rightful place is with their adoptive parents in America."[25]

While the adoptees in *Calcutta Calling* come together through a homeland tour program, the adoptees in *Found* connect because of DNA testing and the kinship forged among adoptees through a secondary, or sometimes even a tertiary, connection as cousins.[26] In tracing the lives of three teenage girls—Chloe Lipitz, Sadie Mangelsdorf, and Lily Bolka—*Found* is reminiscent of *Somewhere Between* (2011), which captures the journey of four Chinese adoptees who grew up across the US. At the outset of production in 2017, Chloe was thirteen years old, Sadie was fourteen years old, and Lily was eighteen years old.[27] *Found* is unique in that it also includes the perspectives of multiple birth parents and Liu Hao, a Chinese genealogy researcher who assists the girls on their birth searches.

The smattering of reflections concerning the operationalization of racial difference in their daily lives highlights the salience of Turner's words across multiple generations. For instance, Sadie discloses, "I honestly don't feel Chinese," and, "I've just always identified myself as an American."[28] These statements are juxtaposed against examples of racial microaggressions provided to viewers—a friend's dad speaking to her in Chinese upon meeting her, and a different friend asking if she spoke Chinese, the latter example captured in the documentary. One of the more heartbreaking moments to see is when Sadie remembers a close friend of hers in middle school who said hurtful things—"like my birth parents not wanting me and that's why they gave me up." Situated alongside Sadie's disclosures are statements by Chloe made in passing: "When you're little, you grow up in your perfect little bubble," which is a reference to the whiteness around her. That recollection of childhood undergirds her previous remark when she notes, "I hadn't really thought of it much that I was one of the only Asians in the communities that I belonged in." There's a clear sense that race became more salient as she grew up, which aligns with Sadie's racist interactions with friends and their families. This does not ignore the racism perpetrated by family; rather, it calls attention to the microaggressions adoptees confront in communities that are ostensibly seen as welcoming.

In contrast, one could view the film and think Lily does not face racism or a dissonance concerning her racial, ethnic, and cultural identities because she does not disclose specific incidents, even as she notes, "I have a lot of questions about my life in China when I was little." I attribute Lily's mediation of her identity to her relationship with her adoptive mother. This understanding stems from her succinct description of the tension surrounding her birth search: "I don't want my mom to kind of feel like I don't love her because I do. I don't want to die where I don't know who my birth parents are." Viewers become privy to adoptees' efforts to not hurt their adoptive parents' feelings. This may mean they delay or forgo birth searches in more extreme cases, or they work to deftly balance their interest in doing so alongside reassurances to their adoptive parents. In her article about the documentary, Tara Adhikari notes that Lily mentions in an interview that "she had a tough time with adoption when she was in high school, because she avoided it when she was younger and didn't want to talk about it."[29]

Thus, I am conscious of the storyline culled from hours of video footage to craft a documentary, which is why my attention is drawn toward the mundane daily interactions with microaggressions. Amanda Lipitz, the filmmaker, presents a slight awareness of what it means to film teens, even as she does not reflect on her subject position as Chloe's aunt. In one interview, Lipitz comments, "In every circumstance, we always put the girls' emotional well-being over any filmmaking. There was no way to compartmentalize in those extremely emotional moments, quite honestly. This film is about the silent trauma that all of our subjects have endured."[30] The recognition of adoption as trauma cannot be overlooked. Her acknowledgement of the reverberating effects of adoption reveals a tacit commitment to exploring adoption as more than an act of humanitarian rescue.

Taken together, the films reveal the fraught nature of adoptee identity, whereby adoptees' reports of racist incidents occur alongside an effort to minimize adoptive families' role as contributors to these moments. Adoptive families' passive or active recognition of our realities as people of color is thus vital. This does not necessarily mean adoptees of color identify as persons of color. It may seem surprising that transnational Asian adoptees neglect to see themselves as Asian, Asian American, or at least nonwhite. However, the ruptures produced by adoption within Asian-adopted families is well documented, as racial, ethnic, and cultural identity formation vexes many adoptees raised against a backdrop of multiculturalism, color blindness, and racial liberalism.[31] To dismiss these adoptee voices or to invoke shame by focusing on when they arrive at an identity fails to acknowledge the effects of transnational, transracial adoption on racial or ethnic identity development.[32] To claim an Asian American identity is an inherently political act for adoptees—not just because of the activist roots of Asian America— since it may mean acknowledging a racial difference that our own families ignore in our everyday lives.

Do You See Us?[33]

Anti-Asian racism isn't something that happens just with strangers; it can and is perpetrated by people who ostensibly know and love us, as well as those in our communities. *Calcutta Calling* and *Found* depict the contradictions inherent in adoption. These documentaries facilitate an interrogation of the intimacy of the adoptive family and propel us to consider what it means to face these hard truths associated with kinship and belonging. What makes the mundane examples of racism in these films significant is the fact that for some Asian adoptees, a public discussion of one's Asian American identity only occurred after the onset of a worldwide pandemic, even as some of our earliest encounters with anti-Asian racism occurred at home. What does this say about the false promises of adoption and the adoptive family? What can we learn about Asian adoptees' internalization of anti-Blackness and Orientalism, among other forms of racism, and how does this question support wider interrogations of broader coalition building? Some of the stronger interracial organizing and solidarities that I have witnessed occur within transracial adoptee communities. As adoptees continue to engage in movements toward transformative social justice, it's imperative that we attend to the heterogeneity of the communities in which we belong while also continuing to push for more nuanced conversations about the messiness of adoption.

Notes

[1] Raleigh, *Selling Transracial Adoption.*

[2] Kim and Park Nelson, "'Natural Born Aliens.'"

[3] McKee, *Disrupting Kinship.*

[4] Willing, "The Adopted Vietnamese Community"; Hübinette, *The Korean Adoption Issue between Modernity and Coloniality*; Nguyen, "Adoption and the Work of Adaptation in Jung's Couleur de Peau"; Wills, Hübinette, and Willing, *Adoption and Multiculturalism*; Wyver, "Exploring Swedish International Adoption Desire"; Hübinette, "The Birth and Development of Critical Adoption Studies from a Swedish and Scandinavian Lens"; Myong and Bissenbakker, "Attachment as Affective Assimilation"; Hübinette, Lundström, and Wikström, *Race in Sweden.*

[5] Jane Jeong Trenka, for example, discloses both her father's anti-Asian racism toward a boyfriend of Southeast Asian descent and multiple encounters with anti-Asian racism in the broader community; Trenka, *The Language of Blood.*

[6] McKee, *Adoption Fantasies.*

[7] Here, I am interested in Sara Ahmed's exploration of willfulness and the willful child; Ahmed, *Willful Subjects.*

[8] McKee, *Disrupting Kinship*, 11; Ahmed, *The Promise of Happiness.*

[9] McKee, *Disrupting Kinship*, 11.

[10] Stanley, "From 'Self-Made Women' to 'Women's Made-Selves?'" 48.

[11] Ibid., 49.

[12] Hong, *Minor Feelings*; Ngai, *Ugly Feelings.*

[13] Gregory Paul Choy and Catherine Ceniza Choy discuss the genre's ability to script narratives that perpetuate the marginalization of its subjects in their analysis of *Daughter from Danang* (2002); Choy and Choy, "What Lies Beneath."

[14] Stanley, "From 'Self-Made Women' to 'Women's Made-Selves?'" 48.

[15] Lee, "20 Years Later." *YELL-OH Girls!* is one of the few examples of Asian American collections featuring the voice of adoptees; see also Bruining, "To Omoni, In Korea"; Kinney, "Seoul Searching."

[16] For instance, I cringe every time I read my use of the word "Caucasian" and not white. And yet, my lack of consciousness around terminology mirrors so many transracial adopted people raised in the suburbs by white parents and reminds me of how I discuss why we use the term "white" with my students more than two decades later. This is not meant to derail my analysis; rather, it's to underscore how these moments offer insights into the worldview adoptees find themselves negotiating even today.

[17] McKee, "The Other Sister," 142–143.

[18] Ibid., 143–144.

[19] Turner, "Planted in the West," 137.

[20] Khoka, dir., *Calcutta Calling*. Additional quotes from the protagonists and their families in *Calcutta Calling* are direct quotations from the documentary.

[21] Lee, "The Transracial Adoption Paradox."

[22] Mani, *Aspiring to Home*, 100, 101.

[23] Cunningham, "Behind the Lens."

[24] Ibid.

[25] Mani, 106.

[26] The use of DNA testing to establish kinship ties is a relatively recent phenomenon among international adopted people; Kopacz, "From Contingent Beginnings to Multiple Ends"; Cai, Kim, and Lee, "Psychological Correlates of Interest in Genetic Testing among Korean American Adoptees and Their Parents"; Suter and Docan-Morgan, "Setting the Agenda"; Kay and Taverner, "Adoptees' Views and Experiences of Direct-to-Consumer (DTC) Genomic Testing."

[27] "Found."

[28] Lipitz, dir., *Found*. Additional quotes from the protagonists in *Found* and their families are direct quotations from the documentary.

[29] Adhikari, "Identity and Adoption."

[30] "Found."

[31] Meier, "Cultural Identity and Place in Adult Korean-American Intercountry Adoptees"; Shiao and Tuan, "Korean Adoptees and the Social Context of Ethnic Exploration"; Lee et al., "Ethnic Identity as a Moderator against Discrimination for Transracially and Transnationally Adopted Korean American Adolescents."

[32] The adoptee consciousness model developed by JaeRan Kim, Susan Branco, Stephanie Kripa Cooper-Lewter, Grace Newton, and Paula O'Loughlin offers a new lens to consider adoptee identity; Newton, "Out of the Fog and into Consciousness: A Model of Adoptee Awareness." This is not to say that I advocate for diagnosing other adoptees on where they are in their journeys. Rather, this is my invitation for non-adopted people to rethink how we understand adoptee identity formation.

[33] This subheading is a direct acknowledgement of the blog post I wrote for KAAN (the Korean American Adoptee Adoptive Family Network) in the wake of the Atlanta, Georgia, spa shootings on March 16, 2021; McKee, "Do You See Me?"

Bibliography

Adhikari, Tara. "Identity and Adoption: 'Found' Follows American Teens as They Return to China." *Christian Science Monitor*, October 27, 2021. https://www.csmonitor.com/The-Culture/Movies/2021/1027/Identity-and-adoption-Found-follows-American-teens-as-they-return-to-China.

Ahmed, Sara. *The Promise of Happiness*. Durham: Duke University Press, 2010.

———. *Willful Subjects*. Durham: Duke University Press, 2014.

Bruining, Mi Ok. "To Omoni, in Korea." In *Making Face, Making Soul/Haciendo Caras*, edited by Gloria Anzaldua, 153–155. San Francisco: Aunt Lute Books, 1990.

Cai, Jieyi, Adam Y. Kim, and Richard M. Lee. "Psychological Correlates of Interest in Genetic Testing among Korean American Adoptees and Their Parents." *Journal of Genetic Counseling* 29, no. 3 (2020): 460–470.

CherryPicks. "'Found': Anita Gou and Amanda Lipitz Piece Together the Past." Accessed April 10, 2023, https://www.thecherrypicks.com/stories/piecing-together-the-past-in-found-with-anita-gou-and-amanda-lipitz/.

Choy, Gregory Paul, and Catherine Ceniza Choy. "White Lies Beneath: Reframing Daughter from Danang." In *Outsiders Within: Writing on Transracial Adoption*, edited by Jane Jeong Trenka, Julia Chinyere Oparah, and Sun Yung Shin, 221–231. Cambridge: South End Press, 2006.

Cunningham, Sachi. "Behind the Lens: Interview with Sasha Khokha." *PBS Frontline World*, January 2006. https://www.pbs.org/frontlineworld/rough/2006/01/india_calcuttaint.html.

Hong, Cathy Park. *Minor Feelings: An Asian American Reckoning*. New York: Oneworld, 2020.

Hübinette, Tobias. "The Birth and Development of Critical Adoption Studies from a Swedish and Scandinavian Lens." *Adoption & Culture* 9, no. 1 (January 2021): 34–38.

———. *The Korean Adoption Issue between Modernity and Coloniality: Transnational Adoption and Overseas Adoptees in Korean Popular Culture*. Sarrbrücken, Germany: Lambert Academic Publishing, 2009.

Hübinette, Tobias, Catrin Lundström, and Peter Wikström. *Race in Sweden: Racism and Antiracism in the World's First "Colourblind" Nation*. Oxford: Taylor & Francis, 2023.

Judd, Melanie and Susan Motamed, dirs. *Girl, Adopted*. iTVS, 2013.

Kay, Alison C., and Nicola V. Taverner. "Adoptees' Views and Experiences of Direct-to-Consumer (DTC) Genomic Testing: An Exploratory Interview Study from the UK." *Journal of Community Genetics* 14, no. 2 (April 1, 2023): 149–162.

Khoka, Sasha, dir., *Calcutta Calling*. PBS, 2006.

Kim, Eleana, and Kim Park Nelson. "'Natural Born Aliens': Transnational Adoptees and US Citizenship." *Adoption & Culture* 7, no. 2 (2019): 257–279.

Kinney, Rebecca J. "Seoul Searching." In *Asian American X: An Intersection of Twenty-First-Century Asian American Voices*, edited by Arar Han and John Y. Hsu, 52–57. Ann Arbor: University of Michigan Press, 2004.

Kopacz, Elizabeth. "From Contingent Beginnings to Multiple Ends: DNA Technologies and the Korean Adoptee 'Cousin.'" *Adoption & Culture* 6, no. 2 (2018): 336–352.

Lee, Christina. "20 Years Later, 'Generation YELL-Oh Girls' Is Still Revolutionary." Mic, November 23, 2021. https://www.mic.com/impact/generation-yell-oh-girls-20-years-later.

Lee, Joyce P., Richard M. Lee, Alison W. Hu, and Oh Myo Kim. "Ethnic Identity as a Moderator against Discrimination for Transracially and Transnationally Adopted Korean American Adolescents." *Asian American Journal of Psychology* 6, no. 2 (2015): 154–163.

Lee, Richard M. "The Transracial Adoption Paradox." *The Counseling Psychologist* 31, no. 6 (November 2003): 711–744. https://doi.org/10.1177/0011000003258087.

Lipitz, Amanda, dir. *Found*. Netflix, 2021.

Mani, Bakirathi. *Aspiring to Home: South Asians in America*. Stanford: Stanford University Press, 2012.

McKee, Kimberly D. *Adoption Fantasies: The Fetishization of Asian Adoptee Girlhood to Womanhood*. Columbus: The Ohio State University Press, 2023.

———. *Disrupting Kinship: Transnational Politics of Korean Adoption in the United States*. Champaign: University of Illinois Press, 2019.

———. "Do You See Me? Us? Asian America?" KAAN, March 26, 2021, https://www.wearekaan.org/post/do-you-see.

———. "The Other Sister." In *YELL-Oh Girls! Emerging Voices Explore Culture, Identity, and Growing up Asian American*, edited by Vickie Nam, 142–144. New York: Harper Collins, 2001.

Meier, Dani I. "Cultural Identity and Place in Adult Korean-American Intercountry Adoptees." *Adoption Quarterly* 3, no. 1 (1999): 15–48.

Myong, Lene, and Mons Bissenbakker. "Attachment as Affective Assimilation: Discourses on Love and Kinship in the Context of Transnational Adoption in Denmark." *NORA—Nordic Journal of Feminist and Gender Research*, March 8, 2021, 1–13.

Newton, Grace. "Out of the Fog and Into Consciousness: A Model of Adoptee Awareness | Red Thread Broken." Red Thread Broken, June 23, 2022. https://redthreadbroken.wordpress.com/2022/06/23/out-of-the-fog-and-into-consciousness-a-model-of-adoptee-awareness/.

Ngai, Sianne. *Ugly Feelings*. Cambridge: Harvard University Press, 2007.

Nguyen, Catherine H. "Adoption and the Work of Adaptation in Jung's Couleur de Peau: Miel." *Adoption & Culture* 8, no. 1 (2020): 55–82.

Opper, Nicole, dir. *Off and Running*. PBS, 2013.

Raleigh, Elizabeth. *Selling Transracial Adoption: Families, Markets, and the Color Line.* Philadelphia: Temple University Press, 2017.

Shiao, Jiannbin Lee, and Mia H Tuan. "Korean Adoptees and the Social Context of Ethnic Exploration." *American Journal of Sociology* 113, no. 4 (2008): 1023–1066.

Stanley, Liz. "From 'Self-Made Women' to 'Women's Made-Selves?': Audit Selves, Simulation and Surveillance in the Rise of Public Woman." In *Feminism and Autobiography: Texts, Theories, Methods*, edited by Tess Cosslett, Celia Lury, and Penny Summerfield, 40–60. New York: Routledge, 2000.

Suter, Elizabeth A., and Sara Docan-Morgan. "Setting the Agenda: A Family Communication Research Agenda for Examining Birth Family Search and Reunion in the Transnational Adoption Context." *Journal of Family Communication* 22, no. 4 (October 2, 2022): 387–395.

Trenka, Jane Jeong. *The Language of Blood*. Saint Paul: Graywolf Press, 2003.

Turner, Kat. "Planted in the West: The Story of an American Girl." In *Voices from Another Place: A Collection of Works from a Generation Born in Korea and Adopted to Other Countries*, edited by Susan Soon-Keum Cox, 132–137. St. Paul: Yeong & Yeong Book Co., 1999.

Willing, Indigo. "The Adopted Vietnamese Community: From Fairytales to the Diaspora." *Michigan Quarterly Review* 43, no. 4 (2004): 648–664.

Wills, Jenny, Tobias Hübinette, and Indigo Willing, eds. *Adoption and Multiculturalism: Europe, the Americas, and the Pacific*. Ann Arbor: University of Michigan Press, 2020.

Wyver, Richey. *Exploring Swedish International Adoption Desire: Transracial Bodies and Nation-Building in the "Goodest" Country*. London: Palgrave Macmillan, 2023.

9

FAR-FLUNG FETISHIZATION

CALLING ASIAN WOMEN TO GLOBALLY TRANSCEND HYPERSEXUALIZATION

Eileen Chung

My earliest consciousness of being fetishized as an Asian woman transpired during my senior year of high school. The San Francisco Giants had just won the 2014 World Series, and my American Democracy class had an urban planning project due the same day of the scheduled parade. My group members were discussing the traffic implications of allowing a left-turning lane into a shopping complex when our white male teacher, Mr. M, came up to me and pulled me aside. He not-so-discreetly proposed that if my group wanted to attend the parade, I could swing by his house to drop off our project portfolio beforehand. "Just make sure my wife's not home!" Mr. M cheekily suggested. I was paralyzed beneath my grimace and too petrified of reprisal to vocalize my discomfort to Mr. M, who had a reputation for being humorous and popular among his students. Throughout the semester, he mentioned that his wife was Taiwanese and that his daughter was a mere three years younger than me. Shockingly (or maybe not), he also joked about having a crush on a Korean student in my graduating class "before [I] came along." The dread sank in. Even though we submitted our project ahead of time, I felt extremely unsettled. In the ensuing months leading up to graduation, Mr. M would message me inappropriately, even when I was no longer in his class. I was reduced to a trope when he sent me these messages: "I think I teased you a little in class, because I assumed you were a party girl that was boy crazy and not intellectual. I don't think I gave you enough credit. . . . You are very outgoing, fashionable, and pretty. You don't fit the stereotype of the Asian girl at [my high school]. Do you like to read?" The admission to stereotyping was flagrant.

Nine years after Mr. M's class, I still grapple with proving myself as a multidimensional person who embodies more depth and range than what's often unilaterally assigned to me. My humanity has been contested each time I'm objectified. Since graduating high school, I gratefully majored in Asian American Studies at UC Santa Barbara, where I cherished acquiring the vocabulary that elucidated these experiences. Becoming educated on "hypersexualization," "exoticization," "sexual politics," and "microaggressions"—among several other terms—galvanized my commitment to social justice. I hadn't realized how severely problematic "having a type" was until my Multiracial Asian Americans course, which delved into the possibilities of racism occurring within romantic encounters. I learned how hypersexualization may potentially (but not always) undergird dynamics of interracial intimacy.[1] Particularly gripping for me was listening to my peers' firsthand accounts as the multiracial offspring of exogamous marriages; some felt as though they were essentially the by-products of one parent fetishizing the other.

I began applying these realizations in retrospect to other relevant micro-aggressions I received when I was younger. One classmate, from my other major, psychology, remarked that he was surprised I was outspoken and opinionated, since he had never met an Asian girl like me before. I felt disoriented, knowing he was assessing me based on his narrow conceptions of Asian women. Although his remark was not explicitly tinged with sexual innuendo, I couldn't help but wonder to what degree sexualized images of Asian women fed into his subsequent ideas about their alleged dispositions as subservient, quiet, meek, submissive, agreeable, acquiescent, and so on and so forth. This instance, and endless others, led me to grow suspicious of the worth I hold in other people's lives and whether it's my intrinsic presence being valued versus a projected ideal of who I am—a reckoning I'm still unpacking to this day. I learned that just because someone desires you as an *object* of racialized sexual desire doesn't mean they value you as a *subject* of humanity.

With more opportunities to travel, I've observed how fetishization functions in (mis)shaping interpersonal dynamics on a global scale. In this essay, I specifically employ my experiences in Cuba and Greece to facilitate commentary on the international scope of the fetishization of Asian women. I acknowledge the many limitations of making observations based on only two countries (which in themselves should not be homogenized), yet the similar experiences of hyper-sexualization across two seemingly disparate regions warrants further exploration. Weaving in the theoretical frameworks of Orientalism and Orientalization as my analytical foundations, I delineate the uncouth microaggressions, lewd stares, and general sense of Sinophobic unease I have encountered. My goal is not to vilify any nation or its people; instead, I aim to convey how Asian women have been misper-ceived in the global imagination, regardless of location. With this in mind, I want to clarify that Cuba and Greece are some of the most remarkable places I've visited; experiences of hypersexualization were not the defining aspect of these travels but only one feature of them.

Moreover, there are also limitations with anchoring these observations from only one person—me; however, I assert that autotheory is a valuable feminist methodological practice that affirms the critical use of autobiographical material in conjunction with theory and philosophy.[2] Autotheory elevates embodied knowledge, enabling the subjectivities of fetishized bodies to come to the fore. Because Western knowledge production generally values conventional empirical objectivity, autotheory challenges dominant perspectives and reveals the immense scholarly value of subjectivity.[3] Although far from representative, and though it is not intended to undermine or invalidate other Asian women's nuanced experiences, I offer mine to generate more dialogue on this topic. I hope this essay will provide elements of relatability and affirmation to fellow Asian women and serve as an invitation to share their own experiences, if compelled. For those who identify otherwise, I wish to provide contextualization of the minor feelings Asian women navigate on a quotidian and international basis.[4] Here, I am catalyzed by Gloria Anzaldúa's use of vulnerability as a source of power—rather than a compromise of it—as we contest the very oppressions that silence us.[5]

I state my positionality as a monoethnic Chinese American woman who is cisgender, heterosexual, young, able-bodied, atheist, and born to working-class immigrant parents. I want to draw heightened attention to the implications of my United States citizenship, which grants me an unearned advantageous position within international discourse, as well as the East Asian privilege I'm conferred, which unjustly obscures Southeast, South, Central, and West Asians from mainstream visibility by those with little familiarity of Asia's expansive diversity. Because autotheory centers the researcher as the instrument of (self-)discovery, any generalizations can only go so far, no matter how intently I practice reflexivity. Due to the centrality of my positionality in driving this essay, I've intentionally foregrounded my method in this introduction rather than in the following sections.

What follows is an overview of key works that align within the theoretical frameworks of Orientalism and Orientalization, an account of my experiences in Cuba and then Greece, and a conclusion on some of the empowering lessons I gleaned from my immigrant mother to trace an intergenerational and transnational resistance from the temporal and spatial omnipresence of fetishization. While unearthing the complexities of fetishization are crucial, emphasizing the dynamic resistance of Asian women within overlapping systems of white supremacy and heteropatriarchy is also urgent. Being reduced to narratives of trauma is an ontological injustice to the multilayered humanity marginalized communities possess; redirecting agency is thus the overarching linchpin of this essay.

Orientalism and Orientalization

Edward Said, cultural critic and founder of postcolonial studies, has theorized Orientalism to highlight how Western scholarship has misrepresented the East ("the Orient") to propagate imperialism, colonialism, and capitalism.[6] In essence, Western discursive practices have depicted Eastern cultures and peoples as possessing incommensurable differences, rendering them as backward civilizations. These misrepresentations have thereby granted Western scholarship continued authority to distort the East as exotic and feminized. Resultantly, Orientalism constructs cultural stereotypes that are more emblematic of Western geopolitical ideologies than anything substantive about the East itself (for all of its heterogeneity, might I add). These influences have infiltrated processes of knowledge production and have caused much epistemic violence, especially toward Asian women, whose lived experiences are often devalued and obscured. I want to emphasize that Western hegemonic discourse has been internalized by other non-Western cultures; that is, non-Western cultures are susceptible to adopting Western attitudes toward Asian women due to the prevailing influence of Western cultural productions.

Aki Uchida extends a gendered critique of Orientalism, coining it "Orientalization." Uchida defines it as "the objectification of Asian women as the 'Oriental Woman'—the stereotypical image of the Exotic Other—in the discursive practices in the United States."[7] This othering dehumanizes Asian women and relegates them to the controlling image of the Oriental Woman in history, popular culture, and general public perception.[8] Tracing various historical influences, Uchida uncovers how Chinese prostitution during the era of restrictive anti-Chinese exclusion laws, picture-bride practices, US military involvement in Asian countries, and the Oriental Woman in cultural texts (e.g., the Lotus Blossom-Dragon Lady dichotomy) have all contributed to the egregious imagery of Asian women in contemporary discourse.[9] Uchida then paints the dangers of how the image of the Oriental Woman has percolated into the interpersonal lives of Asian women, forming treacherous sites of identity negotiation. Uchida writes, "The image of the Oriental Woman as exotic, sexually available, submissive, obedient, domestic, sweet and passive, etc. is also present in everyday conversation; Asian

American women directly receive such messages that attempt to Orientalize them."[10] Needless to say, stereotypes are not innocuous myths that can be easily shaken off by the afflicted persons; they have unforeseen consequences on the livelihoods of Asian women. Therefore, experiences of fetishization should not be trivialized.

Robin Zheng deploys a philosophical approach in debunking yellow fever, the exclusive preference for women of Asian descent that goes hand in hand with the Oriental Woman.[11] Zheng argues that racial fetishes are objectionable "because of the disproportionate psychological burdens it places on Asian/American women, which derive from the part yellow fever plays in a pernicious system of racial meanings."[12] By analyzing testimony from Asian/American women, Zheng incisively illuminates the deleterious effects of fetishizing Asian women. She raises alarming concerns: (1) the depersonalization and fungibility of Asian women inherent in yellow fever seeds doubt as to whether or not they can be loved for their authentic presence rather than as a racialized sexual category; (2) Asian women are faced with a double bind in that their racial difference is a deviation from dominant white standards, or they are only "appreciated" *because* they are different (read: exotic); and (3) the very discomfort Asian women experience while being fetishized is sufficient evidence of the structures of systemic sexual racism, including wrongful representations of Asian women.[13] I emphasize these tenets of Zheng's arguments and situate them with Uchida's theorization of Orientalization to spotlight the emotional and mental toll of the hypersexualization that Asian women experience.

The recent surge of anti-Asian racism in the wake of COVID-19 has spurred further inquiry into Asian women's experiences of fetishization. On March 16, 2021, gunman Robert A. Long murdered Soon Chung Park (seventy-four), Hyun Jung Grant (fifty-one), Suncha Kim (sixty-nine), Yong Ae Yue (sixty-three), Delaina Ashley Yaun (thirty-three), Paul Andre Michels (fifty-four), Xiaojie Tan (forty-nine), and Daoyou Feng (forty-four) in the greater Atlanta area. Six of these victims were women of Asian descent. Known as the Atlanta Spa Shootings, this tragedy brought the abhorrent dangers of hypersexualizing Asian women to the public's consciousness. Long wanted to eliminate the temptation of Asian women, which demonstrates this conflation of them as hypersexual is itself racist and sexist. Maria Hwang and Rhacel Salazar Parreñas have conducted an intersectional racial-gender analysis to convey how these murders can be traced back to a long history of legal and cinematic representations of Asian women as villainous temptresses. The authors maintain that the hypersexualization of Asian women may result in misperceptions of their bodies as disposable receptacles for white male rage.[14] Taken in sum, the lethality of racialized and sexualized violence toward Asian women is rooted in horrific histories of exclusion and imperialism.

However, Asian women have simultaneously been rewriting the script to craft alternative narratives of agency and restoration. Revisiting Uchida, she concludes with how Asian women have been actively resisting Orientalization through their writing, art, and teaching.[15] Joey S. Kim supports the emergence of Asian women writers' works as pivotal to dismantling Orientalist histories. She instills optimism by stating, "The situatedness of our bodies in a capricious world—a world of ever-shifting laws, social restrictions, cultural rituals and new norms—shows us the possibility that the amplified level of today's viral racisms may be temporary."[16] To usher in this new era of authentic portrayals of Asian women, I am a firm believer that outer change begins with inner work; part of the deliberate process of self-reflection includes sharing my experiences.

Chinese Cuban Culture

While obtaining my master's in social work from the University of Pittsburgh in 2019, the Center on Race and Social Problems offered a study abroad course, Cuban Social Policy Issues. I was incredibly fortunate to be accepted to the one-week, fully funded research trip with nine fellow peers and three faculty members. To prepare for our trip, we were assigned course texts that cover some of the racial realities in Cuba.[17] While reading about the predominant trichotomy of racial categorizations in Cuba—white, Black, and mixed—I decided I would discern a correlation between colorism and Cuban mental health outcomes—if there was any—for my research topic.

Upon arriving in Havana, I was immediately cognizant of my identity as an Asian woman. In the span of one week, I was called *chino*, *chinita*, and *china* countless times. These terms respectively translate to "Chinese," "Chinese girl," and "China-woman" from Spanish. The intentions of these terms ranged from cheerful endearments to uncouth catcalls. I couldn't help but notice how all of these identifiers were racially based. Although benign to my physical safety, the fixation on my ethnicity indicated an exoticization of Chinese culture and those of perceived Chinese ancestry.

On our walk to the Malecón one evening, our group passed by Havana's Barrio Chino (Chinatown). I was stunned! How had I not read about this yet? When we got back to our hotel, I looked up the Chinese Cuban diaspora and was thoroughly surprised at the volume of existing scholarship on this subject. I instantly shifted my topic to researching the lingering vestiges of Chinese Cuban culture by utilizing autoethnography. Unbeknownst to many, an estimated 147,000 Chinese indentured servants migrated to Cuba from the Guangdong province of China between 1847 and 1877 to supplement labor demands on sugar plantations alongside enslaved Afro-Cubans.[18] Fundamentally, the history of Chinese Cubans has been subsumed within the trichotomy of current Cuban racial categorizations.

These elisions reminded me of the ways "coolie" labor on the transcontinental railroad has been misremembered in public memory.[19] After having this epiphany, I wondered why the term "American" largely doesn't include a reference to other regions of North America (e.g., Canada, Central America, Latin America, and South America). The issue isn't solely one of nomenclature but of discursive power; the way American exceptionalism has automatically likened "American" to the United States of America warrants more interrogation. For example, how can Chinese Cubans' experiences buttress existing understandings of labor, diaspora, migration, and population studies as well as Asian and Asian American Studies?[20]

With these concurrent streams of thought flooding my head, I could no longer deny the palpable sensation I felt when I was called these racially based identifiers. I had to acknowledge the lewd stares that lingered on me as I was out with my peers carrying out our research agendas. The catcalling was what unnerved me the most; how could I be made a spectacle with my phenotypic markers of difference when Chinese people have been integral to Cuban history? Would these men have felt so emboldened to make these catcalls if I wasn't Asian? To what extent did images of the Oriental Woman circulate in their heads when they appraised me? What if they were made conscious that they might have Chinese ancestry themselves?

I wrestled with how Chinese migrants and their descendants became virtually omitted from Cuban public memory among generations of Sino-Creolization processes. I relayed these musings to a Filipina American medical student at the Latin American School of Medicine, which is located on the outskirts of Havana. She noted that "chino" is the broad identifier for anyone of perceived Asian ancestry, which prompted me to think of the ways Southeast Asian histories are obfuscated by East Asian ones, even at the lexical level. It's critical to note that Sinophobia affects more than just Chinese people and that bigotry doesn't care to make ethnic distinctions. Ultimately, my time in Cuba highlights how nations with robust histories of Asian migration are not immune to the pernicious effects of hypersexualization; this certainly includes the United States, where anti-Asian racism toward Asian women has taken especially graphic forms, despite a proliferating Asian American population.[21] In the end, catcalls and all, I enjoyed my time in Cuba so immensely that it has been my favorite travel destination to date.

Greece Gals

In January 2022, I took my first post-vaccination international trip with three of my Asian girlfriends to Greece. We giddily called ourselves "Greece Gals" as we prepared for our trip to Athens, Mykonos, and Santorini. I savored my first visit to Greece in 2017 so much that I couldn't wait to go back and share the experience with my friends. Although we were visiting Greece in the offseason, I don't think any of us could have predicted the frequency with which we were singled out by our identities. We visited popular tourist destinations, so surely the locals who exoticized us had interacted with Asian women before. The inexplicable air of unease that swirled around us as we were exoticized said otherwise.

On our second day in Athens, we were lightly browsing some souvenir shops on our way to the Acropolis when the owner of an antique store came out to bid us good morning in English. After a friendly exchange of telling him where we were from (San Francisco) and what our plans were, he proceeded to ask what our ethnic backgrounds were—as if that would somehow foster more affiliation with us, when all the question did was alienate us. Basically, it was, "Where are you *really* from?" I can understand the genuine curiosity of wanting to courteously know someone's ethnic background to sensitively inform the next talking point, but the store owner's implication that we should have flown in from Asia and not San Francisco was irritating. We quickly replied, hoping to move on and continue making our way to the Acropolis. When my friend shared her Japanese ancestry, the store owner animatedly sang a Japanese ballad, expecting her to be impressed. She knew the song, given its popularity, but the expectation for us to be ambassadors and experts of our respective cultures felt essentializing. Moreover, the expectation of my friend to find the store owner more appealing because of his singing seemed transactional, and it eerily echoed ideas about Asian women's purported sexual availability.

During our dinner at a nearby restaurant the following evening, we were seated next to a local man dining by himself. He couldn't suppress his intrigue and kept pestering us with questions about our ethnicities. After nearly two days of feeling fatigued from these questions, we decided not to engage with him. Our joint agitation must have been visible given how swiftly the waitstaff intervened and castigated the man for making us feel uncomfortable. His desire to know where we hailed from made me feel as though we were objects to be classified within a precarious racial system. In a region where there isn't a sizable amount of Asians, it makes complete sense that we would raise this intrigue. However, what we took issue with was the man's aggression and the entitlement that led him to feel he could harass us. With limited exposure to the lives of Asian women, what schemas of us was he referring to? What dominant image of Asian women made the cut and found its way to his cultural consumption? Our reluctance to answer his questions seemed to intensify his persistence, as he likely did not expect that we would challenge his notions of Asian women's demeanors.

At one point, he asked about our relationship to one another, assuming we were sisters. This assumption perturbed me (well, they all did), as it harkened back to erroneous ideas that "all Asians look alike." So what if we were different compositions of Japanese, Malaysian, Vietnamese, and Chinese ancestry? What difference would that have made to him if his fabrication of the Orient and the Oriental Woman was monolithic? If only he could fathom the idiosyncrasies among all of our personalities. This was a common theme that recurred throughout our trip; the sense of interchangeability, which Zheng asserts is racist in its depersonalization, radicalized me so much that I applied to my current PhD program with the goal of studying the detrimental impact of fetishization.

While the presence of four Asian girls traveling in Greece in the offseason was understandably novel for the locals, I couldn't pinpoint why we faced the sensationalism we did. Factoring in how colossal Asia and the Asian diaspora are, Asian women aren't rare. Yet an influential minority of the world's population has curated false representations of Asian women for the rest of the world to interpellate. As distressing as these fetishized encounters were for me, the support of my friends on this trip, and our joint abilities to relate to one another while unpacking these interpersonal exchanges, truly strengthened the potential of collective solidarity to me. After our still-magical trip concluded, I contemplated the necessity of community in uplifting one another while traversing unrelenting systems of white supremacy and heteropatriarchy. I am beyond appreciative of the sheer support fellow Asian women—and our generous allies—have gifted me.

Toward Intergenerational and Transnational Resistance

My sense of gratitude is deepened knowing that my mother is one of my earliest role models of resistance against fetishization. She offers me a glimpse into what intergenerational and transnational resistance looks like when I reflect on how Asian women across time and space have had to create their own counternarratives to resist dehumanization. My mother immigrated to the US in 1992 and gave birth to me in 1997, making me the only US-born member of our immediate family. That same year, she started working at the United States Postal Service. Although I was far too young to comprehend the tribulations and acculturative stress she navigated at the time, I cherished learning more about her early history in the US when I matured. I came to grasp the enormity of her sacrifices through the Asian American Studies courses I took at UC Santa Barbara. I sympathized when she told me her coworkers doubted she could lift heavy parcels given her petite frame, winced when she told me they chalked her up as too ignorant in her monolingualism to understand their flirtatious remarks (the salacious stares said it all), and fretted when she told me she feared I would face similar realities in this nation.

Despite these pain points, my mother has taught me invaluable lessons about dynamically resisting the effects of discrimination. First, be selective about giving your educational and emotional labor. People who are committed to misunderstanding you will likely be unreceptive to your stances and burn you out.

I don't want to sound cynical or immediately cast educational efforts as ineffectual, but there's usually a clear difference between someone intent on unlearning the biases they've been engrained with and someone who insidiously engages in intellectual debate as a hobby and thinks invalidating your traumas is a theoretical game for their superiority.

Second, self-care is not selfish; it's necessary to recalibrate, and it helps you recharge so that you may more effectively show up for others. My mother has always been adamant about rest and insists that nothing is worth exhausting your output to the point of unwellness. In fact, rest and resilience aren't mutually exclusive; resilience requires rest, and rest is likewise a form of resilience in systems that viciously deplete Asian women's reserves. There should be no shame attached to reveling in restful activities that recenter yourself. The feelings of guilt attached to practicing self-care are usually a sign of internalized capitalism. Admittedly, I'm still working on untying my sense of self-worth to my productivity.

Lastly, you are not alone. I'm forever grateful to have a mother who recognizes the value of mental health and who holds space for my experiences. I'm indebted to several Asian women before and around me who have enabled the courage to share these reflections on the global advent of fetishization. I invite you to share your stories too; there is always someone who's not only willing but overjoyed to listen. It is because others have told their stories that I've finally made sense of my own; their demonstrations of agency unlocked mine.

Oh, by the way, yes, I do like to read.

Notes

[1] See Chou for an extensive qualitative study on this topic.

[2] Fournier, *Autotheory as Feminist Practice in Art, Writing, and Criticism.*

[3] Tuhiwai Smith, *Decolonizing Methodologies: Research and Indigenous Peoples.*

[4] Hong, *Minor Feelings: An Asian American Reckoning.* Hong's book title arises from the emotions that marginalized groups feel while traversing a predominantly white society; these feelings are often dismissed and viewed as disproportional.

[5] Anzaldúa, "El Mundo Zurdo: The Vision."

[6] Said, *Orientalism.*

[7] Uchida, "The Orientalization of Asian Women in America."

[8] Ibid., 171. Uchida is referencing Patricia Hill Collins's use of controlling images outlined in *Black Feminist Thought* (1991). Hill Collins, Patricia. *Black Feminist Thought: Knowledge, Consciousness and the Politics of Empowerment.* New York: Routledge, 1990.

[9] Ibid., 167.

[10] Ibid., 169.

[11] Robin Zheng, "Why Yellow Fever Isn't Flattering: A Case Against Racial Fetishes." While yellow fever primarily applies to women of East and Southeast Asian descent, Zheng's overall argument in elucidating how racial fetishes operate is still immensely valuable.

[12] Ibid., 401.

[13] Ibid., 408–410.

[14] Hwang and Parreñas, "The Gendered Racialization of Asian Women as Villainous Temptresses."

[15] Uchida, 173.

[16] Kim, "Orientalism Restated in the Era of COVID-19."

[17] Morales Domínguez, *Race in Cuba: Essays on the Revolution and Racial Inequality.*

[18] Yun and Larémont, "Chinese Coolies and African Slaves in Cuba, 1847–74."

[19] Chang, *Ghosts of Gold Mountain: The Epic Story of the Chinese Who Built the Transcontinental Railroad.*

[20] Various scholars, such as Evelyn Hu-Dehart, Sean Metzger, and Susan Thananopavarn— among others—are working on these exact intersecting areas. Many thanks to Jennifer Ho for pointing me toward these scholars' works. Ho's own coedited volume with Jenny Heijun Wills for MLA, *Teaching Approaches on Asian North American Texts* (2022), dismantles the hegemony of "America" as being equated with the US.

[21] In addition to the 2021 Atlanta Spa Shootings, Michelle Alyssa Go was pushed to her death in front of an oncoming New York City subway train on January 15, 2022. A few weeks later, also in New York City, Christina Yuna Lee was stalked and found fatally wounded in her bathtub on February 13, 2022.

Bibliography

Anzaldúa, Gloria. "El Mundo Zurdo: The Vision." In *This Bridge Called My Back: Writings by Radical Women of Color*, edited by Cherríe Moraga and Gloria Anzaldúa, 195–196. Latham: Kitchen Table/Women of Color Press, 1983.

Chang, Gordon H. *Ghosts of Gold Mountain: The Epic Story of the Chinese Who Built the Transcontinental Railroad.* Boston: Mariner Books, 2019.

Chou, Rosalind S. *Asian American Sexual Politics: The Construction of Race, Gender, and Sexuality.* Lanham: Rowman & Littlefield, 2012.

Fournier, Lauren. *Autotheory as Feminist Practice in Art, Writing, and Criticism.* Cambridge: MIT Press, 2022.

Ho, Jennifer, and Jenny Wills. *Teaching Approaches on Asian North American Texts.* New York: Modern Language Association Press, 2022.

Hong, Cathy P. *Minor Feelings: An Asian American Reckoning.* New York: Penguin Random House, 2020.

Hwang, Maria, and Rhacel Salazar Parreñas. "The Gendered Racialization of Asian Women as Villainous Temptresses." *Gender & Society* 35, no. 4 (2021): 567–576.

Kim, Joey S. "Orientalism Restated in the Era of COVID-19." *Asian American Literature: Discourses & Pedagogies* 11, no. 4 (2022): 1–22.

Morales Domínguez, Esteban. *Race in Cuba: Essays on the Revolution and Racial Inequality.* New York: Monthly Review Press, 2012.

Said, Edward W. *Orientalism.* New York: Parthenon Books, 1978.

Smith, Linda Tuhiwai. *Decolonizing Methodologies: Research and Indigenous Peoples.* London: Zed Books, 1999.

Uchida, Aki. "The Orientalization of Asian Women in America." *Women's Studies International Forum* 21, no. 2 (March/April 1998): 161–174.

Yun, Lisa, and Ricardo René Larémont. "Chinese Coolies and African Slaves in Cuba, 1847–74." *Journal of Asian American Studies* 4, no. 2 (2001): 99–122.

Zheng, Robin. "Why Yellow Fever Isn't Flattering: A Case Against Racial Fetishes." *Journal of the American Philosophical Association* 2, no. 3 (Fall 2016): 400–419.

10

TRANSLATING GULING

TECHNOLOGIES OF LANGUAGE, RACE, AND RESISTANCE IN SWEDEN

Jennifer Hayashida

["Asian American"] may be conceived as a mediating presence that links bodies to the knowledge regimes of the U.S. nation. "Asian American" is in this sense a *metaphor* for resistance and racism.

—Kandice Chuh, *Imagine Otherwise: On Asian Americanist Critique*

I understand language to be a regulatory technology. To be fluent in a language is to have access to that technology, but fluency is also a means for the technology to colonize and regulate you. What we do, enact, with a word in one language is determined by the context in which the doing is situated, but what happens to the word's performative power when it is resituated in another language?

I sometimes joke that at least in New York, they'd get it right and say *konichiwa*.

Swedish has no language for *Asian American*, *mixed race*, or *hapa*.[1] In translation, foreign terms are often italicized, and so, in Swedish, I italicize these words. Jag är *hapa*. Jag är *mixed race*. And when I do that—italicize the words that speak an important metaphor for me—I have no choice but to perform my own foreignness.

But perhaps you are reading this with English as your first language, or with one of many Englishes as the language that grants you access to the academy. Then I should invert the italicization: *Jag är* hapa. *Jag är* mixed race.

Asian American is a speech act, I would tell my students in the US, after explaining what a speech act is. In its utterance—its enactment of how bodies are entangled with politics and language—it simultaneously does and undoes "identity." And while *Asian American* fetters us to the chronic infection of the racial capitalist US nation-state, it also bonds us to a proposition of what can be made better in that festering wound.

How to translate into Swedish:

She suffer so much

For so much her life[2]

Hailed, I would say. You are *hailed*. In Swedish, *to hail* becomes *anropa*, which is closer to *to call* and would, more directly, be translated as *to summon* or *to invoke*. *Asian American* is a summoning. *Asian American* is an invocation.

A *sansei* father from Honolulu, Hawai'i. A mother from Vaxholm, Sweden. *Lau lau*, *strömming*, *bento* beneath the giant monkey pod tree, how lilies of the valley brighten each clearing of birch.

Roman is the antonym of *italic*, *upright* the antonym of *oblique*—type that is slanted. *Asiatisk*, in Swedish, still connotes East Asian, but a pan-Asian/American metric would hold that nearly eight hundred thousand people, almost 10 percent of the Swedish population, are Asian. Early Asian immigrants arrived from Turkey, Lebanon, and Iran; more recent ones have fled Yemen, Syria, and Iraq. Thus, many Asians in Sweden live the consequences of direct and indirect US warfare.

I am a translator. I was always a translator, even before I understood how I live between languages, between public and private regimes of belonging to states and families. Today, I translate mostly Asian American and Asian diaspora poetry to and from American English and Swedish, but my training is in translating the oblique: glances, questions, how someone cuts ahead of you in line or pulls their purse close as you walk by. For many of us, translation is the art of suspicion, where we eavesdrop on the periphery of words.

Inference is to go beyond the information given, while deduction is understanding based on evidence. But evidence to me may be inference to you.

If a language cannot hold you, if its words do not, with precision, metaphorize essential aspects of how you move through the world—to whom you are "of consequence," and how—then what do you do?[3] Borrow from a distant well of words that provides language for not merely what you look like but also for the experiences imprinted on your skin and memory, even from before you were born? Or can you force yourself into this *other* language, bend it to hold a history, a politics, a potential future? But how, when this language is inscribed with another history and politics, where you have no choice but to engage in wayward translation?

****

How does translation scatter language? *Shrapnel*, a noun, is named for General Henry Shrapnel, a man who invented a thing that explodes into sharp metal fragments intended to injure and kill. In Swedish, *shrapnel* is translated into *splitter*, meaning shards or bits. Here, the connection to a man and the invention that bears his name is severed, and fragments of the thing scatter, etymologically severed.

Shrapnel is not italicized, for it is both here and there: here, with grenade launchers produced and exported by Swedish companies such as Bofors and SAAB, and there, with Swedish shrapnel scattered in, among others places, Syria and Myanmar. As shrapnel scatters, as it flies through the hypermilitarized multiverse of forever war, the doing of words, how and what they name, is inflected by whose experiences they enact or redact, how they metaphorize. *Shrapnel*, a word that names military injury, scatters: instead of death by a thousand cuts, it is metaphorized into the thousand pieces of a shattered vase.

A shattered tongue speaks borders, utters a body's belonging. Language speaks lives into incomplete being. Languages may reject a body through silence and mistranslation. If language can be shelter, translation is the memory of crouching beneath bare sky.

> Sinew of muscle memory, tonguing words
> I knew and heard, how they started   something
> within   an alertness   Every public space a stage
> potential offense   glance or word
> and I am translated   aslant

I dream that the strength of my tongue is maintained through strength-training, lifelong resistance exercises. How the strength of the tongue builds through exercises in race as well as resistance. The tongue lifts, lilts, is pulled and drawn out in alien and familiar sounds.

To translate a racialized body between histories is a political and linguistic riddle, so my tongue and I hunt through archives of the pejorative.

How to translate: "Don't pay any attention to those little fuckers"?

How to translate: ". . . like he was swinging for a home run"?[4]

If, as Chuh argues, "the political may be animated by difference, not identity," then what politics are animated when the linguistic flux of difference is read as the fixity of identity?[5] What kind of political resistance becomes possible if you have to italicize these and other words: *war on terror, Chinatown, Pidgin, perpetual foreigner, community, model minority, racial formation, yellow power, passing, person of color, Brown*?

To put it plain: How to map Asian America onto a language where the vocabulary to chart its victories and defeats does not exist?

How to translate those words if the act of translation, of carrying them, tenderly, from American English to Swedish—from Daly City or Queens to Rinkeby or Rosengård—also scrubs them of their resistance, leaves them overflowing with race? Or, if always leaving them in their English locates the questions they utter *there*, not *here*? Or, if to insist on their Englishness is to also insist on the righteousness of US empire?

****

The term *Pidgin* (1807) derives from the Chinese pronunciation of the English word "business" and was the language of trade in Guangzhou.[6] The Pidgin I know is the language my father's family spoke at dinners and on the phone back in Honolulu and around the table in the Bay Area. I think of Pidgin as an argument, as a refusal to smooth the seams between languages, a fugitive assemblage of words uttered, and then inherited, by both colonizer and colonized. This Pidgin taught me how history and power come alive in language, that we summon the past and the future every time we open our mouths.

From "The Future of the White Race," my English translation of Swedish author Viktor Rydberg's 1895 foreword to the Swedish translation of Benjamin Kidd's *Social Evolution*:[7]

It is in this condition that the whites of Europe meet the yellows of Asia in the battle that will decide their fate. In its first and most important stage, the battle is of a purely economic nature and will be fought on the worker and labor market. If no other motivations than the purely economic ones prevail, the whites will fight this battle divided among themselves. The class of whites, whose material prosperity depends on procuring as cheap labor as possible, must become the allies of the yellows. This is because the yellow worker can sell his muscular energy, nearly tireless, at a lower price than the white worker is able to. For a long time, in the struggle between industrialism and manual labor, the idea appeared and, as well as it could thus far, sought to be realized, to replace the white working class with a yellow one. If the Aryan instinct for self-preservation does not succeed in resisting the plan here at the gate, then Europe will first have:

> a white upper class and a yellow lower class;
>
> then a largely yellow upper class and a yellow lower class,
>
> finally yellow capitalists and mandarins and a yellow underclass,
>
> in other words, a Chinese stock instead of an Aryan.

The Swedish Society for Racial Hygiene was founded in 1909. Titles of some of their publications include *On Fertilization as Well as Fertility and Sterility from the Perspective of Race; The Hazards of Degeneration and Guidelines for Its Prevention; The Sterilization Question: Some Social-Medical and Ethical Perspectives.*[8]

The Swedish State Institute for Racial Biology was founded in 1922, with the mission to study and publish findings regarding genetics, heredity, and the characteristics of various racialized groups, including archetypal white Swedes but also—as subjects of a white supremacist project—Indigenous peoples and others who had immigrated to Sweden. The institute was one of the first of its kind in the world, and many of its researchers provided material that the Nazis subsequently mobilized as evidence in their genocidal undertaking.

Karesuandolappar: Postcard from Herman Lundborg (1868–1943), director of the State Institute for Racial Biology, to his wife, Thyra Lundborg (1868–1931).

Indigenous Sami people from Karesuando, referred to as *lappar*, which derives from the Finnish. Recently, the term *Sami* has become more ubiquitous, in line with the practice of no longer referring to groups of people using terms they do not themselves deploy and which have, historically, been pejorative. *Lapp* can also mean: a slip of paper or fabric, a patch, a small plot of arable land. A large swath of northern Sweden bears the name *Lappland*.

A sudden change of mind can be called a *lappkast*, which refers to the ability to, on parallel skis, jump from one position to its 180-degree opposite.

The formalization of the institute, its status as a state-run institution, but also the long shadow it casts across twentieth-century Sweden—a more general mainstreaming of eugenics, forced sterilization of those considered mentally inferior (women in distress, Roma, and Indigenous peoples), the aforementioned complicity with Third Reich logics of extermination—means that Swedish public debate often distinguishes between "biological" and "cultural" racism, a squeamishness regarding the entanglement of the two, how they animate one another.

The institute operated independently from 1922 to 1958, when it was incorporated into Uppsala University and renamed, or metaphorized, the Institute for Medical Genetics.

In the few existing contemporary academic commentaries on Rydberg's text, readings emphasize his attention to that era's moral hygiene, that his analysis is prescient in light of contemporary labor and market relations between *the West* and China, and that his assessment of the Chinese (here, a nineteenth-century American would most likely say "Chinaman") is complimentary enough that it cannot be considered too problematic.[9]

What kind of resistance, but also what kind of injury, can be performed when words of anti-racist refusal are not built into a language? When the language of race is de facto the language of eugenics? When a history of welfare state-sponsored eugenics continues to stink up how language that performs anti-racism is taught and spoken?

The historical fact of the State Institute for Racial Biology is maybe what renders the mere utterance of the Swedish word for "race" a speech act. By saying *ras*, you are, according to many Swedes, making race. Thus, the anti-racist swiftly becomes a racist, since in order to speak against something, we must also name what we are in opposition to.

I am not "that way" is a common way of saying that one is not racist. To simply say *rasist* is to risk enacting racial animus. I look at Swedes who say they aren't "that way," who have occasion to say such a thing, and am reminded of Ron Ebens being interviewed in *Who Killed Vincent Chin?*[10]

The small Swedish city of Norrköping (pop. 137,000) operates yellow streetcars nicknamed *Gula faran*, the yellow peril.

Afrosvenskar are Swedes of African descent, and the word is included in SAOB, the dictionary of the Swedish Academy—the OED of Swedish. In many ways, the construction of the word follows the hyphenated logics of US English and contains both race and resistance.

But if I search for *antisvart* ("anti-Black"), the only word that comes up in the dictionary, obliquely, is *ramsvart*: "black as a raven, completely black, raven's black, coal black; historically said in reference to horses."[11]

Any linguistic acknowledgment of racism being a structural practice has a very limited official Swedish vocabulary.

That same dictionary today defines the word *guling* ("yellow one") as follows:[12]

1. (pejorative) person with yellow skin, esp. from China and Japan

2. (pejorative) strike-breaker, scab

The playground rhyme I often heard as a child:

Mamma kines (use fingertips to pull eyes in an upward slant)

Pappa japan (use fingertips to pull eyes in a downward slant)

Stackars lilla barn (use fingertips to pull one eye up, one eye down)

To return to a place that was once home is to accept time as chronic double exposure, a density to each interaction since it invokes a *then* and a *now* and the static of remembering, but never fully. The ebb and flow of my view of the schoolyard from a swing, the sour scent of candy and tobacco in a Swedish corner store, the wood bench where I ate egg sandwiches with my *Mormor*.

I return to Sweden after almost twenty-five years. Seven election cycles, nearly each one a gentle toggle to the right regardless of the victor.

I grew up in Sweden in the 1970s and 1980s and knew that the state operated the trains we rode on, the pharmacies where we purchased faintly scented soaps, toothbrushes, cotton to be pulled out in wooly wads and not in individual balls. Lines outside the state-run liquor store on Friday afternoons: the great equalizer, a socioeconomic cross section of mostly white Swedes in a queue to buy booze.

I also grew up in the US in the 1970s and 1980s and knew that Jimmy Carter had been raised on a peanut farm and that he lost to Ronald Reagan, whom my parents held responsible for the fact that homeless vets lined Telegraph Avenue. Quarters in the ashtray of our car, to be swiftly deposited in the hands of Bay Bridge toll workers. The deeply xenophobic and anti-Black policies enacted via Clinton-era welfare *reform*, a word that is identical in both Swedish and English.

It is the mid-1990s. I am a teenager, old enough to take public transportation on my own, travel to and from the Stockholm suburb where I live with my white Swedish mother. I know to move to another train car when I see the skinheads board.

In the nineties, my Japanese American father lives in the Bay Area: he is a third-generation *sansei* from Honolulu, and it is through his family I have learned that I am hapa. But in Sweden, there are mostly mistranslations for someone like me: at best, I am a Korean adoptee named Anna Larsson, the slightly older girl whose ID I borrow to get into clubs. The young men on the train raise their arms in a familiar salute.

As a teen, I saw it spray-painted in underpasses and on garbage cans: BSS, an acronym for *Bevara Sverige Svenskt*, or "Keep Sweden Swedish," the slogan of that era's neo-Nazi movement. BSS would later become a mainstream political party, the Sweden Democrats, or SD. Until the late 1990s, SD maintained *Bevara Sverige Svenskt* as its slogan.

Utlänningslag (2005:716)—directly translated as "Foreigner Legislation," contextually as "Foreigner Bill"—is the central piece of legislation that structures migration to Sweden. Initially passed in 1927, the foreigner legislation's restrictions speak to nationalist ideologies in motion following World War I.

Modified in 1938, this law required a *J* to be stamped in passports belonging to Jews in an effort to minimize the entry of refugees fleeing Nazi Germany. Once Sweden began to consider a more lenient policy toward Jewish refugees in 1941, Germany had severely restricted Jewish emigration, and any performance of mercy was rendered moot.

Today, the anti-Black logics of US policing and carcerality structure the dominant political language of Swedish migration policy—especially, now, an endlessly surging Islamophobia that mobilizes Sweden's ruling right-wing coalition, carried to victory by SD, a party supported by one in five Swedish voters.

SD deploys standard populist messaging: lower gas prices, law and order, closed borders. They are now the second-largest political party in Sweden, after the historical monolith the Social Democrats.

In August of 2022, almost one month before the national elections, SD purchases advertising space that covers the entirety of one of Stockholm's subway trains. Every train car is swathed in SD's party symbol, a blue anemone, with the slogan "Welcome to the Victory Train" and "SD 22."

SD's legal spokesperson tweets an image of the train along with the comment, "Welcome to the repatriation train. You have a one-way ticket. Next stop, Kabul!"[13]

The train workers' union files a complaint on the basis that the advertising places workers at risk of violence, given that commuters have no choice but to enter a train plastered in a political message they may find offensive.

****

When I first returned to Sweden one election cycle earlier, I spotted a center-right Liberal Party campaign poster which urged, "Jalla, Sverige!" It featured Robert Hannah, L party member, human rights attorney of Assyrian descent, raised in so-called Million Program housing in Gårdsten and Tynnered. The title of Hannah's 2018 autobiography is *Potatisskallen*, that is, *The Potato Head*.

Let me translate: *svartskalle* is a Swedish pejorative but also a potential expression of solidarity, depending on whose tongue is talking. Translated verbatim, this compound word means "black" + "head." A potato head in Sweden may, for Hannah, be an affirmative liberal take on someone who, in the US, might be called a banana or an Oreo.

I try to translate US solidarities of resistance while the state translates US racisms. I have been trying to identify the shades of my difference.

Blatte, in English pronounced *bluhtteh*. No one knows, but maybe from the French *blatte*, meaning cockroach. The first modifying half of the compound *blattesvenska*, a form of Swedish spoken by a dark-skinned person residing in southern Sweden. Potentially pejorative, also a *samlingsbegrepp*—literally, a "gathering word"—for all of us who are italicized on a daily basis. Sometimes also a reclaimed expression of solidarity, depending on whose tongue is talking, and I will say that my heart warms when I am called *blatte* by a friend from Macedonia or Iran or Yemen or Turkey. A white Swede would never call me *blatte*: they just call me *kines*.

The Social Democrats of the sixties and seventies promised, and delivered, one hundred thousand homes per year over the course of a decade. Hence the term *Million Program*—not a metaphor but literally a million homes to house labor migrants from Turkey, Greece, Poland, Romania. Today they are the homes of mostly refugees from Syria, Afghanistan, Iraq, Yemen, Eritrea, Somalia.

> The Swedish boom years were marked by a relocation of large swaths of the population. In 1955 approximately 2.5 million people resided in the countryside. Twenty years later, only one million remained. At the same time, the populations in the cities and urban areas increased from four to nearly seven million. In order to manage industry's need for labor, extensive labor migration was required. Workers were recruited from,

primarily, Italy, former Yugoslavia, and Finland. This, along with a large youth population, aggravated the housing shortage, which once again became a hot political topic.[14]

The housing queues of the sixties and seventies nearly disappeared, but those who were not as competitive on the housing market—read: your income but also your last name and the size of your family—were relegated to the least desirable of the less desirable areas.

Million Program Construction i Saltskog, Södertälje.

Construction of Saltskog was initiated in 1970. The buildings were rapidly built thanks to advanced mechanization. The apartments were well-built and the standard high. But there were too many apartments in a limited area. And small apartments were lumped together, so that many single residents lived in the same building. The social structure was not very successful.[15]

Orten, in English is pronounced the way it's spelled. Second half of the word *förorten*—geographically, the suburbs, but, metaphorically, not an American suburb. *Orten* is the site of Million Program housing, and the regulatory terminology of the state now calls many of these neighborhoods *utsatta områden*, meaning areas where crime rates and subsequent police enforcement have surged.

Campaign promises made by today's triumphant right wing: *visitationszoner*, a metaphor for legally sanctioned geographic boundaries around stop and frisk. Foreign gang members could be deported even without suspicion of crime. Wiretaps without a warrant. Anonymous witnesses. I am reminded of Manu Uch, Mohamed Yousry, the word *impunity*.

Utsatt means vulnerable or exposed, but also subject or prone to—that is, subject to crime and therefore also subject to biopolitical surveillance and policing. But also the subject of public discourse on crime, and those living there are subjectivized into abject forms of citizenship where they play the part of the refugee, the parasite, the criminal. Also: the Robert Hannahs struggling to get out from under the thumb of purportedly homophobic, anti-feminist, and backward communities, groups living in supposedly self-imposed isolation from Swedish liberal values.

In *The Karma of Brown Folk*, Vijay Prashad urges South Asian Americans to "commit model minority suicide!" in order to stand in solidarity with Black Americans.[16] Deployed as a solution to US racial conflict—the project of Black liberation demanding racial justice and sovereignty of a white supremacist nation—Prashad takes Desis to task for undermining Black Americans' struggle in an effort to belong. This conditional belonging at the hands of white America is not a prize, according to Prashad, but a form of indentured servitude.

I suspect that Robert Hannah did not read Prashad while he studied at Georgetown.

There is no word for *model minority* in Swedish, and so I simply try to explain the concept of "the good immigrant." Not only do I lose the alliteration, but it also has no political history, or future, since Sweden's immigrants are not all called minorities, and its minorities are not always immigrants.

How do you kill off a concept that has no name?

Minoritetsspråk, minority languages, are five legally protected languages: Yiddish, Romani Chib, Sami, Finnish, and Meänkieli. It is estimated that perhaps 350,000 people in Sweden speak these languages.

Invandrarspråk, immigrant languages, include Arabic (four hundred thousand speakers), Kurdish (eighty-four thousand), and Farsi (seventy-four thousand).

There were Swedish-only schools for Sami and Finnish children. Roma children were prohibited from attending Swedish schools until 1959. Consider the colonial segregationist policies of state-run Sami schools in particular: in order to preserve the nomadic nature of the Sami who kept reindeer, their children attended so-called nomad schools, drafty tents as classrooms for Sami language and culture. Meanwhile, children of settled Sami, who did not keep reindeer, were required to attend Swedish-only schools, since their Sami lifestyle, according to the Swedish colonizers, no longer metaphorized a minoritarian Indigenous race that warranted preservation. A neocolonial order emerged between nomadic and settled Sami, while both remained under the colonial thumb of the Swedish state.

Sweden's current minister of education is also the head of Robert Hannah's Liberal Party, a party that recently made the cataclysmic decision to align itself with the right-wing coalition, including SD, in order to squeak past the 4 percent barrier, maintain its seats in parliament, and thus become part of the ruling block.

In the lead-up to the most recent election, public debates rendered language an effective populist metaphor for discussing race. If preschool teachers did not speak Swedish well enough, then how would immigrant children ever learn to speak properly? How could they ever become fully integrated? If they did not become integrated, would these multilingual children by default end up in criminal gangs?[17] Language and multilingualism suddenly presented a cosmos—perhaps even a multiverse—of potentially disastrous, alternately lifesaving fates for children born of parents from Syria, Guinea, Yemen.

In her 2022 essay in the *Washington Post* regarding the multiversal blockbuster *Everything Everywhere All at Once*, Anne Anlin Cheng proposes that the film be read through the lens of "Asian-pessimism," an Asian American borrowing or invocation of Afro-pessimism. If Afro-pessimism is a framework to, among other critical errands, articulate the transhistorical terror of social death that many consider inherent to Blackness, then Asian-pessimism, according to Cheng, "pushes back with a vengeance against the narrative paucity of the same old stories we tell about Asian American lives."[18] The origins of such pessimism, Cheng argues, include legal exclusion, model minoritization, kung fu-Orientalism, contemporary anti-Asian hate—and, I would add, Islamophobia, in its consolidation of anti-Asian xenophobia and anti-Black carcerality.

I saw *Everything* on my own in a cineplex in downtown Stockholm, with mostly white teens in the small audience. Only one major Swedish review of the film had even mentioned race, and then in relation to the relationship between Evelyn and Joy—the conflict that arises between the mother born in China and her American-born daughter.[19] Other white Swedish critics either lauded the film's over-the-top-ness or lamented that very same quality, complaining that there was no there there, that it was all chaos for the sake of spectacle.

I read the poet Bao Phi's essay on watching the film—also alone at a cineplex, his in Minnesota, home to, among others, refugees from US wars in Southeast Asia as well as fifth- and sixth-generation Swedish settlers—where he continuously returns to a question I share: How Eurocentrism makes it possible to dismiss the film on the basis of a white gaze trained to not see what Cheng simply terms "Asian American concerns"—a training structured by legal exclusion, Orientalism, model minoritization.[20] In other words, it is the very material that animates the film that also makes it possible for white viewers to not see the existential and political concerns being set in furious motion.

From *White Blight*, my translation of Iranian-Swedish poet Athena Farrokhzad's 2013 debut, *Vitsvit*:

> My brother said: Some day I want to die in a country
>
> where people can pronounce my name[21]

I was born in 1973 in Oakland, California. From 1970 to 1984, "Jennifer" was ranked the number one name for girls in the United States, and there was inevitably another Jennifer—or Jen or Jenny—in my elementary school class in California. The editor of this volume is also named Jennifer. My mother has said that she and my father named me Jennifer so that I would have a name that no one would struggle to pronounce, and they succeeded. When my mother and I moved to Sweden in the late seventies, there was, astonishingly, a Jennifer right across the way, and then another Jennifer in my second-grade class. My name, an export, metaphor for all-American empire.

In Swedish, the *J* in my name sounds like a *Y*, without the hard consonantal edge of English. As a result, when I lived in Sweden as a child, I was "Yennifer," and when my mother and I returned to the US in the early 1990s, I became "Jen." When I moved back to Sweden in 2018, I introduced myself as "Jen" in an effort to maintain some continuity of self, the consequence of which is that I am today called "Yen," a name which seems to prompt people to assume that I am, after all, from Japan.

I mention this phonetic genealogy not because my all-American name has been translated into Japanese currency but because, as Solmaz Sharif writes in *Look*, "it matters what you call a thing." Together with the Swedish poet Ida Börjel, I cotranslated Sharif's debut into Swedish, and we struggled with how to translate the poetic scaffold of the book: key terms from the *Dictionary of Military and Associated Terms* published by the US Department of Defense. What, if not *Look*, were we to title this book, prismatic in its ability to be both infinitive and imperative as well as, according to the DoD, "a period during which a mine circuit is receptive of an influence"?[22] It mattered that we let the shrapnel of the word scatter, something we did not think we could accomplish with as much brutality in Swedish, a language for a nation that has not officially been at war (unless you count vigorous arms exports) for more than two hundred years. This is not to say that Swedish has no language for militarism, but those words—and how they fertilize athletics and video games—are generally borrowed, Duchampian readymades, from American English. *Ceci n'est pas une guerre.*

I may very well die in a country where my name sounds like Japanese currency. A country where I become seen as the aggressor when I mention yellow power or wonder at the absence of a term for those of us, the more and more of us, who are *mixed race*. Still, although my Swedish life is largely muted by this absence of a language to name experience, memory, and body, translation is increasingly affording me a borderlands and language to think and enact a poetics of insurgence.

Despite, or perhaps even thanks to, critiques regarding the way nation structures the concept of Asian America, it is also a hard-won technology to situate Asian experience outside "Asia."

For as much as translation from American English is an enterprise animated by empire, translating Asian American poetry from American English into Swedish is a method for me to borrow from North American anti-racist struggles—as enacted in poetry as well as politics—and then explore how those struggles can contaminate or infect the Swedish.

To translate Asian American poetry is to translate the oblique, the fugitive, the margins. To translate Asian American poetry is to translate David Palumbo-Liu's "Asian/American" beyond America, with not merely another nation as substitute.[23] Translation lets me populate Asian/America otherwise, toward fugitive futures in contestation of the nation-state. It allows me to graft victories onto current struggles, to hack technologies that seek to redact and refuse me. This language carved from birch shall not contain me.

Notes

[1] Given that italicization is one of the phenomena analyzed in my contribution, I've been given editorial permission to use italics rather than double quotation marks—a Chicago-style standard—in relevant sections.

[2] Kim, *Commons*, 78.

[3] Diaz, "Workshop."

[4] In 1981, Ronald Ebens, together with his stepson Michael Nitz, beat Chinese American autoworker Vincent Chin to death with a baseball bat in the parking lot of a Detroit McDonald's. Ebens repeatedly bludgeoned Chin in the head while Nitz held him down, and the two were ultimately sentenced to three years' probation and a $3,000 fine, with Judge Charles Kaufman stating, "These weren't the kind of men you send to jail. . . . You don't make the punishment fit the crime; you make the punishment fit the criminal." Chin's killing mobilized a local and national movement against anti-Asian racism, documented in the 1987 film *Who Killed Vincent Chin?* by Christine Choy and Renee Tajima-Peña. In the film, Ebens states, "And I didn't even do it on purpose. You know, I didn't walk up and shoot somebody." According to Starlene, one of the dancers at the Fancy Pants Club, Ebens told her, "Don't pay any attention to those little fuckers," as a shouting match between the three men began. "Like he was swinging for a home run" is how another witness, an off-duty police officer, described Ronald Ebens's use of a baseball bat to bludgeon Chin in the head.

[5] Chuh, *Imagine Otherwise*, 147.

[6] Mufwene, "Pidgin."

[7] Kidd, *Den sociala utvecklingen*, xiv.

[8] Wikipedia, "Svenska sällskapet för rashygien."

[9] Hedberg, *En strid för det som borde vara*, 161–162.

[10] See note 4.

[11] SAOB, "Ramsvart."

[12] Ibid., "Guling."

[13] Amanda Lindholm, "Moderat kritik mot SD:s tunnelbanetweet."

[14] Allmännyttan, "1946–1975."

[15] Ibid.

[16] Prashad, *The Karma of Brown Folk*, 2001.

[17] Prekopic, "Hur kan vi rättfärdiga."

[18] Cheng, "Everything Everywhere."

[19] Lundström, "Livskänslan är maxad."

[20] Phi, "When Something Is Nearly 'Everything.'"

[21] Farrokhzad, *White Blight*, 19.

[22] Department of Defense Dictionary, "Look."

[23] Palumbo-Liu, *Asian/American*.

Bibliography

Allmännyttan. "1946–1975 Allmännyttan byggs ut och bostadsbristen byggs bort." Accessed April 7, 2023. https://www.allmannyttan.se/historia/historiska-epoker/1946-1975-%20allmannyttan-byggs-ut-och-bostadsbristen-byggs-bort/.

Cheng, Anne Anlin, "'Everything Everywhere All at Once' Is a Deeply Asian American Film." *Washington Post*, May 4, 2022. https://www.washingtonpost.com/outlook/2022/05/04/everything-everywhere-asian-american-pessimism/.

Chuh, Kandice. *Imagine Otherwise: On Asian Americanist Critique*. Durham: Duke University Press, 2003.

Department of Defense Dictionary of Military and Associated Terms. "Look." Accessed April 7, 2023. https://irp.fas.org/doddir/dod/dictionary.pdf.

Diaz, Natalie. "Workshop: Glossary of Consequence with Natalie Diaz." Nottingham Contemporary. February 9, 2022. Video. https://www.nottinghamcontemporary.org/whats-on/five-bodies-workshop-natalie-diaz-glossary-of-consequence/.

Farrokhzad, Athena. *White Blight*. Translated by Jennifer Hayashida. Brooklyn: Argos Books, 2016.

Hedberg, Andreas. *En strid för det som borde vara: Viktor Rydberg som moderniseringskritiker 1891–1895*. Möklinta: Gidlunds Press, 2012.

Kidd, Benjamin, *Den sociala utvecklingen. Med en inledande afhandling "Den hvita rasens framtid" af Viktor Rydberg*. Stockholm, 1895.

Kim, Myung Mi, *Commons*. Berkeley: University of California Press, 2002.

Lindholm, Amanda. "Moderat kritik mot SD:s tunnelbanetweet." *Svenska Dagbladet*, August 17, 2022.

Lundström, Jakob. "Livskänslan är maxad i spexiga 'Everything Everywhere All at Once,'" *Dagens Nyheter*, May 19, 2022. https://www.dn.se/kultur/livskanslan-ar-maxad-i-spexiga-everything-everywhere-all-at-once/.

Mufwene, Salikoko Sangol. "pidgin," *Encyclopedia Britannica*, February 24, 2023. Accessed April 7, 2023, https://www.britannica.com/topic/pidgin.

Palumbo-Liu, David. *Asian/American: Historical Crossings of a Racial Frontier*. Redwood City: Stanford University Press, 1999.

Phi, Bao. "When Something Is Nearly 'Everything." *The Nerds of Color*, March 16, 2023. https://thenerdsofcolor.org/2023/03/16/when-something-is-nearly-everything/.

Prashad, Vijay. *The Karma of Brown Folk*. Minneapolis: University of Minnesota Press, 2001.

Prekopic, Vesna. "Hur kan vi rättfärdiga att det i Sverige bor svenska barn som inte kan svenska?" *Dagens Nyheter*, February 3, 2022. https://www.dn.se/kultur/vesna-prekopic-hur-kan-vi-rattfardiga-att-det-i-sverige-bor-svenska-barn-som-inte-kan-svenska/.

SAOB. *Ordbok över svenska språket*, utgiven av Svenska Akademien. Lund 1893–, accessed April 7, 2023, https://www.saob.se/.

Wikipedia. "Svenska sällskapet för rashygien." Accessed April 7, 2023. https://sv.wikipedia.org/wiki/Svenska_s%C3%A4llskapet_f%C3%B6r_rashygien.

About the Editor

The daughter of a refugee father from China and an immigrant mother from Jamaica, whose own parents were, themselves, immigrants from Hong Kong, **JENNIFER HO** is the director of the Center for Humanities & the Arts at the University of Colorado Boulder, where she also holds an appointment as Professor of Ethnic Studies. She is past president of the Association for Asian American Studies and the author of three scholarly books and two edited collections. In addition to her academic work, Ho is active in community engagement around issues of race and intersectionality, leading workshops on anti-racism and how to talk about race in our current social climate.

About the Contributors

Listed in Chapter Order

CHRISTINE R. YANO, Professor of Anthropology at the University of Hawaiʻi, has conducted research on Japan and Japanese Americans with a focus on popular culture. In 2020–2021 she served as the President of the Association for Asian Studies. Her publications include *Tears of Longing: Nostalgia and the Nation in Japanese Popular Song* (2002), *Airborne Dreams: "Nisei" Stewardesses and Pan American World Airways* (2011), and *Pink Globalization: Hello Kitty and its Trek Across the Pacific* (2013). Her latest book is *Straight A's: Asian American College Students in Their Own Words* with Neal Akatsuka (2018). Since 2023 until 2025, Yano serves as President of the Society for East Asian Anthropology (American Anthropological Association).

RAHUL K. GAIROLA, PhD (University of Washington, Seattle) is The Krishna Somers Senior Lecturer in English & Postcolonial Literature and a Fellow of the Indo-Pacific Research Centre (IPRC) at Murdoch University, Western Australia. He has published six books, and is an Area Editor for *Oxford Bibliographies in Literary & Cultural Studies* and Editor of the *Routledge/Asian Studies Association of Australia (ASAA) South Asian Book Series*. He holds Digital Humanities certificates from the University of Oxford, the University of Victoria (Canada), and Leipzig University; in 2019, The Digital Studio of the University of Melbourne appointed him a Digital Champion for the State of Western Australia. He was thrice a German Academic

Exchange (DAAD) fellow at Leipzig University, a Macmillan Center South Asian Studies Scholar at Yale University, a Ministry of Human Resource Development (MHRD) Research Fellow at the Indian Institute of Technology Roorkee, a School of Criticism & Theory Scholar at Cornell University, and a Pembroke Fellow at the University of Cambridge, among other funded distinctions. In January 2023, he was a Visiting Professor at ArtEZ University of the Arts, The Netherlands, and is a matriculated, lifetime Member of Pembroke College, Cambridge.

SARA DJAHIM is an independent researcher based in Berlin. Her research interests include be/longing, identity, and community organizing around anti-racism. She has worked extensively with migrant organizations throughout Germany on issues of political participation and solidarity. Sara holds a BA in Asian Studies and an MA in International Development Studies.

ÉRIKA TIEMI W. FUJII is a fourth-generation Japanese Brazilian and a fourth-generation Chinese Brazilian. She has a bachelor's degree from the University of São Paulo (USP) School of Law and is a specialist in Public Law and Constitutional Law. **GABRIEL AKIRA** is Brazilian and Japanese. He has a bachelor's degree from USP School of Law and teaches Japanese language. His lines of research include nationality, the Marxist theory of law, and nation-state. In 2023, he presented his undergraduate thesis entitled "Against Brasilianness: Japanese Immigration and Legal Form." **MARIA VICTÓRIA RUY**, or Mavi, is third-generation Chinese Brazilian and a historian on anti-Asian racism and Chinese immigration by Universidade Federal do Paraná. She is currently a Ph.D. student in the Ethnic Studies Department at the University of California, Berkeley. **MARIANA MITIKO NOMURA** is a third-generation Japanese Brazilian and lawyer with a bachelor's degree from the USP School of Law. They are a Master's student in Law and Development at FGV Sao Paulo Law School, and an awardee of the Graduate Support Program for Private Education Institutions (Prosup) – CAPES and the Mario Henrique Simonsen Scholarship for Teaching and Research. Their line of research is within Public International Law and Antidiscrimination Law. We are members of **Coletivo Dinamene**, an Asian-Brazilian activism collective founded in early 2020, named after a forgotten Asian female character by Portuguese poet Luís de Camões, who is told to have abandoned her in order to save the manuscript of "The Lusiads." Our group is composed of young descendants of Japanese and Chinese immigrants, who met each other at universities, social movements, or on social media. We gather at Dinamene with the common goal of weaving a safe space to share and understand our racial experiences, to study and debate existing works, and to create content under the principle of anti-racist solidarity with Black and Indigenous peoples.

RICHARD AIDOO is a Professor of Political Science in the Department of Political Science at Coastal Carolina University where he teaches international politics and African political and economic development. His research work on China's political-economic engagements with Sub-Saharan African countries, and other economic development issues in Sub-Saharan Africa has appeared in journals, book chapters, as well as several media outlets such as *The Washington Post, CNN, Real Clear World, The National Interest,* and more. He co-authored *Charting the Roots of Anti-Chinese Populism in Africa* (2015) with Steve Hess and edited a volume titled *The Politics of Economic Reform in Ghana* (2019).

RIVI HANDLER-SPITZ is associate professor and chair of Asian Languages and Cultures at Macalester College and a former fellow at the National Humanities Center. Her monograph, *Symptoms of an Unruly Age: Li Zhi and Cultures of Early Modernity* (University of Washington Press, 2017), compares writings by the sixteenth-century Chinese maverick intellectual Li Zhi to works by several of his best-known European contemporaries including Montaigne, Shakespeare, and Cervantes. Her drawings have appeared in *Inside Higher Ed* and in the award-winning *COVID Chronicles: A Comics Anthology* (Penn State University Press, 2021). Her current project is a book-length work of graphic scholarship titled *Savage Script: How Chinese Writing Became Barbaric.*

XUENING KONG is a Ph.D. candidate in the Department of History at Purdue University. Her research interests include modern Chinese history, transnational studies, Asian diaspora, Global Asias, borderland studies, and women and gender. She is currently working on her dissertation, entitled "Identity Formation in Displacement: Chinese Migrants on the U.S.-Mexico Border, 1899–1945." Her book reviews appear in the *Journal of Asian Studies, The Chinese Historical Review,* and *The PRC History Review.* She lives and studies in West Lafayette, Indiana, and actively engages in local educational events related to Asian, Asian American, and Latino cultures and experiences. In February 2022, she gave a talk "Herlinda Chew: A Chinese Mexican Woman Negotiating among Powers on the U.S.-Mexico Border" at the Purdue University Asian American and Asian Resource and Cultural Center.

IRMAK YAZICI is a fellow and lecturer in the Civic, Liberal, Global Education (COLLEGE) Program at Stanford University. She is a political scientist by training and her research broadly focuses on religion in global and comparative politics. Prior to her appointment at Stanford, she was a lecturer in the Department of Political Science at the University of Hawaiʻi at Mānoa.

KIMBERLY D. MCKEE is an associate professor and chair of the Integrative, Religious, and Intercultural Studies Department at Grand Valley State University. She is the author of *Disrupting Kinship: Transnational Politics of Korean Adoption in the United States* (University of Illinois Press, 2019) and co-editor of *Degrees of Difference: Reflections of Women of Color on Graduate School* (University of Illinois Press, 2020). McKee serves as a co-chair of the executive committee for the Alliance of the Study of Adoption and Culture. She received her Ph.D. in Women's, Gender, and Sexuality Studies from The Ohio State University.

EILEEN CHUNG is a Multicultural Women's and Gender Studies PhD student at Texas Woman's University. She graduated from the University of California, Santa Barbara with degrees in Asian American Studies and Psychology and received her Master of Social Work from the University of Pittsburgh. Eileen harbors an avid interest in Asian American women's advancement made possible through women of color coalition movements. Eileen's research interests span Asian American feminisms, Asian American Mental Health, Black-Asian solidarity, critical mixed-race studies, and qualitative feminist methodology. She is currently studying the mental health ramifications of fetishization experienced by self-identified Asian women and how these women subsequently demonstrate dynamic resistance in spaces overlaid by white supremacy and heteropatriarchy.

JENNIFER HAYASHIDA is a poet, translator and artist. She was born in Oakland, California, and spent her childhood in the suburbs of Stockholm and San Francisco. She has a B.A. in American Studies from the University of California, Berkeley, and an MFA in writing from the Milton Avery Graduate School of the Arts at Bard College. She is currently a PhD candidate in artistic research at the Academy of Art and Design at the University of Gothenburg, where her research examines autoethnographic ontologies of translation vis-a-vis multilingualism, dislocation, and racialized narratives of the nation-state. From 2009 to 2017, Hayashida served as Director of the Asian American Studies Program at Hunter College, The City College of New York. She has also held contingent positions at universities including the University of California, Davis; Montclair State University; and Columbia University. Her debut collection, *A Machine Wrote This Song*, was published by Gramma/Black Ocean in 2018. She is the recipient of awards from the New York Foundation for the Arts, PEN, and the Jerome Foundation, among others. Her translations between English and Swedish include work by Athena Farrokhzad, Don Mee Choi, Merima Dizdarević, and Kim Hyesoon.